American Christmases

John F. Blair, Publisher

Winston-Salem, North Carolina

American Christmases

Firsthand Accounts of Holiday Happenings From Early Days to Modern Times

Compiled by
Joanne Martell

*The paper in this book meets the guidelines
for permanence and durability of the Committee on
Production Guidelines for Book Longevity
of the Council on Library Resources.*

COVER IMAGE
Christmas Eve—Santa Claus Waiting for the Children to Get to Sleep
by Thomas Nast

Library of Congress Cataloging-in-Publication Data

American Christmases : firsthand accounts of holiday happenings from early days to
modern times / compiled by Joanne Martell.
p.   cm.
Includes bibliographical references (p.   ) and index.
ISBN-13: 978-0-89587-319-4 (alk. paper)
ISBN-10: 0-89587-319-2
1. Christmas—United States—History. 2. United States—Social life and customs.
I. Martell, Joanne, 1926–
GT4986.A1A64 2005
394.2663'0973—dc22   2005019404

DESIGN BY DEBRA LONG HAMPTON

Printed in Canada

For Sally and Susie and Nancy

Table of Contents

Introduction

*A*s a former Philadelphia court reporter, who recorded people's actual words for a living, I have a natural liking for verbatim accounts. Looking back, however, I realize that my research for this book—to discover what real people had to say about American Christmases—began a long time ago.

I was six years old, growing up in Ashtabula, Ohio. That Christmas Eve at bedtime, Mother and Dad let me hide behind our davenport to see for myself whether or not there really was a Santa Claus.

Unfortunately, the carpet was soft, the room was warm and dark, and the next thing I knew, it was Christmas morning and I was in my own bed.

If only I had been able to stay awake, what a fascinating firsthand account I could have brought to this book! To make up for that early dozing-off, I have located a great many people who managed to stay awake through a great variety of Christmas experiences. In these pages, they share their authentic accounts of holiday happenings from early days to modern times.

For reading ease, I changed 17th-century spelling to modern spelling in the opening pieces by John Smith and William Bradford. For example, "salvages" was changed to savages; "beere," to beer. Otherwise, I have kept misspellings as they occurred in their original formats.

The accounts begin with Captain John Smith in Virginia in 1608 and close with Major Carrie Acree in Iraq in 2004.

1539

In Excelsis Gloria

*Hernando De Soto's Spanish expeditionary force—
six hundred soldiers and five Franciscan priests—took over a
Florida Indian village for their winter encampment. There in
Anaica Apalache, six miles from present-day Tallahassee, they
celebrated the first Christmas Mass in what would become the
United States of America.*

No firsthand account survives.

1600s

1608

Never More Merry

*John Smith, of the English colony at Jamestown, Virginia, left this first written
account of Christmas in America. The struggling settlers were bracing for their
second winter. In late December, Captain Smith volunteered to find the
great Indian Powhatan and acquire much-needed supplies. Marooned in the wilds by
winter storms, Smith and his party celebrated a new-world Christmas in a native
village near present-day Hampton, Virginia.*

The next night being lodged at Kecoughtan 6 or 7 days, the extreme wind, rain, frost, and snow caused us to keep Christmas among the Savages, where we were never more merry, nor fed on more plenty of good oysters, fish, flesh, wild fowl, and good bread, nor never had better fires in England than in the dry warm smoky houses of Kecoughtan.[1]

1620

Now and Then
Some Beer

Englishman William Bradford, newly arrived in Massachusetts on the Mayflower, left the next account. The ship anchored at Plymouth harbor four days before Christmas 1620. The new settlers were Puritans, and if they had their way, there would be no such thing as an American Christmas. They regarded holiday celebrations as un-Christian, pagan, and sinful. They made December 25 a work day like any other, and began constructing Plymouth Plantation's first house.

The Master Caused Us to Have Some Beer
By Howard Pyle
Harper's New Monthly Magazine, December 1883

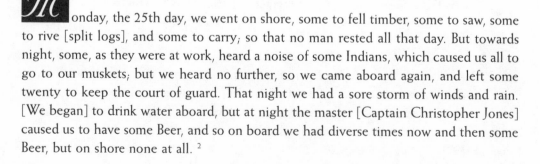

Monday, the 25th day, we went on shore, some to fell timber, some to saw, some to rive [split logs], and some to carry; so that no man rested all that day. But towards night, some, as they were at work, heard a noise of some Indians, which caused us all to go to our muskets; but we heard no further, so we came aboard again, and left some twenty to keep the court of guard. That night we had a sore storm of winds and rain. [We began] to drink water aboard, but at night the master [Captain Christopher Jones] caused us to have some Beer, and so on board we had diverse times now and then some Beer, but on shore none at all. [2]

The Puritan Governor Interrupting the Christmas Sports
By Howard Pyle
Harper's New Monthly Magazine, December 1883

1 6 2 1

A Matter of Conscience

*By Plymouth Plantation's second Christmas, thirty-five new settlers
had arrived on the ship* Fortune—*"most of them were lusty young men,
and many of them wild enough," Governor William Bradford noted.
Worse, they shocked their Puritan neighbors by celebrating the Christmas holiday.
In a year-end report to England, Bradford told how he handled the situation.*

And herewith I shall end this year. Only I shall remember one passage more, rather of mirth than of weight. On the day called Christmas Day, the Governor called them out to work as was used. But the most of this new company excused themselves and said it went against their consciences to work on the day. So the Governor told them that if they made it matter of conscience, he would spare them till they were better informed; so he led away the rest, and left them. But when they came home at noon from their work, he found them in the street at play, openly; some pitching the bar, and some at stool-ball [a game like cricket] and such like sports. So he went to them and took away their implements and told them that was against his conscience, that they should play and others work. If they made the keeping of it matter of devotion, let them keep their houses; but there should be no gaming or reveling in the streets. Since which time nothing hath been attempted that way, at least openly.[3]

1659

Pay For Every Such Offense

Puritan patience finally came to an end. Christmas was banned in Boston. In 1659, the Massachusetts Bay Colony legislature enacted the following anti-Christmas law that would remain on the books for the next twenty-two years.

For preventing disorders arising in several places within this jurisdiction, by reason of some still observing such festivals as were superstitiously kept in other countries, to the great dishonor of God and offence of others, it is therefore ordered by this Court . . . that whosoever shall be found observing any such day as Christmas or the like, either by forbearing of labor, feasting, or any other way . . . every such person so offending shall pay for every such offence five shillings, as a fine to the county.[4]

Rejoicing, Dancing, and Feasting

Half a continent away from Puritan decrees,
Father Louis Hennepin explored the upper Mississippi Valley
with a French expedition. He left this account, in which
he rejoiced over a miraculous (if muddy) meal during Christmas week.

The last of December, 1679, on the banks of the river, we killed only a buffalo and some wild turkeys, because the Indians had set fire to the dry grass of the prairies along our route. The deer had fled; and in spite of the effort made to find game, we subsisted merely through the providence of God, who grants aid at one time that he withholds at another. By the greatest good fortune in the world, when we had nothing more to eat we found a huge buffalo mired at the river's edge. It was so big that twelve of our men using a cable had difficulty in drawing it onto firm ground. . . .

After spending the day rejoicing, dancing, and feasting, we assembled the chiefs of the villages on either side of the river. We let them know through our interpreter that we Franciscans had not come to them to gather beavers, but to bring them knowledge of the great Master of Life and to instruct their children. We told them that we had left our country beyond the sea (or, as the Indians call it, the great lake) to come live with them and be their good friends. We heard a succession of loud voices saying "Tepatoui Nicka," which means "That is a good thing to do, my brother; you did well to have such a thought."[5]

1687

Mad Mirth

Meanwhile, back in Boston, Reverend Increase Mather,
Congregationalist pastor of North Church, published
A Testimony against Several Prophane and Superstitious
Customs, Now Practiced by Some in New-England,
which included his opinion of Christmas festivities.

The generality of Christmas-keepers observe that festival after such a manner as is highly dishonourable to the name of Christ. How few are there comparatively that spend those holidays (as they are called) after an holy manner. But they are consumed...in playing at Cards, in Revellings, in excess of Wine, in mad Mirth.[6]

This month the Cooks do very early rise,
To roast their meat, & make their
Christmas pies.
Poor men at rich men's tables their guts
forage
With roast beef, mince-pies, pudding
& plum porridge.

—*John Tully Almanac* (Boston 1688)

1702

Driving of Great Nails

*In Williamsburg, Virginia, rampaging schoolboys tried to
extort a Christmas holiday by barricading the schoolhouse and forcibly
"barring-out" their teacher. When schoolmaster James Blair
tried to break in, he narrowly escaped serious injury.*

bout a fortnight before Christmas 1702 . . . I heard the School boys about 12
o'clock at night, a driving of great nails, to fasten & barricade the doors of the Grammar
School. . . . made haste to get up & with the assistance of 2 servant men . . . I had
almost forced open one of the doors before they sufficiently secured it, but while I was
breaking in, they presently fired off 3 or 4 Pistols & hurt one of my servants in the eye
with the wadd . . . of one of the Pistols.

[W]hile I pressed forward, some of the boys, having a great kindness for me, call'd
out, "for God's sake sir don't offer to come in, for we have shot, and shall certainly fire
at any one that first enters." . . . [I then] resolved to let them alone till morning, and then
getting all the other masters together & calling for workmen to break open the doors.[1]

1711 and *1712*

Rude Reveling

By 1711, Cotton Mather shared the North Church pulpit
in Boston with his father, Increase. Father and son also shared a distaste
for Christmas frolics, as evidenced in this diary entry from December 30, 1711,
and an excerpt from one of his books, published in 1712.

I hear of a number of young people of both sexes, belonging, many of them, to my flock, who have had on the Christmas-night, this last week, a Frolick, a revelling feast, and Ball.[2]

[T]he Feast of Christ's Nativity is spent in Reveling, Dicing, Carding, Masking, and in all Licentious Liberty . . . by Mad Mirth, by long Eating, by hard Drinking, by lewd Gaming, by rude Reveling.[3]

Strong-Beer Stout Syder and a good fire
Are Things this season doth require
Now some with feasts do crown the day,
Whilst others loose their coyn in play.

—Titan Leeds from Philadelphia
The American Almanack for . . . 1714

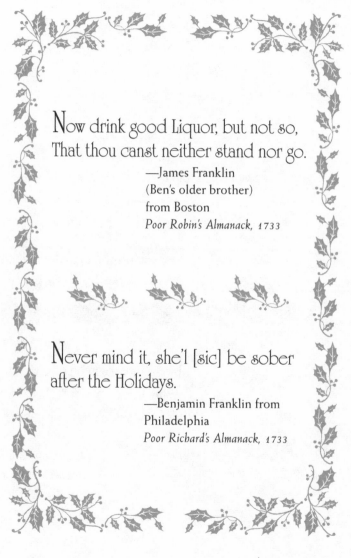

Now drink good Liquor, but not so,
That thou canst neither stand nor go.
—James Franklin
(Ben's older brother)
from Boston
Poor Robin's Almanack, 1733

Never mind it, she'l [sic] be sober
after the Holidays.
—Benjamin Franklin from
Philadelphia
Poor Richard's Almanack, 1733

O blessed Season! Lov'd by Saints
    and Sinners,
For long Devotions, or for longer Dinners.

—Benjamin Franklin
Poor Richard's Almanack, 1739

How many observe Christ's Birth-day! How few, his Precepts! O! 'tis easier to keep Holidays than Commandments.

—Benjamin Franklin
Poor Richard's Almanack, 1743

1747

All Decorated With Candles

*Moravian Brethren from Central Europe
brought their old-country Christmas "pyramids"
(four-sided frame structures) to frontier Pennsylvania,
as recorded in 1747 Bethlehem church records.*

For this occasion several small pyramids and one large pyramid of green brushwood had been prepared, all decorated with candles and the large one with apples and pretty verses.[4]

In Christmas feasting pray take care,
Let not your table be a Snare,
But with the Poor God's
  Bounty share.

—Benjamin Franklin
Poor Richard Improved, 1748

This is a Time for Joy and Mirth
When we consider our Saviour's Birth.

—Nathanael Ames in Boston
An Almanack for... 1760

1764

He Hopes You'll Not His Hopes Destroy

The Boston Evening Post *printed
this poem in 1764 to urge subscribers to tip their
newsboys at Christmas.*

The Boy who Weekly Pads the Streets,
With all the freshest News he meets,
His Mistresses and Masters greets.
Christmas and New-Year, Days of Joy,
The Harvest of your Carrier Boy,
He hopes you'll not his Hopes destroy. . . .
His generous Patrons may inspire,
By filling up his Pockets higher! [5]

1765

Drank Tea at Grandfather Quincy's

John Adams, who was 30 years old and the
newly appointed city counsel for Boston, spent a peaceful Christmas day
with his in-laws, his wife Abigail, and his baby daughter.
That night, he wrote in his diary about possible future
violence and rebellion in the colony.

ecr. 25th. 1765. Christmas.

At Home. Thinking, reading, searching, concerning Taxation without Consent, concerning the great Pause and Rest in Business. By the Laws of England Justice flows, with an uninterupted Stream: In that Musick, the Law knows of neither Rests nor Pauses. Nothing but Violence, Invasion or Rebellion can obstruct the River or untune the Instrument. . . .

Went not to Christmas. Dined at Home. Drank Tea at Grandfather Quincys. The old Gentleman, inquisitive about the Hearing before the Governor and Council . . . and about the final Determination of the Board. The old Lady as merry and chatty as ever, with her Stories out of the News Papers. . . .

Spent the Evening at Home, with my Partner and no other Company.[6]

1769

Fortune Changed the Scene

*Frontiersman Daniel Boone told his life story to Gilbert Imlay, who
dressed up Boone's language, but stuck to the facts. For example, this
excerpt from Imlay's book described a very unmerry Christmas week that
Boone spent among the Indians in the Kentucky wilderness.*

22nd day of December . . . This day John Stewart and I had a pleasing ramble, but
fortune changed the scene in the close of it. . . . —In the decline of the day, near
Kentucky river, as we ascended the brow of a small hill, a number of Indians rushed out
of a thick cane-brake upon us, and made us prisoners. The time of our sorrow was now
arrived, and the scene fully opened. The Indians plundered us of what we had, and kept
us in confinement 7 days, treating us with common savage usage. During this time we
discovered no uneasiness or desire to escape, which made them less suspicious of us; but
in the dead of the night, as we lay in a thick cane-brake by a large fire, when sleep had
locked up their senses, my situation not disposing me for rest, I touched my companion,
and gently awoke him. We improved this favourable opportunity, and departed, leaving
them to take their rest, and speedily directed our course towards our old camp.[7]

1769

The Good Sauce of Hunger

*On the Pacific coast, England and Russia challenged Spain's hold
on upper California. In 1769, Spain sent "Holy Expeditions" of soldiers, settlers,
and missionaries from Mexico to forge a chain of California missions.
In his role as the expedition diarist for the party traveling with
Captain Gaspar de Portolá, Franciscan priest Juan Crespi,
wrote of his first Christmas in California, near present-day Ventura.*

ore than two hundred heathen of both sexes came to visit us in this place, bringing us Christmas gifts, for many of them came with baskets of pinole [ground, leached acorn meal] and some fish, with which everybody supplied himself, so that we had something with which to celebrate Christmas Day. Blessed be the providence of God, who succors us more than we deserve! Their gifts were returned with beads, which greatly pleased them.

The cold is so biting that it gives us good reason to meditate upon what the Infant Jesus, who was this day born in Bethlehem, suffered for us. We made three leagues and a half, and went to stop a little farther to the south of the estuary of Santa Serafinia close to a small village of Indian fishermen, from whom a great deal of fish was obtained, in exchange for beads, with which all provided themselves. So we celebrated Christmas with this dainty, which tasted better to everybody than capons and chickens had tasted in other lands, because of the good sauce of . . . hunger which all had in abundance. And there was not lacking a Christmas gift of good baskets of pinole and atole [ground-up seeds].[8]

Christmas is come, hang on the Pot,
Let Spits turn round, and Ovens be hot;
Beef, Pork, and Poultry, to provide
To feast thy Neighbours at this Tide;
Then, wash all down with good Wine and Beer
And so with Mirth conclude the Year.
                    —*Virginia Almanack, 1765*

Now Christmas comes, 'tis fit that we
Should feast and sing, and merry be.
Keep open House, let Fiddlers play
A Fig for Cold, sing Care away.
And may they who thereat repine
On brown Bread and on small Beer dine.
                    —*Virginia Almanack, 1766*

We wish you health and good fires; drink, and
Good stomachs; innocent diversion, and good company;
Honest trading, and good success; loving courtship, and
Good wives; and lastly, a merry CHRISTMAS and a
Happy New Year.
                    —*Virginia Almanack, 1771*

1773

Never Learn'd to Dance

*In 1773, Philip Vickers Fithian, Princeton graduate and aspiring
Presbyterian minister, went South to tutor the eight children of
Mr. and Mrs. Robert Carter III. He lived with the family in Nomini Hall, a
mansion overlooking the Potomac and Nomini rivers. In these letters and selections
from his journal, the young teacher from New Jersey described his
enjoyment of Christmas on the Virginia tidewater plantation, but also showed how
much he missed his sweetheart, Laura, back home.*

From his journal:

Saturday 18 December: . . . Nothing is now to be heard of in conversation,
but the *Balls*, the *Fox-hunts*, the fine *entertainments*, and the *good fellowship*, which
are to be exhibited at the approaching *Christmas.*— . . . Mr. Goodlet was barr'd
out of his School last Monday by his Scholars, for the Christmas Holidays,
which are to continue til twelfth-day; But my Scholars are of a more quiet nature, and have consented to have four or five Days now, and to have their full

Holiday in May next, when I propose by the permission of Providence to go Home, where I hope to see the good and benevolent *Laura* . . .

From a letter to Laura:

Nominy-Hall Virginia. Decem: 21.1773.
. . . Laura, . . . tho, we have fine Ladies; Gay Fellows, charming Music; rich & I may say luxurious Entertainment; to all which I am almost every Week strongly invited; Yet I find greater Pleasure at Home, where I have every genteel Accomodation I could wish. . . . every one is now speaking of the approaching Christmas.—The young Ladies tell me we are to have a Ball, of selected Friends in this Family—But I, hard Lot, I have never learn'd to dance!

I am, however, . . . thine
Phi: V. Fithian.

As Christmas dawned at Nomini Hall,
Fithian poured out all his spare change for holiday tips,
which he described in this excerpt from his journal.

Saturday 25. I was waked this morning by Guns fired all round the House. The morning is stormy, the wind at South East rains hard Nelson the Boy who makes my Fire, blacks my shoes, does errands &c. was early in my Room, drest only in his shirt and Breeches! He made me a vast fire, blacked my Shoes, set my Room in order, and wish'd me a joyful Christmas, for which I gave him half a Bit.—Soon after he left the Room, and before I was Drest, the Fellow who makes the Fire in our School Room, drest very neatly in green, but almost drunk, entered my chamber with three or four profound Bows, & made me the same salutation; I gave him a *Bit*, and dismissed him as soon as possible.—Soon after my Cloths and Linen were sent in with a message for a Christmas *Box*, as they call it; I sent the poor Slave a Bit, & my thanks.—I was obliged for want of small change, to put off for some days the Barber who shaves & dresses me.—I gave *Tom* the Coachman, who Doctors my Horse, for his care two Bits, & am to give more when the Horse is well.—I gave to *Dennis* the Boy who waits at Table half a *Bit*—So that the sum of my Donations to the Servants, for this Christmas appears to be five Bits, . . .

Our Dinner was no otherwise than common, yet as elegant a *Christmas Dinner* as I ever sat Down to.[9]

Fithian returned home, was ordained, and married his sweetheart.
All too soon, he rode off with General Washington's Continental Army
and died in camp from sickness and exposure.

1776

"Battle of Trenton"
Author Unknown

On Christmas day in seventy-six
Our ragged troops with bayonets fixed
　　For Trenton marched away.
The Delaware see! the boats below!
The light obscured by hail and snow!
　　But no signs of dismay.

Our object was the Hessian band
That dared invade fair freedom's land
　　And quarter in that place.
Great Washington he led us on,
Whose streaming flag, in storm or sun,
　　Had never known disgrace.

In silent march we passed the night,
Each soldier panting for the fight,
　　Though quite benumbed with frost.
Greene, on the left, at six began.
The right was led by Sullivan,
　　Who ne'er a moment lost.

Their pickets stormed, the alarm was spread
That rebels risen from the dead
　　Were marching into town.
Some scampered here, some scampered there,
And some for action did prepare,
　　But soon their arms laid down.

Twelve hundred servile miscreants,
With all their colors, guns and tents,
　　Were trophies of the day.
The frolic o'er, the bright canteen
In centre, front and rear was seen
　　Driving fatigue away.

Now, brothers of the patriot bands,
Let's sing deliverance from the hands
　　Of arbitrary sway.
And as our life is but a span,
Let's touch the tankard while we can,
　　In memory of that day. [10]

1776

Our Attempt on Trenton

*General Washington's Continental Army was at low ebb as the second
wartime Christmas approached. In a report to the commander of the Hessian garrison
at Trenton, New Jersey, on December 21, one British general described Washington's soldiers,
who were camped on the Pennsylvania side of the ice-clogged Delaware River, as "almost
naked, dying of cold, without blankets, and very ill supplied with provisions."
The next two entries describe how Washington's troops spent this particular Christmas.*

23 December 1776, General George Washington to Colonel Joseph Reed—

The bearer is sent down . . . to inform you, that Christmas-day at night, one hour before day is the time fixed upon for our attempt on Trenton. For Heaven's sake keep this to yourself, as the discovery of it may prove fatal to us, our numbers, sorry am I to say, being less than I had any conception of: but necessity, dire necessity, will, nay must, justify an attempt. . . .

> I am, dear Sir, Your obedient servant
> Geo. Washington [11]

Elisha Bostwick, Seventh Connecticut Regiment—

[Our] army passed through Bethleham and Moravian town and so on to the Delaware which we crossed 9 miles north of Trenton and encamped on the Pennsylvania side and there remain to the 24ᵗʰ December. [O]ur whole army was then set on motion and toward evining began to recross the Delaware but by obstructions of ice in the river did not all get across till quite late in the evening, and all the time a constant fall of snow with some rain, and finally our march began with the torches of our field pieces stuck in the exhalters. [They] sparkled and blazed in the storm all night and about day light a halt was made, at which time his Excellency and aids came near to front on the side of the path where the soldiers stood.

I heard his Excellency as he was comeing on speaking to and encourageing the soldiers. The words he spoke as he passed by where I stood and in my hearing were these:

"Soldiers, keep by your officers. For God's sake, keep by your officers!" Spoke in a deep and solemn voice.

While passing a slanting, slippery bank his Excellencys horse's hind feet both slipped from under him, and he seized his horse's mane and the horse recovered. Our horses were then unharnessed and the artillery men prepared. We marched on and it was not long before we heard the out centries of the enemy both on the road we were in and the eastern road, and their out gards retreated fireing, and our army, then with a quick step pushing on upon both roads, at the same time entered the town. Their artillery taken, they resigned with little opposition, about nine hundred all Hessians, with 4 brass field pieces; . . .

When crossing the Delaware with the prisoners in flat bottom boats the ice continually stuck to the boats, driving them down stream; the boatmen endevering to clear off the ice pounded the boat, and stamping with their feet, beconed to the prisoners to do the same, and they all set to jumping at once with their cues* flying up and down, soon shook off the ice from the boats. [*Bostwick said the Hessians wore their hair "cued as tight to the head as possible, sticking straight back like the handle of an iron skillet."][12]

1777

Fire Cake and Water

*A few days before Christmas 1777, General Washington
and his Continental Army retreated from Germantown, Pennsylvania,
and straggled into Valley Forge, where they began setting up winter
encampment. "To go into the wild woods . . . in such a weak, starved and naked
condition was appaling, . . ." said one soldier. Army surgeon Albigence Waldo of the
Connecticut Line, voiced the following complaints in his diary.*

Dec. 21—Preparations made for hutts. Provisions Scarce . . . Heartily wish myself at home, my Skin and eyes are almost spoil'd with continual smoke. A general cry thro' the Camp this Evening among the Soldiers, "No Meat! No Meat!" . . .

What have you for your Dinners Boys? "Nothing but Fire Cake & Water, Sir." At night, "Gentlemen the Supper is ready." What is your Supper Lads? "Fire Cake & Water, Sir."

Dec. 22—Lay excessive Cold & uncomfortable last Night—my eyes are started out from their Orbits like a Rabbit's eyes, occasion'd by a great Cold & Smoke.

What have you got for Breakfast, Lads? "Fire Cake & Water, Sir." The Lord send that our Commissary of Purchases may live on Fire Cake & Water, 'till their glutted Gutts are turned to Pasteboard.[13]

On December 23, General Washington begged the President of Congress for help.

I am now convinced, beyond a doubt that unless some great and capital change suddenly takes place in [the Commissary department] this Army must inevitably be reduced to one or other of these three things. Starve, dissolve, or disperse, in order to obtain subsistence in the best manner they can; rest assured Sir this is not an exaggerated picture. . . .

What then is to become of the Army this Winter?

I can assure those Gentlemen that it is a much easier and less distressing thing to draw remonstrances in a comfortable room by a good fire side than to occupy a cold bleak hill and sleep under frost and Snow without Cloaths or Blankets; however, although they seem to have little feeling for the naked, and distressed Soldier, I feel superabundantly for them, and from my Soul pity those miseries, wch. It is neither in my power to relieve or prevent.[14]

From Dr. Waldo's diary, again:

December 24.— . . . Hutts go on Slowly—Cold & Smoke make us fret. . . . I don't know of any thing that vexes a man's Soul more than hot smoke continually blowing into his Eyes, & when he attempts to avoid it, is met by a cold and piercing Wind.

December 25, Christmas.—We are still in Tents—when we ought to be in huts— the poor Sick, suffer much in Tents this cold Weather.[15]

1797
Great Cake and Eggnog for Christmas

In 1797, President Washington refused a third term,
bade farewell to public service, and returned to Mount Vernon
in time for Christmas. Martha Washington's "Great Cake" was the type of
dessert traditionally served on Epiphany (January 6), the last of the twelve days
of Christmas. January 6 was also the Washingtons' wedding anniversary.
This original "receipt" was copied down by Mrs. Washington's granddaughter.

Martha Washington's Great Cake

Take 40 eggs & divide the whites from the youlks & beat them
to a froth then work 4 pounds of butter to a cream & put the whites of
eggs to it a Spoon full at a time till it is well work'd. Then put 4 pounds
sugar finely powder'd to it in the same manner then put in the Youlks of
eggs & 5 pounds of flower & five pounds of fruit. 2 hours will bake it
add to it half an ounce of mace, one nutmeg, half a pint of wine & some
frensh brandy. [16]

Although no authentic recipe exists for
George Washington's eggnog, this robust concoction, often attributed to him,
is worthy of a Virginia-born president's Christmas toast.

Virginia Eggnog

1 quart cream
1 pint brandy
1 quart milk
½ pint rye whiskey
1 dozen eggs
¼ pint sherry
1 dozen tablespoons sugar
¼ pint Jamaica or New England rum

Combine the liquors, then separate the eggs into yolks and whites. To the yolks, when beaten, add the sugar and mix. To this slowly add the combined liquors, very lightly while you beat very slowly. Then add the milk and cream, again working slowly. Beat the egg whites until they are stiff and fold into the mixture, then set for several days in a cool place until ready to serve.

1800~1850

c. 1800

The Orphan Found Kind Friends

Bethlehem Female Seminary, founded by Moravians in Pennsylvania,
was the first and most distinguished female boarding school in the country.
During his second term, President Washington enrolled two of his nieces there.
A New York schoolgirl, who attended the seminary about that time,
described Christmas in Old House, where the younger girls lived.

or a month before Christmas, we commenced saving our pocket-money; a dollar a month was the allowance. Happy they were whose friends remembered them in time to send a remittance. . . . On the morning of Christmas-eve, we of the younger rooms were gathered round the closet in the wall, wherein were deposited our little money-boxes, to receive a portion of their contents. Away we flew to the "Sisters' House," to make our purchases. A dollar went a great way in those days. Behold us returning across the corner of the green, hands and aprons full!

Let me see what you have there? Gingerbread, wafers, doughnuts, a bunch of small wax candles, exquisitely moulded wax figures of a cat, deer, sheep, and *apropos* to the

time, a cradle with its little occupant imbedded in moss; bundles of candy, dried fruits, and branches of fragrant box! We gather round dear Sister Caroline Shubb, and to her confide our treasures.

Out into the play-ground we hasten, our comfortable and spacious room is too circumscribed in limit for the exuberance of our spirits, a game at snow-balls, and then, with or without gloves, no mittens, we Philadelphians and New Yorkers begin to build snow cities in different corners of the yard. Drawing a circle we pile up a wall, in the centre a mound, on which we plant a flag, round this we rally, and then, as boys say at marbles, the "hardest fend off." Incessantly fly the balls, until one or the other fort is destroyed, the victors proclaiming their city preeminent in every excellence. With glowing cheeks and stinging hands we assemble at the sound of the dinner-bell, in procession the three rooms move on to the refectory, the youngest in each room leading. Silently we stand in our places, on either side of the three tables, a word is spoken, and a handful [of] youthful voices chant forth praise to the Giver of all Good, and implore his blessing on their food. The meal is taken in silence; in order we move back to our rooms, to prepare for the evening service in church.

In the next excerpt, the young student described the
activities on Christmas Day at the Bethlehem Female Seminary.

At the earliest dawn, the morning-bell roused us. . . . Descending, . . . we stood in the dim twilight on either side of the closed door; at a given signal, the Christmas Hymn arose, triumphantly proclaiming "Glory to God in the highest, and on earth peace and good will to men." The door is opened, our eyes are dazzled with sudden brilliancy. Hundreds of wax-tapers, arranged in lines of light, mark out the portion of the long table allotted to each girl—within these bright enclosures our purchases of the previous day are fancifully displayed. Beneath the tiny box-tree reposes, on a diminutive bed of moss, the speckled deer; in an opposite corner, a little, old-fashioned shepherd tends his

 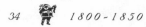

patient flock; a portly Dutch doll watches over the safety of the Lilliputian cradle. Bundles of tapers are in readiness to continue the illumination through the day; for, until the appearance of to-morrow's sun, our shutters remained unopened. Walls of gingerbread impart a substantial look to each little domain, while raisins, almonds, sugerplums, and an endless variety of cake, promise full employment to every happy proprietor. Our kindhearted sisters have decorated the walls with wreaths of evergreen and bright win-ter-berries. The delicious Christmas breakfast, who can forget the triangular piece of Moravian suger-cake, a feast for an epicure.

Happy days! happy days! The orphan found kind friends in the dear Old House—where are ye now? [1]

Below is a recipe for Moravian sugar cake, which is a traditional pastry, popular at Christmastime. This particular recipe appeared in The Moravian *newspaper on April 30, 1863.*

Moravian Sugar Cake

To gratify one of our lady subscribers, and in compliance with other re-peated solicitations, we furnish herewith a recipe for making the genuine home-made sugar cake which we have taken down from the lips of several experi-enced housekeepers.

Recipe: Of well-risen wheaten bread dough take about two pounds. Work into it a tea-cupful of brown sugar, quarter of a pound of butter and a beaten egg. Knead well and put into a square pan dredged with flour. Cover it and set it near the fire for half an hour to rise. When risen, wash with melted butter, make holes in the dough to half its depth, two inches apart, fill them with sugar and a little butter. Then spread ground cinnamon and a thick layer of brown sugar over the whole surface. Sprinkle with a little essence of lemon. Put into the oven and bake in fifteen minutes.[2]

1804

I Had to Thank the Indians

*By 1804, Daniel Boone's family had moved to Missouri.
Nathan Boone, Daniel's tenth and youngest child, was twenty-four years old
and a chip off the old block. In a later interview with historian Lyman Draper,
Nathan described his adventures leading to his return home for Christmas.*

In 1804 Matthias Van Bibber [Nathan's brother-in-law] and I started on a winter's hunt, aiming to go to the Kansas [River]. I had caught fifty-six beavers and twelve otters when a party of twenty-two Osage Indians came to our camp one day. They took our three horses and what furs we had and told us we had better clear out, as there was another party hunting for us, and then they departed. . . .

As soon as the Indians were out of sight over a ridge, Van Bibber and I struck off at a run and kept running till after dark. We had only five bullets between us. . . . We had

lost our blankets and coats, which were on the horses the Indians took, but we felt it wiser not to try to recover them. We were now in shirtsleeves. The next morning we shot a turkey.

Soon snow began to fall. We traveled two days and struck the Missouri River. We managed to cross on the ice and continued on down. It snowed for two or three days and became knee-deep. We shot away our remaining four balls but killed nothing, as our guns seemed to be affected by the cold weather. . . . We finally came to an old Indian camp and found where the Indians had shot at a mark. We cut enough lead out of the tree to make four balls. Two or three miles further we came to some old Indian cabins, which were perhaps half a mile below where Rocheport now stands. It was getting on towards night, so we decided to go into one of the cabins, make a fire, and stay till morning. . . .

On entering the Indian cabin, I was in the lead and spied a huge panther lying on his belly, some ten feet distant. I shot and killed it, skinned it, and roasted it on stick spits. The animal had a sweet and cattish taste. I cut the skin into two pieces, and we each made a vest, cutting holes for inserting our arms and wearing the fur side next to our bodies. We fastened our fur vests with strings, and though our arms were still exposed, they added vastly to our comfort. We were now greatly revived, and hoppusing up [tying onto our backs] the balance of our meat, the next morning we started again. We had only traveled three or four miles when we discovered a person's tracks in the snow. We decided to follow them to their camp, regardless of whether they were white or Indian.

In a mile and a half we came to the weather-bound camp of a party of white hunters consisting of my nephew, James Callaway, and three or four other friends. . . . This was a time of inexpressible joy for the two hapless wanderers. We had, from time to time, as our moccasins were worn through by the frozen snow and ice, cut off a sufficiency of the lower part of our deerskin leggings for patch-leather—until finally our leggings were nearly gone and our legs entirely exposed to the severity of the weather. At this camp we obtained good buffalo and deer meat, clothing, blankets, and ammunition from this group. We recruited for a week with them, then resumed our hundred-mile journey home. . . . I reached home on December 24 and spent Christmas with my family and parents.

Olive Boone (Nathan's wife) added: It was the first Christmas he [Nathan] had spent at home since our marriage, and I had to thank the Indians for that.[3]

A year after Nathan's ordeal, Daniel Boone himself, age 71, accompanied his son and a friend on a winter hunt, during which Daniel slipped and plunged up to his neck into the icy Missouri River. They thawed him out and carried him home for Christmas on a litter slung between two horses.

1804

Firing, Dancing, & Frolicking

The Corps of Discovery, led by Meriwether Lewis and William Clark, shoved off on their mission to explore the uncharted West from the mouth of the Missouri in May 1804. By winter, they had reached Dakota Territory, where they raised the American flag (which consisted of 15 stars and 15 stripes at this time) and celebrated Christmas. The three accounts below are entries from journals kept by members of the expedition.

Fort Mandan, 1804—

December 24: Some snow fell this morning; about 10 it cleared up, and the weather became pleasant. This evening we finished our fortification. Flour, dried apples, pepper and other articles were distributed in the different messes to enable them to celebrate Christmas in a proper and social manner.

—Sergeant Patrick Gass

25th December: We ushred [in] the morning with a discharge of the Swivvel [keelboat cannon], and one round of Small arms of all the party, then another from the Swivel. then Capt. Clark presented a glass of brandy to each man of the party. we hoisted the american flag, and each man had another Glass of brandy. the men prepared one of the rooms and commenced dancing. at 10 oC we had another Glass of brandy, at one a gun was fired as a Signal for diner. half past two another gun was fired to assemble at the dance, and So we kept it up in a jovel manner untill eight oC. at night, all without the compy. of the female Seck, except three Squaws the Intreptirs wives and they took no part with us only to look on.

—Private Joseph Whitehouse

December 25: . . . we had the Best to eat that could be had, & continued firing dancing & frolicking dureing the whole day. the Savages did not Trouble us as we had requested them not to come as it was a Great medician day with us. we enjoyed a merry cristmas dureing the day & eveing untill nine oClock—all in peace & quietness.

—Sergeant John Ordway[4]

1805

Still Keep in Good Spirits

*By 1805, Lewis and Clark's Corps of Discovery had trekked
over the Rockies and reached the Pacific coast, crossing a territory
that would be called the Oregon Territory. This area would eventually
be divided into ten states. On December 24, they roofed their winter
huts and moved in for Christmas. The next two journal selections
described how the group spent their Christmas.*

ort Clatsop, 1805—

25th December: At day light this morning we we[re] awoke by the discharge of the fire arm[s] of all our party & a Selute, Shouts and a Song which the whole party joined in under our windows, after which they retired to their rooms were chearfull all the morning. after brackfast we divided our Tobacco which amounted to 12 carrots one half of which we gave to the men of the party who used tobacco, and to those who doe not use it we make a present of a handkerchief. the Indians left us in the evening. all the party Snugly fixed in their huts. I recved a presnt of Capt. L. of a fleece hosrie Shirt Draw and Socks, a pr. Mockersons of Whitehouse a Small Indian basket of Gutherich, two Dozen white weazils tails of the Indian woman, & some black root of the Indians before their departure. . . . The day proved Showerey wet and disagreeable. we would have Spent this day the nativity of Christ in feasting, had we anything either to raise our Sperits or even gratify our appetites, our Diner concisted of pore Elk, so much Spoiled that we eate it thro' mear necessity, Some Spoiled pounded fish and a fiew roots.

—Captain William Clark

 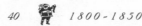

25 December: rainy and wet. disagreeable weather. we all moved in to our new Fort, which our officers name Fort Clatsop after the name of the Clatsop nation of Indians who live nearest to us. . . . we have no ardent Spirits, but are all in good health which we esteem more than all the ardent Spirits in the world. we have nothing to eat but poor Elk meat and no Salt to Season that with, but Still keep in good Spirits as we expect this to be the last winter that we have to pass in this way.

—Sergeant John Ordway [5]

1805

We Were Sorely Disappointed

*Charles Ball, born into slavery in Maryland, was separated
from his wife and sold to a South Carolina cotton plantation
owner. In 1836, Ball published a narrative about his days as a slave.
In it, he described how the plantation overseer used King Cotton
as a good excuse to cancel Christmas in 1805.*

The richest and best part of the crop has been secured . . . but large quantities of cotton still remain in the field, and every pound that can be saved from the winds, or the plough of the next spring, is a gain of its value, to the owner of the estate. For these reasons, which are very powerful on the side of the master, there is but little Christmas on a large cotton plantation. In lieu of the week of holiday, which formerly prevailed even in Carolina, before cotton was cultivated as a crop, the master now gives the people a dinner of meat, on Christmas-day, and distributes among them their annual allowance of winter clothes. . . . As Christmas of the year 1805 approached, we were all big with hope of obtaining three of four days, at least, if not a week of holliday; but when the day at length arrived, we were sorely disappointed, for on Christmas eve, when we had come from the field with our cotton, the overseer fell into a furious passion, and swore at us all for our laziness, and many other bad qualities. He then told us that he had intended to give us three days, if we had worked well, but that we had been so idle, and had left so much cotton yet to be picked in the field, that he found it impossible to give us more than one day; but that he would go to the house, and endeavor to procure a meat dinner for us, and a dram in the morning. . . . We went to work as usual the next morning, and continued our labor through the week, as if Christmas had been stricken from the calendar.[6]

*In 1809, Ball escaped from the plantation in South Carolina and made his way
back to Maryland. He lived there as a fugitive for twenty-one precarious years.
He was recaptured and returned South. Again he escaped, and at last
found safety in the free state of Pennsylvania.*

1814
Treaty of Peace, Signed and Sealed

*Beginning in August 1814, John Quincy Adams was in Ghent,
Belgium, negotiating an end to the War of 1812 between
England and the United States. In his Memoirs, Adams noted that on the
day before Christmas, negotiators from both sides reached agreement
on "a firm and universal Peace" between His Britannic Majesty
and the United States.*

*D*ecember 24th. . . A few mistakes in the copies were rectified, and then the six copies were signed and sealed by the three British and the five American Plenipotentia-

 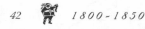

ries. Lord Gambier delivered to me the three American copies of the treaty, which he said he hoped would be permanent; and I told him I hoped it would be the last treaty of peace between Great Britain and the United States. . . .

25th. Christmas-day. The day of all others in the year most congenial to proclaiming peace on earth and good will to men.[7]

1821

At the Foot of the Rocky Mountains

In 1832, fur trader Ross Cox published a book about his six adventurous years roaming the wild territory west of the Rocky Mountains. As this excerpt shows, at Christmas even the most intrepid wanderer dreamt of home and Christmases past.

 thought of my preceding Christmas off Cape Horn, and was puzzled to decide which was the most enviable—a tempestuous storm in the high southern latitude, after losing a couple of men—or a half-inundated island, without fire, at the foot of the rocky mountains covered with sheets of snow. In my slumbers, I imagined I was sitting at my father's table surrounded by the smiling domestic group, all anxious to partake of a smoking sirloin, and a richly dotted plumb-pudding, while the juvenile members recounted to each other with triumphant joy the amount of their Christmas boxes; but alas! "Sorrow returned with the dawning of morn, And the voice in my dreaming ear melted away!"[8]

1822

'Twas the Night Before Christmas

*On Christmas Eve 1822, Clement C. Moore
(Professor of Oriental and Greek Literature, as well as Divinity and Biblical Learning,
at the Theological Seminary of the Protestant Episcopal Church in New York City)
delighted his family when he read aloud the new poem
he had written for his children.*

A Visit From St. Nicholas

Twas the night before Christmas, when all through the house
Not a creature was stirring, not even a mouse;
The stockings were hung by the chimney with care,
In hopes that St. Nicholas soon would be there;
The children were nestled all snug in their beds,
While visions of sugar-plums danced in their heads;
And Mamma in her 'kerchief, and I in my cap,
Had just settled our brains for a long winter's nap;
When out on the lawn there arose such a clatter,
I sprang from the bed to see what was the matter.
Away to the window I flew like a flash,
Tore open the shutters and threw up the sash.

A Visit From Saint Nicholas, *Harper's New Monthly Magazine*, December 1857

The moon on the breast of the new-fallen snow,
Gave the lustre of mid-day to objects below,
When, what to my wondering eyes should appear,
But a miniature sleigh, and eight tiny rein-deer,
With a little old driver, so lively and quick,
I knew in a moment it must be St. Nick.
More rapid than eagles his coursers they came,

And he whistled, and shouted, and called them by name:
"Now, *Dasher!* now, *Dancer!* now, *Prancer!* and *Vixen!*
On, *Comet!* on, *Cupid!* on, *Donder* and *Blitzen!*
To the top of the porch! to the top of the wall!
Now dash away! dash away! dash away all!"
As dry leaves that before the wild hurricane fly,
When they meet with an obstacle, mount to the sky;
So up to the house-top the coursers they flew,
With the sleigh full of toys, and St. Nicholas too.
And then, in a twinkling, I heard on the roof,
The prancing and pawing of each little hoof—
As I drew in my head, and was turning around,
Down the chimney St. Nicholas came with a bound.
He was dressed all in fur from his head to his foot,
And his clothes were all tarnished with ashes and soot

A bundle of toys he had flung on his back,
And he looked like a peddler just opening his pack.
His eyes—how they twinkled! his dimples how merry!
His cheeks were like roses, his nose like a cherry!
His droll little mouth was drawn up like a bow,
And the beard of his chin was as white as the snow;
The stump of a pipe he held tight in his teeth,
And the smoke it encircled his head like a wreath;
He had a broad face and a little round belly,
That shook, when he laughed, like a bowlful of jelly.
He was chubby and plump, a right jolly old elf,

 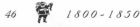

And I laughed when I saw him, in spite of myself;
A wink of his eye and a twist of his head,
Soon gave me to know I had nothing to dread;
He spoke not a word, but went straight to his work,
And filled all the stockings; then turned with a jerk,
And laying his finger aside of his nose,
And giving a nod, up the chimney he rose;
He sprang to his sleigh, to his team gave a whistle,
And away they all flew like the down of a thistle.
But I heard him exclaim, ere he drove out of sight,
"Happy Christmas to all, and to all a good-night!" [9]

1823

Parisian Styles and Buckskin Coats

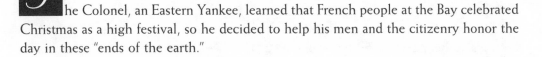

*In 1823, United States Army Colonel John McNeil commanded Fort Howard,
on the frontier at Green Bay, Wisconsin. A friend,
General Albert G. Ellis, later recorded his recollections of a gala Christmas ball
hosted by McNeil at this "outpost of the Western wild."*

The Colonel, an Eastern Yankee, learned that French people at the Bay celebrated
Christmas as a high festival, so he decided to help his men and the citizenry honor the
day in these "ends of the earth."

He sent formal invitations for dinner and a ball to everyone. Food was prepared for one hundred guests, and on December 25, 1823, a big hall at the fort was filled with French, Indians, and Americans sharing holiday greetings.

Clothing ran from the latest Parisian styles to buckskin coats, pants, petticoats, and moccasins.

None of the elite considered himself over-dressed nor none of the citizens . . . reproached himself with the least want of etiquette, or of intended disrespect to their host, on account of costume or manner.

The dinner equalled one expected in a more civilized setting in quantity if not in kind. Venison, bear meat, porcupine, geese, ducks, and many fish headed by that kind of all the fish tribe, the sturgeon, were offered for the main course. Dinner, dancing, and revelry lasted . . . throughout Christmas night.

Thus did this big-hearted man of war delight to transform this outpost of the Western wild, hitherto in its winters especially a place of desolation, solitude, ennui, and almost despair, to one of unalloyed happiness, animated life, and real pleasure.[10]

1823

Christmas-Tide on Mackinac

In her memoir, Contes Du Temps Passe,
*Therese Fisher Baird told of French-American Christmases
on Mackinac Island, Michigan.*

 was particularly fond of the Island of Mackinac in winter with its ice-bound shore. . . . Mackinac, or Michilimackinac, (the name used when there was more time in the world than there is today—it means "great turtle") was the fur trade center of the West. . . .

Since the Catholic faith prevailed, it followed as a matter of course that the special holidays of the church were always observed. They were celebrated in one's own home, often with some friends and neighbors participating. Some weeks before Christmas, for instance, the dwellers on the island met in turn at each other's homes and read prayers, chanted psalms, and unfailingly repeated the litany of the Saints. On Christmas Eve both sexes would read and sing, the service lasting until midnight. After this a midnight treat would be partaken of by all.

The last meeting of this sort that I attended on the island was at our own home in 1823. This affair was considered the occasion for the high feast of the season, and no pains were spared to make the meal as good as the island afforded. The cooking was done at an open fire. I wish that I could recall the bill of fare in full. We will begin with the roast pig; then followed roast goose, chicken pie, and round of beef a la mode; pattes d'ours—bear's paws, so-called from their shape, and made of chopped meat baked in a crust; sausage; head-cheese; souse; small fruit preserves; many small cakes. Such was the array. No one was expected to partake of each dish, unless he so chose.

Christmas, itself, was observed as a holy-day. The children were kept at home and from play until nearly night-time, when they were permitted to run out and bid their friends a "Merry Christmas". The evening was spent at home. . . .

As soon as la fête de Noel, or Christmas-tide, had passed, all the young people were set to work to prepare for New Year's. Christmas was not the day set to give or to receive presents; this was reserved for New Year's.[11]

1828

Cast-Off Dresses

*While visiting New Orleans on Christmas Day 1828,
Mrs. Mary S. Helm from New York marveled to see highly
stylish slaves enjoying Fête de Noel festivities.*

I never at one time had seen so many nice dresses, and was told they were the cast-off dresses of their owners of the previous year, and that quite a rivalry existed as to whose slaves should be best dressed during the Christmas holidays. The men equaled, if they did not excel the women, in their shining broadcloth and stovepipe hats, and as I listened to their pleasant salutations and jovial conversation, I changed my opinion in regard to the condition of the down-trodden slave. It all seemed like a fairy dream to me, being surrounded by this strange race in a country where all nature was clothed in summer attire—roses everywhere, with an endless variety of other flowers, and fruits brought from a tropical climate and seen now for the first time.[12]

1830

A Famous Christmas Tree

*The Dorcas Society of York, Pennsylvania, an association
of ladies formed "for the truly charitable purpose of clothing
the poor widow and the friendless orphan," exhibited what may have been
the first decorated Christmas tree ever seen on public display.
This advertisement for the society's money-raising Christmas fair
appeared in the* Republican and Anti-Masonic Expositor *on December 14, 1830.*

he Society has . . . made preparation for a FAIR, which will be held in the front room of the house lately occupied by Genl. Spangler.

We are particularly requested to invite our country friends, as the goods will be sold low, and comprise the greatest variety of fancy articles, as well as the exhibition of a famous CHRISTMAS TREE. The fair will be open day before Christmas, closed on Christmas day, and open in the evening, and from thence until the articles are disposed of. . . .

Tickets will be sold for 6¼ cents, which will admit the bearers to the 'Christmas Tree!' during the time it remains for exhibition.[13]

1832

One Doll's Petticoat Caught Fire

English writer Harriett Martineau helped to decorate
Boston's first Christmas tree while visiting her German-born
friend, Harvard professor Charles Follen. Her description of the
delightful result was published in a penny pamphlet distributed
by the American Sunday School Union of Boston.

My little friend Charley [Follen's son] and three companions had been long preparing for this pretty show. The cook had broken eggs carefully in the middle for some weeks past, that Charley might have the shells for cups; and these cups were gilded and coloured very prettily. We were all engaged in sticking on the last seven dozen of wax tapers, and in filling the gilded egg-cups and gay paper cornucopiae with comfits, lozenges, barley sugar. The tree was the top of a young fir, planted in a tub, which was ornamented with moss. Smart dolls and other whimsies glittered in the evergreen, and there was not a twig which had not something sparkling upon it.

It really looked beautiful; the room seemed in a blaze, and the ornaments were so well hung on that no accident happened, except that one doll's petticoat caught fire. There was a sponge tied to the end of a stick to put out any supernumerary blaze, and no harm ensued. I mounted the steps behind the tree to see the effect of opening the doors. It was delightful. The children poured in, but in a moment every voice was hushed. Their faces were upturned to the blaze, all eyes wide open, all lips parted, all steps arrested. Nobody spoke, only Charley leaped for joy. The first symptom of recovery was the children's wandering around the tree. At last, a quick pair of eyes discovered that it bore something eatable, and from that moment the babble began again. . . . I have little doubt the Christmas tree will become one of the most flourishing exotics of New England.[14]

 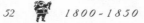

1833

The Streets Were Very Lively

When the German immigrant family of Gustave Körner
found no Christmas evergreens growing around their new home
in Belleville, Illinois, they made do with a sassafras tree. Körner,
who would later become a legislator and friend of Abraham Lincoln,
wrote of this occasion in his memoir.

 day or two before Christmas I went, on terribly bad roads and in a disagreeable drizzle of half snow and half rain, to St. Louis to buy a present for Sophie, and for myself, *Blackstone's Commentaries on the English Law*, a classic book, for which I paid five dollars.

On my return from St. Louis on the evening of the twenty-fourth, I passed through Belleville after dark. In spite of the mud in the streets they were very lively. The Americans celebrate Christmas in their own way. Young and old fired muskets, pistols and Chinese fire-crackers, which, with a very liberal consumption of egg-nog and tom-and-jerry, was the usual, and in fact, the only mode of hailing the arrival of the Christ-Child (Christ-Kindchen).

On Christmas day, 1833, we had a Christmas tree, of course. In our immediate neighborhood we had no evergreen trees or bushes. But Mr. Engelmann had taken the top of a young sassafras tree, which still had some leaves on it, had fixed it into a kind of pedestal, and the girls had dressed the tree with ribbons and bits of colored paper and the like, had put wax candles on the branches, and had hung it with little red apples and nuts and all sorts of confectionery, in the making of which Aunt Caroline was most proficient. Perhaps this was the first Christmas tree that was ever lighted on the banks of the Mississippi.[15]

1833

The Demon of Disorder

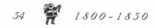

This report appeared in the Philadelphia Daily Chronicle *on December 26, 1833.*

Throughout almost the whole of Tuesday night—Christmas Eve—riot, noise, and uproar prevailed, uncontrolled and uninterrupted in many of our central and most orderly streets. Gangs of boys and young men howled and shouted as if possessed by the demon of disorder. Some of the watchmen occasionally sounded their rattles; but seemed only to add another ingredient to the horrible discord that murdered sleep. It is undoubtedly in the power of our city police to prevent slumbering citizens from being disturbed by the mad roars of such revelers.[16]

1 8 3 0 s

"Barring-Out"

*Earlier in this book, the schoolboy prank of
"barring-out" the teacher was described in a firsthand account from
Virginia, written in 1702. The excerpt below, from newspaper editor
Horace Greeley's* Recollections of a Busy Life, *showed that
the same mischief was still occurring in the 1830s
when he was a New Hampshire schoolboy.*

here was an unruly, frolicsome custom of "barring-out" in our New Hampshire common schools. . . . [On] the day that the big boys chose to consider or make a holiday, the forenoon passed off as quietly as that of any other day; but, the moment the master left the house in quest of his dinner, the little ones were started homeward, the door and windows suddenly and securely barricaded, and the older pupils, thus fortified against intrusion, proceeded to spend the afternoon in play and hilarity. I have known a master to make a desperate struggle for admission; but I do not recollect that one ever succeeded,—the odds being too great.[17]

c. 1830

The Blockade Was Complete

 *Professor Henry Harbaugh, who was a Pennsylvania schoolboy
in the 1830s, wrote this verse about a successful barring-out.*

Old Christmas brought a glorious time—
Its memory still is sweet!
We barred the Master firmly out,
With bolts, and nails, and timbers stout—
The blockade was complete.[18]

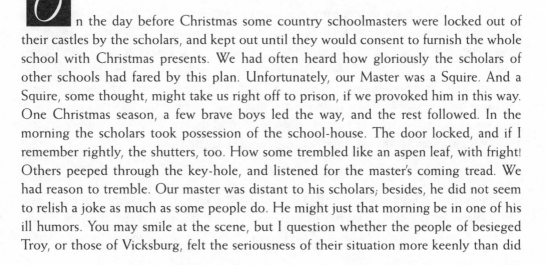

c. 1834

We Had Reason to Tremble

*Other Pennsylvania country schoolboys also dared
to try an old-time Christmas barring-out. Later in their lives,
two such students described two separate incidents, which resulted
in two entirely different outcomes.*

On the day before Christmas some country schoolmasters were locked out of their castles by the scholars, and kept out until they would consent to furnish the whole school with Christmas presents. We had often heard how gloriously the scholars of other schools had fared by this plan. Unfortunately, our Master was a Squire. And a Squire, some thought, might take us right off to prison, if we provoked him in this way. One Christmas season, a few brave boys led the way, and the rest followed. In the morning the scholars took possession of the school-house. The door locked, and if I remember rightly, the shutters, too. How some trembled like an aspen leaf, with fright! Others peeped through the key-hole, and listened for the master's coming tread. We had reason to tremble. Our master was distant to his scholars; besides, he did not seem to relish a joke as much as some people do. He might just that morning be in one of his ill humors. You may smile at the scene, but I question whether the people of besieged Troy, or those of Vicksburg, felt the seriousness of their situation more keenly than did that group of children in a besieged country school-house.

At length we heard his tread. "Hush," was whispered round. Silent as the grave, was the school, for once. Such order the master had perhaps never produced before. In vain he tried to open the barred door. He commanded us to open. To disobey his command usually brought a storm about our ears. Such an act of disobedience, refusing to let him enter his own school-house, was a daring feat. A paper was slipped out under the door, solemnly setting forth our demands—candies, cakes, nuts and the little nick-nacks that make up the ordinary Christmas presents of country children. It was a fearful suspense. . . . What could we do if he should fly into a passion, force the door open, and lay about him with the rod! There was no way to retreat left open, no open window through which to leap out! . . . At length the Master proposed to surrender, upon our terms, as specified in the paper. The door was opened. He entered with a smile, and we hardly knew whether to smile or scream from fear, lest after all he might visit us with dire punishment. He ordered us to our seats, wrote a note containing a list of the articles promised, and sent a few of the larger boys to the village to buy and bring them. Studying was impossible during their absence. The joy was too tumultuous to be bottled up, even for an hour. And the kind-hearted Master was as mirthful as we. At length the boys came, with great baskets, full of the spoils of our victory. Each one got a nice Christmas present. Never before had our Master seemed to us such a good man. For months this great siege in our school-house, and the grand victory of the besieged, was the daily topic of talk among the scholars. And in all the country round about, it was soon noised abroad, that Squire S. had been locked out by his school. And the scholars, even the most timid and worst frightened, shared the glory and renown of the victory.

—Reverend Benjamin Bausman [19]

On or near Christmas it was the custom of the children to lock the door and bolt the shutters of the school house, in the morning, or at noon, while the master was absent, in order to extort candy and cakes from him. This was done of the day before

 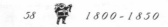

Christmas at the Humberger school house, William Stewart, master. When he arrived in the morning and found it closed against him he was not slow to take in the situation, and to turn the tables in his naughty scholars. From a nearby worm fence he got a sufficient number of rails which he set up against the door and shutters, and imprisoned boys and girls until late in the afternoon, and this was the last time this little trick was played on their schoolmaster.

—Reverend U. Henry Heilman [20]

1834

The Shops Are Preparing

This description of the Christmas season,
from a letter in Boston's Christian Register *on December 20, 1834,*
showed how early Christmas was commercialized.

The days are close at hand when everybody gives away something to somebody. . . . All the children are expecting presents, and all aunts and cousins to say nothing of near relatives, are considering what they shall bestow upon the earnest expectants. . . . I observe that the shops are preparing themselves with all sorts of things to suit all sorts of tastes; and am amazed at the cunning skill with which the most worthless as well as most valuable articles are set forth to tempt and decoy the bewildered purchaser. . . . and often have I been pained to observe the perplexity of some kind parent or friend, who wished to choose wisely, but knew not how, and after long balancing took something at random, perhaps good, perhaps worthless. [21]

1834

I Hated Slavery

*In 1834, Frederick Bailey was a 16-year-old slave worker around Fell's Point, Baltimore.
By 1838, Fred broke free of slavery when he slipped aboard a train headed north.
Soon after, he emerged as Frederick Douglass, the powerful, persuasive, and popular
abolitionist writer and orator. In this excerpt from his autobiography,
Douglass described the longstanding tradition of Christmas marking a new
work year for hired-out slaves. He also voiced strong
opinions about the way slaves celebrated the Christmas holiday.*

My term of service with Edward Covey expired on Christmas Day, 1834. . . .
My home for the year 1835 was already secured, my next master selected. . . . I had
become somewhat reckless and cared little into whose hands I fell. The report got abroad
that I was hard to whip; that I was guilty of kicking back, and that, though generally a
good-natured Negro, I sometimes "got the devil in me." . . . One bad sheep will
spoil a whole flock. I was a bad sheep. I hated slavery, slaveholders, and all pertain-
ing to them; . . . A knowledge also of my ability to read and write got pretty widely
spread, which was very much against me.

The days between Christmas and New Year's day are allowed as holidays; and, ac-
cordingly, we were not required to perform any labor, more than to feed and take care
of the stock. This time we regarded as our own, by the grace of our masters; and we
therefore used or abused it nearly as we pleased. Those of us who had families at a

 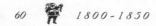

distance, were generally allowed to spend the whole six days in their society. This time, however, was spent in various ways. The staid, sober, thinking and industrious ones of our number would employ themselves in making corn-brooms, mats, horse-collars, and baskets; and another class of us would spend the time in hunting opossums, hares, and coons. But by far the larger part engaged in such sports and merriments as playing ball, wrestling, running foot-races, fiddling, dancing, and drinking whisky; and this latter mode of spending the time was by far the most agreeable to the feelings of our masters. A slave who would work during the holidays was considered by our masters as scarcely deserving them. He was regarded as the one who rejected the favor of his master. It was deemed a disgrace not to get drunk at Christmas; and he was regarded as lazy indeed, who had not provided himself with the necessary means, during the year, to get whisky enough to last him through Christmas.

From what I know of the effect of these holidays upon the slave, I believe them to be among the most effective means in the hands of the slaveholder in keeping down the spirit of insurrection. Were the slaveholders at once to abandon this practice, I have not the slightest doubt it would lead to an immediate insurrection among the slaves. These holidays serve as conductors, or safety-valves, to carry off the rebellious spirit of enslaved humanity. But for these, the slave would be forced up to the wildest desperation; and woe betide the slaveholder, the day he ventures to remove or hinder the operation of those conductors! I warn him that, in such an event, a spirit will go forth in their midst, more to be dreaded than the most appalling earthquake. . . .

The fiddling, dancing, and "jubilee beating" was going on in all directions. This latter performance was strictly southern. It supplies the place of a violin or of other musical instruments and is played so easily that almost every farm had its "Juba" beater. The performer improvises as he beats, and sings his merry songs, so ordering the words as to have them fall pat with the movement of his hands. Among a mass of nonsense and wild frolic, once in a while a sharp hit is given to the meanness of slaveholders. Take the following for an example:

We raise de wheat,
Dey gib us de corn:
We bake de bread,
Dey gib us de cruss;
We sif de meal,
Dey gib us de huss;
We peel de meat,
Dey gib us de skin;
And dat's de way
Dey take us in;...[22]

1830s and 1840s

Music to Dance By

*Lewis Paine spent six years in a Georgia prison for helping
a fugitive slave escape. In a book about his experiences, he included
a good account of the kind of "Jubilee beating" Douglass mentioned.*

Some one calls for a fiddle—but if one is not to be found, some one "pats juber."
This is done by placing one foot a little in advance of the other, raising the ball of the
foot from the ground, and striking it in regular time, while, in connection, the hands are
struck slightly together, and then upon the thighs. In this way they make the most
curious noise, yet in such perfect order, it furnishes music to dance by. . . . It is really
astonishing to witness the rapidity of their motions, their accurate time, and the preci-
sion of their music and dance. I have never seen it equaled in my life. [23]

1835

The First Christmas in My Den

In 1835, Harriet Jacobs was a 22-year-old fugitive slave. She left a new owner, whom she detested, and hid herself in a secret loft at her grandmother's home in Edenton, North Carolina. In this passage, taken from her own written narrative, Jacobs described how she spent her first Christmas season as a fugitive.

Christmas was approaching. Grandmother brought me materials, and I busied myself making some new garments and little playthings for my children. Were it not that hiring day is near at hand, and many families are fearfully looking forward to the probability of separation in a few days, Christmas might be a happy season for the poor slaves. Even slave mothers try to gladden the hearts of their little ones on that occasion. Benny and Ellen had their Christmas stockings filled. Their imprisoned mother could not have the privilege of witnessing their surprise and joy. But I had the pleasure of peeping at them as they went into the street with their new suits on. I heard Benny ask a little playmate whether Santa Claus brought him any thing. "Yes," replied the boy; "but Santa Claus ain't a real man. It's the children's mothers that put things into the stockings."

"No, that can't be," replied Benny, "for Santa Claus brought Ellen and me these new clothes, and my mother has been gone this long time."

How I longed to tell him that his mother made those garments, and that many a tear fell on them while she worked! . . .

Christmas is a day of feasting, both with white and colored people. Slaves, who are lucky enough to have a few shillings, are sure to spend them for good eating; and many a turkey and pig is captured, without saying, "By your leave, sir." Those who cannot obtain these, cook a 'possum, or a raccoon, from which savory dishes can be made. My grandmother raised poultry and pigs for sale; and it was her established custom to have both a turkey and a pig roasted for Christmas dinner.

On this occasion, I was warned to keep extremely quiet, because two guests had been invited. One was the town constable, and the other was a free colored man, who tried to pass himself off for white, and who was always ready to do any mean work for the sake of currying favor with white people. My grandmother had a motive for inviting them. She managed to take them all over the house. All the rooms on the lower floor were thrown open for them to pass in and out; and after dinner, they were invited up stairs to look at a fine mocking bird my uncle had just brought home. There, too, the rooms were all thrown open, that they might look in. When I heard them talking on the piazza, my heart almost stood still. I knew this colored man had spent many nights hunting for me. Every body knew he had the blood of a slave father in his veins; but for the sake of passing himself off for white, he was ready to kiss the slaveholders' feet. How I despised him! As for the constable, he wore no false colors. The duties of his office were despicable, but he was superior to his companion, inasmuch as he did not pretend to be what he was not. Any white man, who could raise money enough to buy a slave, would have considered himself degraded by being a constable; but the office enabled its possessor to exercise authority. If he found any slave out after nine o'clock, he could whip him as much as he liked; and that was a privilege to be coveted. When the guests were ready to depart, my grandmother gave each of them some of her nice pudding, as a present for their wives. Through my peep-hole I saw them go out of the gate, and I was glad when it closed after them. So passed the first Christmas in my den.

Because she could never be seen, Harriet missed the carousing "Johnkannaus" of coastal North Carolina Christmas week. The original "Johnkannaus" arrived on the Carolina coast from Africa by way of Jamaica. One historian reported tall, robust fellows on Jamaica in 1774, during Christmas holidays, dressed in grotesque costumes, with a pair of ox horns sprouting from the top of a horrid mask, and large boar tusks about the mouth, dancing from door to door, bellowing out "John Connu!" In this excerpt from her memoir, Harriet described the tradition.

 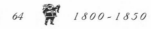

Every child rises early on Christmas morning to see the Johnkannaus. Without them, Christmas would be shorn of its greatest attraction. They consist of companies of slaves from the plantations, generally of the lower class. Two athletic men, in calico wrappers, have a net thrown over them, covered with all manner of bright-colored stripes. Cows' tails are fastened to their backs, and their heads are decorated with horns. A box, covered with sheepskin, is called the gumbo box. A dozen beat on this, while others strike triangles and jawbones, to which bands of dancers keep time. For a month previous they are composing songs, which are sung on this occasion. These companies, of a hundred each, turn out early in the morning, and are allowed to go round till twelve o'clock, begging for contributions. Not a door is left unvisited where there is the least chance of obtaining a penny or a glass of rum. They do not drink while they are out, but carry the rum home in jugs, to have a carousal. These Christmas donations frequently amount to twenty or thirty dollars. It is seldom that any white man or child refuses to give them a trifle. If he does, they regale his ears with the following song—

Poor massa, so dey say;
Down in de heel, so dey say;
Got no money, so dey say;
Not one shillin, so dey say;
God A'mighty bress you, so dey say.[24]

1837

Enough to Frighten Our Horses

*A Northern woman was startled, shocked, and embarrassed by some rowdy
"Jonny Cooners" she encountered during a Christmas visit in the South.
William Lloyd Garrison later printed her observations in the May 26, 1837,
issue of his abolitionist newspaper,* The Liberator.

I was passing to church on this morning, with a party of ladies in an open carry-all, when we perceived a rabble advancing. The sound of bells, clashing of tin plates, and blowing of stage horns, were all heard, accompanying a loud screaming voice to these words, sung in the peculiar negro accent:—"We bees Jonny Cooner; good masser, missus, chink, chink, and we drink to Jonny Cooner, Cooner." The gesture to these words was the extending and passing round a hat for the collection of pence.

John Cooner was represented by a slave in a mask, with a tall, hideous figure, twice the length of a natural man, with patches of every shade and color hanging from him, and bells attached to him to gingle at all his grotesque motions.

Such uncouth gestures, shrieking, dancing, and fighting of boys, who were ragged and without hat or shoes, were enough to frighten our horses as they passed. We were filled with pity and disgust, and felt it a relief, when our little black driver turned down a bye-way, for very shame at the sight. There are grades amongst the slaves, as in all other classes of society; and those who rank highest, will not join in this species of beggary and frolic combined. . . . My heart sickened when I thought to myself, "Is this the happiness of slaves at Christmas?"[25]

 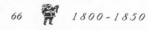

1838

Mirth and Cheerful Joy

The Jonkonnu parades amused most people.
Dr. James Norcom of Edenton wrote the following letter to his daughter,
mentioning his enjoyment of the "Koonah" entertainers. Dr. Norcom was
the master that Harriet Jacobs fled from three years earlier.

*H*ad it not been for the John Koonahs that paraded through the town in several successive gangs Christmas day would have pass'd without the least manifestation of mirth cheerful joy or hilarity.[26]

1838

Ribbons, Rags, and Feathers

Another North Carolina doctor, Dr. Edward Warren from Somerset Place,
a plantation near the eastern coast, wrote in his autobiography of watching
Somerset slaves performing their American version of the African ritual.

*O*ne of their customs was playing at what they called "John Koonering" . . . on Christmas day. The leading character is the "ragman," whose "get-up" consists of a costume of rags, so arranged that one end of each hangs loose and dangles; two great ox horns, attached to the skin of a raccoon, which is drawn over the head and face, leaving apertures only for the eyes and mouth; sandals of the skin of some wild "varmint"; several cow or sheep bells or strings of dried goats' horns hanging about their shoulders, and so arranged as to jingle at every movement; and a short stick of seasoned wood, carried in his hands.

The second . . . carried in his hand a small bowl or tin cup, while . . . half a dozen other fellows, each arrayed fantastically in ribbons, rags, and feathers, bear between them several so-called musical instruments or "gumba boxes," which consist of wooden frames covered over with tanned sheepskin. These are usually followed by a motley crowd of all ages, dressed in their ordinary working clothes, which seemingly comes as a guard of honor to the performers.

Coming up to the front door of the "great house," the musicians commenced to beat their gumba-boxes violently, while characters No. 1 and No. 2 enter upon a dance of the most extraordinary character—a combination of bodily contortions, flings, kicks, gyrations, and antics of every imaginable description, seemingly acting as partners, and yet each trying to excel the other . . . while the whole crowd joined in the chorus, shouting and clapping their hands in the wildest glee.[27]

In contemporary times, Tryon Palace Historic Sites & Gardens, in New Bern, North Carolina, presents a Jonkonnu Celebration each December, with a festive procession that brings to life a 19th-century yuletide blend of African, Caribbean, and English music, dance, and song.

1830s and 1840s

Considered Great Fun in Those Days

In Pennsylvania Dutch country, delightfully scary "Belsnickels"
made the rounds on Christmas Eve. They were described in an article on
Christmas customs among the Pennsylvania Dutch, printed in the
Philadelphia Public Ledger *on December 24, 1891.*

The Belsnickles were generally young men of the neighborhood dressed in fantastic garbs, and wearing masks, with bags of candies and nuts slung over their shoulders. They always received a hearty welcome from parents and children, and travelled from house to house, distributing their gifts. Often they would scatter them over the floor, while there would be a lively scampering among the children to get them, the visitors at the same time applying to their bodies long thin switches, which was considered great fun in those days.[28]

1840s

Belsnickel Carries His Whip

*In an article by Benjamin Bausman, "An Old-Time Christmas in a Country Home,"
printed in the* Guardian *in January 1871, he recalled a childhood
visit from the Belsnickel. He also recalled wondering how the Belsnickel
knew the bad children from the good.*

What a fearful fuss the dogs are making! Watch runs barking about the house, as if he would tear some one to pieces.

Hist! Somebody's knocking.

"Come in," says father. And in they come, such as they are: A half dozen jovial fellows, led by a so-called Belsnickel.

"O ma!" scream a group of us smaller children, and seize hold of her dress, like an affrighted brood rush under the wings of the mother hen, when the hawk is after them. Belsnickel may either mean a fur-clad Nicholas, or a flogging Nicholas. In the wintry nights, he is usually robed in furs, and carries his whip with him.

Our Belsnickel is most likely some well-known neighbor friend. Under his ugly mask . . . and an outlandish dress, such as no child ever saw mortal wear before, no one can tell who he is. We children tremble as in the presence of an unearthly being. Really, the Nickel tries to be pleasant, jabbers in some unknown tongue, and takes a few chestnuts and candies out of his vast bundle on his back, and throws them on the floor for the larger boys. One after another shyly picks up a gift. Among these older boys is a self-willed fellow, who sometimes behaves rudely. Whenever he picks up something, Nickel thwacks a long whip across his back—across his only. Whereupon the little ones scream and hold on to their mamma with a firm grip, and the older ones laugh aloud. The guilty boy puts his hand where the whip has made an impression. Again the unknown being puts his large working hand into the bag and scatters gifts, and again cracks his whip on the bad boy. How does this ugly man know who has been naughty?[29]

 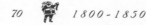

c. 1845

I Don't Believe
in Such Foolishness

In his reminiscences, published in the Weekly Eagle *in
Reading, Pennsylvania, on December 28, 1895, Matthias Mengel
recalled how he and other foolish young fellows once tried Belsnickeling
in a non-"Dutch" neighborhood.*

Particularly vivid in my memory is a Christmas eve when I was one of three or
four lads who started out to act the "Belsnickel." Well, each of us boys carried a switch
in his hand. We dressed in the clothing we could find at home, tied handkerchiefs over
our faces and filled our pockets with chestnuts and hickory nuts. We went to the house
of a neighbor where there were children, and expected to have some fun by frightening
the children by our singular appearance, throwing the nuts on the floor, and belsing the
children if they should pick up any of the nuts. We tinkled our bells, entered the house
and began jumping about and throwing nuts, when the head of the family, who was an
old Amish, said very sternly, "I don't believe in such foolishness, clear out!" and we
cleared. You see that was an English and Amish neighborhood. The English did not
observe the German customs of Christmas and the Amish were a very plain people like
the Quakers and had no festive occasions as had the Germans of other denominations
in other sections of Berks.[30]

1840

The Eating Commenced

*In his journal, fur trapper Osborne Russell recorded
this description of a Christmas feast in the Weber River country of Utah.*

It was agreed on by the party to prepare a Christmas dinner but I shall first endeavor to describe the party and then the dinner. I have already said the man who was the proprietor of the lodge in which I staid was a Frenchman with a flat head wife and one child. The inmates of the next lodge was a halfbreed Iowa, a Nez Percey wife and two children his wife's brother and another halfbreed; next lodge was a halfbreed Cree, his wife (a Nez Perce) two children and a Snake Indian. The inmates of the third lodge was a halfbreed Snake, his wife (a Nez Percey and two children). The remainder was 15 lodges of Snake Indians. Three of the party spoke English but very broken therefore that language was made but little use of as I was familiar with the Canadian French and Indian tongue.

About 1 o'clk we sat down to dinner in the lodge where I staid, which was the most spacious being about 36 ft. in circumference at the base, with a fire built in the center around this sat on clean Epishemores all who claimed kin to the white man (or to use their own expression all that were gens D'esprit), with their legs crossed in true Turkish style—and now for the dinner.

The first dish that came on was a large tin pan 18 inches in diameter rounding full of Stewed Elk meat. The next dish was similar to the first heaped up with boiled Deer meat (or as the whites would call it Venison a term not used in the Mountains). The 3rd and 4th dishes were equal in size to the first, containing a boiled flour pudding prepared with dried fruit accompanied by 4 quarts of sauce made of the juice of sour berries and sugar. Then came the cakes followed by six gallons of strong Coffee ready sweetened

 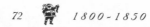

with tin cups and pans to drink out of large chips or pieces of bark supplying the place of plates. On being ready, the butcher knives were drawn and the eating commenced at the word given by the landlady. As all dinners are accompanied with conversation this was not deficient in that respect. The principal topic which was discussed was the political affairs of the Rocky Mountains the state of governments among the different tribes, the personal characters of the most distinguished warrior Chiefs, etc. One remarked that the Snake Chief, *Pahdahewakumda* was becoming very unpopular and it was the opinion of the Snakes in general that *Moh-woomba* his brother would be at the head of affairs before 12 ms as his village already amounted to more than 300 lodges. . . . Dinner being over the tobacco pipes were filled and lighted while the squaws and children cleared away the remains of the feast to one side of the lodge where they held a Sociable tite a tite over the fragments. After the pipes were extinguished all agreed to have a frolic shooting at a mark which occupied the remainder of the day.[31]

1842

Exhilarating Hilarity

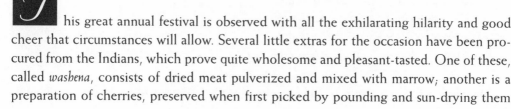

In his autobiography, another roaming mountain man,
Rufus Sage, described his Christmas celebration
in the White River region of the Rockies.

This great annual festival is observed with all the exhilarating hilarity and good cheer that circumstances will allow. Several little extras for the occasion have been procured from the Indians, which prove quite wholesome and pleasant-tasted. One of these, called *washena*, consists of dried meat pulverized and mixed with marrow; another is a preparation of cherries, preserved when first picked by pounding and sun-drying them (they are served by mixing them with *bouillie*, or the liquor of fresh-boiled meat, thus giving to it an agreeable winish taste); a third is marrow-fat, an article in many respects superior to butter; and, lastly, we obtained a kind of flour made from the *pomme blanc* (white apple), answering very well as a substitute for that of grain.

The above assortment, with a small supply of sugar and coffee, as well as several other dainties variously prepared, affords an excellent dinner,—and, though different in kind, by no means inferior in quality to the generality of dinners for which the day is noted in more civilized communities.[32]

1842

I Gladden All Hearts

In 1841, a live Santa attracted customers when he stationed himself on the roof of Parkinsons' shop in Philadelphia during the Christmas shopping season. The next year he was back. The illustration pictured here appeared in a front-page advertisement in the morning newspaper Spirit of the Times *(price one cent), on December 21, 1842. The following text appeared with the drawing.*

Kriss Kingle's Head Quarters
Parkinsons', 180 Chestnut St., Between Seventh and Eighth Streets

I come to you with the closing year,
To all with a smile, to none with a tear,
I banish all care from the passing day,
I gladden all hearts, and then hasten away.

We most respectfully inform the citizens of Philadelphia, and the public in general,

 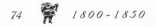

Kriss Kingle's Head Quarters.

PARKINSONS', 180 CHESTNUT ST.,
BETWEEN SEVENTH AND EIGHTH
STREETS.

I come to you with the closing year,
To all with a smile, to none with a tear,
I banish all care from the passing day,
I gladden all hearts, and then hasten away.

We most respectfully inform the citizens of
Philadelphia, and the public in general, that we
have just received from our friend and patron,
St. Nicholas, a large and extensive assortment of articles suited for the approaching festivities, and that the above named good-natured and jolly little SAINT, with his well accoutered person, hoary head, laughing face, and load of presents for the little ones, will himself preside, ready to greet all who may call, offering them a rich and splendid assortment of Fancy Articles, recently selected with great care in Paris—Consisting in part of Baskets, Boxes and Caskets of paper, wood, silk and velvet; also, Bags for Sugar Plumbs, which he has taken care to ornament in a manner peculiar and pleasing. All of which will be exposed for sale on Wednesday morning, 21st inst., at PARKINSONS'.

Saloon open at 10 o'clock. d20-1w

that we have just received from our friend and patron, St. Nicholas, a large . . . assortment of articles suited for the approaching festivities, and that the above named good-natured and jolly little SAINT, with his well accoutered person, hoary head, laughing face, and load of presents for the little ones, will himself preside, ready to greet all who may call, offering them a rich and splendid assortment of Fancy Articles, recently selected with great care in Paris— Consisting in part of Baskets, Boxes and Caskets of paper, wood, silk and velvet; also, Bags for Sugar Plumbs, which he had taken care to ornament in a manner peculiar and pleasing. All of which will be exposed for sale on Wednesday morning, 21st inst., at

PARKINSONS

Saloon open at 10 o'clock[33]

Philadelphia (Penn.) Spirit of the Times *newspaper,*
December 21, 1842
Courtesy of Nannette Rod

1842

Almost Endless Variety of Things

Another rooftop Santa made an appearance at a store in Albany, New York.
This advertisement from Pease's Great Variety Store accompanied
the drawing, pictured on page 77 in an article in the
Daily Albany Argus on December 23, 1842.

SANTA CLAUS

In the act of descending a Chimney to fill the Children's Stockings, after supplying himself with FANCY ARTICLES, STATIONERY, CUTLERY, PERFUMERY, GAMES, TOYS, &C.

AT PEASE'S GREAT VARIETY STORE, No. 50 Broadway, Albany,

Where can be found an almost endless variety of "Things to use and things for sport," suitable for CHRISTMAS AND NEW-YEAR'S PRESENTS, such as

Work boxes, furnish'd & unfurnh'd
Dressing cases, toilet cases
Writing desks, papeteries
Card receivers, portfolios
Card cases, purses
Velvet and silk bags
Rich paper boxes, guard chains
Gold and silver pencils
Infants' rattles of gold, silver, ivory
Gold and silver thimbles
Napkin rings, segar cases

Music boxes, hair brushes
Combs and tooth brushes
Gold and silver toothpicks

Penknives, inkstands
Gloves in a nut shell, watch stands
Bouquet holders of silver and gilt
Breast pins, rings, bracelets
Hair pins, shawl pins, cuff pins
Gilt combs, fans, work baskets
Perfumery in great variety
Games and toys
Splendid and common chess men
Backgammon boards and men
Battledoore, graces, cups and balls
Skipping ropes, dissected maps
Building blocks and alphabets
Mosaic puzzles, panoramas

Magic lanterns, wax dolls
Kid and jointed dolls, tea sets
Nine pins, doll's heads
Rocking horses, whips, swords, guns
Soldiers, pistols, drums and flags
Masks, accordions, sheep and dogs
Printing presses, whistles, rattles
Arks, magnetic fishes, livery stables
Horses and carriages, dominoes, dice

Albany (N.Y.), Daily Albany Argus
Friday, December 23, 1842
Courtesy Nannette Rod

Wheelbarrows and wagons
Cradles, cooking stoves
Kitchens, tea sets
Rocking horses, sofas, tables
&. &. &c.[34]

1843

Fresh Indian Tracks

*In 1843, Lieutenant John Charles Fremont, a member of the
Army Corps of Topographical Engineers, was on the second
of five expeditions to map the vast Oregon Territory. With Kit Carson
scouting the way, the party pitched their Christmas camp in Oregon,
where Fremont recorded the following entry for his official report to the Senate.*

ecember 25.—We were roused, on Christmas morning, by a discharge from the small arms and howitzer, with which our people saluted the day, and the name of which we bestowed on the lake. It was the first time, perhaps, in this remote and desolate region, in which it had been so commemorated. Always, on days of religious or national commemoration, our voyageurs expect some unusual allowance; and, having nothing else, I gave them each a little brandy, (which was carefully guarded, as one of the most useful articles a traveller can carry,) with some coffee and sugar, which here, where every eatable was a luxury, was sufficient to make them a feast. The day was sunny and warm; and, resuming our journey, we crossed some slight dividing grounds into a similar basin, walled in on the right by a lofty mountain ridge. The plainly beaten trail still continued, and occasionally we passed camping grounds of the Indians, which indicated to me that we were on one of the great thoroughfares of the country. . . . There were fresh Indian tracks about the valley, and last night a horse was stolen.[35]

 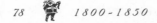

1844

A Great and Glorious Day in the Rocky Mountains

Dressed in a long black robe with a shining crucifix,
Belgian missionary Pierre-Jean DeSmet, who was known
as the "Apostle of the Rocky Mountains," was a familiar figure from the
Oregon coast to Jackson's Hole, the Teton Mountains, and the Yellowstone country.
"He is a Blackrobe, a man who speaks with the Great Spirit," his interpreter
told the Blackfeet, Flat-Heads, and Coeur d'Alenes they encountered and
converted. In his Oregon Missions and Travels Over the Rocky
 Mountains *in 1845-46, Father DeSmet described Christmas amongst the Indians.*

I shall always remember with pleasure the winter of 1844-45, which I had the happiness of spending among these good Indians. The place for wintering was well chosen, picturesque, agreeable, and convenient. The camp was placed near a beautiful waterfall, caused by Clark river's being blocked up by an immense rock, . . . We were encircled by ranges of lofty mountains, whose snow-clad summits reflected in the sun, their brightness on all the surrounding country.

The place for wintering being determined, the first care of the Indians was to erect the house of prayer. While the men cut down saplings, the women brought bark and mats to cover them. In two days this humble house of the Lord was completed—humble and poor indeed, but truly the house of prayer, . . .

The great festival of Christmas, the day on which the little band was to be added to the number of the true children of God, will never be effaced from the memory of our good Indians. The manner in which we celebrated midnight mass, may give you an idea of our festival. The signal for rising, which was to be given a few minutes before midnight, was the firing of a pistol, announcing to the Indians that the house of prayer would soon be open. This was followed by a general discharge of guns, in honor of the birth of the Infant Saviour, and three hundred voices rose spontaneously from the midst of the forest, and entoned in the language of the Pends d'Oreilles, the beautiful canticle: *"Du Dieu puissant tout annonce la gloire."*—"The Almighty's glory all things proclaim." In a moment a multitude of adorers were seen wending their way to the humble temple of the Lord—resembling indeed, the manger in which the Messiah was born. . . . Of what was our little church of the wilderness constructed? I have already told you—of posts fresh cut in the woods, covered over with mats and bark; these were its only materials. On the eve, the church was embellished with garlands and wreaths of green boughs; . . . The interior was ornamented with pine branches. The altar was neatly decorated, bespangled with stars of various brightness, and covered with a profusion of ribbons—things exceedingly attractive to the eye of an Indian. At midnight I celebrated a solemn Mass, the Indians sang several canticles suitable to the occasion. . . . A grand banquet, according to Indian custom, followed the first Mass. Some choice pieces of the animals slain in the chase had been set apart for the occasion. I ordered half a sack of flour, and a large boiler of sweetened coffee to be added. . . .

About 3 o'clock in the afternoon, the solemn benediction of the blessed sacrament was given for the first time, immediately after which, upwards of fifty couples, many of whom were eighty years old, came forward to renew before the Church, their marriage promises. I could not help shedding tears of joy at witnessing this truly primitive simplicity, and the love and affection with which they pledged again their faith to each other. . . .

The Christmas of 1844 was, therefore, a great and glorious day in the Rocky Mountains.[36]

1845

Dined To-day on One of Our Mules

*Edward M. Kern, the topographer for John C. Fremont's
third expedition exploring the West, wrote in his journal about the
Christmas they spent while on a clandestine side trip into Mexican California.
He found little to celebrate.*

Our Christmas was spent in a most unchristmas-like manner. Our camp was made on the slope of the mountain, at some Indian wells of good water. The yuca tree is here in great abundance, furnishing us a plentiful supply of fuel. The camp-fires blazed and cracked joyously, the only merry things about us, and all that had any resemblance to that merry time at home. The animals, on account of [lack of] grass, were guarded about a quarter of a mile from camp, higher up the mountains. . . .

Dined to-day, by way of a change, on one of our tired, worn mules, instead of a horse.[37]

1845

I, Santa Claus

*By 1845, Santa Claus had not yet struck out for the West. However,
the following two newspaper articles indicated that he made appearances
at two confectionary shops in Reading, Pennsylvania.*

I, Santa Claus, hereby announce, I will be found at my *Depot des Coniseur*, No. 46, West Penn Street, a full and complete assortment of Christmas and New Year's Presents.

The whole has been prepared and selected by me Santa Claus in person, and will be presented to the good burghers of Reading, by my own hand, this being the first visit I shall have ever made to this place. My only wish is that I may meet with a cordial reception by one and all of my juvenile subjects. So that I may not regret leaving the more populous cities, to pay this *pop* visit to the place where many natives of the Vaterland dwell, with my panniers well laden with all kinds of niceties.

Signed, Santa Claus, or St. Nicholas.
—Reading *Gazette*, December 20, 1845[38]

Old Santa Claus, in front of the Messrs. Souders' Confectionary, was the observed of all observers during the day. His *tout ensemble* was quite ingenious, and in our opinion, made a finer display than his prototype which attracted so much attention at Parkinson's in Philadelphia, a year or two ago.

—Reading *Gazette*, December 27, 1845[39]

1845

Christmas Trees

Philadelphia publisher E. Ferrett & Co. cashed in on the Christmas tree craze with a popular book titled, Kriss Kringle's Christmas Tree. In a second edition of the book, printed in 1847, the publisher recommended that everyone who desired "to conform to the most approved fashion" should buy several copies.

Fashions change, and of late Christmas Trees are becoming more common than in former times. The practice of hanging up stockings in the chimney corner for Kriss

 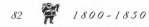

Kringle to fill with toys, pretty books, bon-bons, &c., for good children, and rods for naughty children, is being superseded by that of placing a Christmas Tree on the table to await the annual visit of the worthy Santa Klaus. He has, with his usual good nature, accommodated himself to this change in the popular taste, and having desired a literary gentleman to prepare his favourite Christmas present in accordance with this state of things, the following volume is the result of the new arrangement, and all parents, guardians, uncles, aunts, and cousins, who are desirous to conform to the most approved fashion, will take care to hang one, two, or a dozen copies of the book on their Christmas Tree for 1847. [40]

1846

A Splendid Assortment of Fancy Articles

This advertisement, offering firecrackers and ice cream for Christmas, appeared in the Pittsburgh Daily Commercial Journal *on December 17, 1846.*

FIRE CRACKERS FOR CHRISTMAS—Decidedly the best ever imported, the report is like that of a pistol, loud and clear, for sale by the box or pack, at the EAGLE BAKERY, No. 42 Diamond Alley, and at the SALOON on Wood street.

Also, a great variety of Fancy Cake and Confectionary, Pyramids, Nuts, Mince Pies, Oranges, and other fruits,—A splendid assortment of fancy articles at the Saloon on Christmas Day. Orders promptly attended to.

N.B. Ice Cream for parties in forms.[41]

1846

The Prospect is Appalling

While emigrating west in 1846, the Donner Party took a bad shortcut
off the Oregon Trail. The party totaled sixty people—nineteen men, twelve women,
and twenty-nine children, six of them babies. By Christmas, they were snowbound
and huddled in cabins built at Truckee Lake in the Sierra Nevada Mountains.
One member of the group, Irish immigrant Patrick Breen, made these entries
in the only surviving diary.

Wend. 23rd   Snowed a little last night clear to day & thawing a little. Milt took some of his meat to day   all well at their camp   began this day to read the Thirty days prayer, may Almighty God grant the request of an unworthy sinner that I am. *Amen*

Thursd. 24th   rained all night & still continues to rain   poor prospect for any kind of Comfort Spiritual or temporal, wind S: may God help us to spend the Christmass as we ought considering circumstances

Friday 25th   began to snow yesterday about 12 o clock snowed all night & snows yet rapidly wind about E by N Great difficulty in getting wood John & Edwd.[14 and 13] has to get [it] I am not able offered our prayers to God this Cherimass morning the prospect is apalling but hope in God *Amen*[42]

Patrick and Peggy Breen, with their seven children, survived the winter
and made their way to Sutter's Fort in California without losing a single family
member. Like all Donner Party survivors, they brought horrifying tales of the thirty-four
people who perished—some of whom were butchered and eaten by their starving companions.

 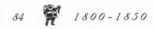

<h1 style="text-align:center">1848</h1>

<h2 style="text-align:center">Camp Dismal</h2>

*John C. Fremont's Fourth Expedition, which began in St. Louis, was supposed to
locate a route that the transcontinental railroad could take through the
central Rocky Mountains, but it met with disaster.
By Christmas, every pack mule was dead or dying, and the men had to haul
all their supplies on their own backs. They camped at a "desolate looking place,"
as expedition member Benjamin Kern wrote in his diary. "A raven floating thro the
cold air gave the music of its hoarse notes a perfect addition to camp dismal."
In an 1896 book titled* The Story of a Famous Expedition, *Thomas Breckenridge—the last living survivor—was finally able to joke
about their dreadful ordeal.*

 will never forget that Christmas breakfast. We had no luxuries, but plenty of variety in meats.

BILL OF FARE, CAMP DESOLATION
December 25, 1848
Menu
Mule
Soup
Mule Tail
Fish
Baked White Mule
Boiled Gray Mule
Meats
Mule Steak, Fried Mule, Mule Chops, Broiled Mule, Stewed Mule,
Boiled Mule, Scrambled Mule, Shirred Mule, French-Fried Mule,

Minced Mule, DAMNED Mule, Mule on toast (without the toast),
Short Ribs of Mule with Apple Sauce (without the Apple Sauce)
Relishes
Black Mule, Brown Mule, Yellow Mule, Bay Mule,
Roan Mule, Tallow Candles
Beverages
Snow, Snow-water, Water[43]

1849

A Candy Pull

*Sallie Hester's family left Indiana and crossed the country
on the Oregon Trail with a covered wagon party, hoping that the clear Western air
would improve Mrs. Hester's poor health. Fourteen-year-old Sallie kept a
diary of their journey, and their arrival in Fremont, California, just as the
rainy winter season began. As her December entries indicate, the family's
bright hopes for California had begun to dim.*

December 20—Have not written or confided in thee, dear journal, for some time. Now I must write up. My father returned from Sacramento with a supply of provisions. Everything is enormously high. Carpenter's wages sixteen dollars per day; vegetables scarce and high; potatoes the principal vegetable; onions, fifty cents each; eggs, one dollar apiece; melons, five dollars, and apples, one dollar each. . . . The rain is pouring down. River very high.

Christmas, 1849—Still raining. This has been a sad Christmas for mother. She is

 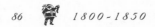

homesick, longs for her old home and friends. It's hard for old folks to give up old ties and go so far away to live in a strange land among strange people. Young people can easily form new ties and make new friends and soon conform to circumstances, but it's hard for the old ones to forget. Was invited to a candy pull and had a nice time. Rather a number of young folks camped here. This is a funny looking town anyway. Most of the houses are built of brush. Now that the rains have set in, people are beginning to think of something more substantial. Some have log cabins, others have clapboards like ours.[44]

1849

Worldly Pleasure

On December 22, 1840, the St. Paul,
Minnesota Chronicle and Register *suggested that its readers celebrate to suit themselves.*

Christmas will be with us next Tuesday, and every one is preparing to enjoy it as seemeth best to suit them. The grave and devout will be at church. Those that love worldly pleasure will be at the several balls, or out upon sleighing, and eating and drinking parties. The great centre of attraction for this class is the ball at the "Minnesota House," Stillwater, on Christmas night, on which occasion "mine host," Hartshorn, expects to "lay himself out," and surpass every thing of the kind yet got up in the Territory.[45]

1849

Not a *Lady* to be Seen

In his A Western Journal, 1849-50, *naturalist John Woodhouse Audubon,*
son of the well-known naturalist and bird artist, grumbled about a
gloomy Christmas in San Francisco.

Happy Christmas, Merry Christmas! Not that here, for me at any rate, in this pandemonium of a city. Not a *lady* to be seen, and the women, poor things, sad and silent—except when drunk or excited. . . . *[A day like any other]* except for a little more drunkenness and a little extra effort by the hotel keepers to take in more money.[46]

1849

I Climbed Upon the Roof

In his book, Hunting for Gold, *Major William Downie*
described the winter of the Gold Rush of 1849, when he and his
gold-seeking partners lived in a strong, warm, and watertight cabin they
built at the Forks of the Yuba River (later to become the town
of Downieville), in California.

It was on the 10th of December, 1849, that we moved into our new quarters, and then came Christmas. We were determined to make the best of the festive season, even though we were in the midst of the wilds, far away from friends and relations. Our greatest trouble was, that we had but one bottle of brandy in camp, and it took us some

time before we could decide whether we would drink it on Christmas or New Years day. The discussion, pro and con, was very animated and resulted in the drawing of the cork on Christmas morning. It was quite early, when this important event took place, and we made punch with the liquor, using hot water and nutmeg. We drank to absent friends, to wives and sweethearts and to the great American Nation. Gradually as the sun rose higher in the heavens and the brandy got lower in the bottle, we became more enthusiastic. I had a small representation of the stars and stripes in my possession, and we determined that on this day it should adorn our house. So I climbed upon the roof with the flag in one hand, a pistol in the other. I made a short speech, waved the flag and fired a few shots and finished up by giving three cheers for the American Constitution. Then I fixed the flag on the gable point, and we all shouted for joy when we saw it unfurled to the breeze for the first time in the fastnesses of the Sierras. . . .

I must admit with every due respect to the temperance cause and its advocates, that our brandy proved, "the staff of life" to us, notwithstanding all that has been said to the contrary. It is true, no doubt, that there are circumstances and conditions of life, when liquor is not absolutely necessary, but let every honest temperance preacher try a little starving in the mountains with nothing to drink but snow water, and it is just possible that the whole fraternity will feel called upon to change opinion.[47]

1851

The Perfect Saturnalia

*Louise Clappe, who spent a rainy winter with her husband
in the California gold diggings, wrote of the miners' Christmas celebration
in this letter to her sister Molly, back home in Massachusetts.*

From our Log Cabin, Indian Bar,
January 27, 1852

I wish that it were possible, dear M., to give you an idea of the perfect Saturnalia, which has been held upon the river. . . .

The Saturnalia commenced on Christmas evening, at the Humboldt, which on that very day, had passed into the hands of new proprietors. The most gorgeous preparations were made for celebrating the two events. The bar was re-trimmed with red calico, the bowling alley had a new lining of the coarsest and whitest cotton cloth, and the broken lamp-shades were replaced by whole ones. All day long, patient mules could be seen descending the hill, bending beneath casks of brandy and baskets of champagne, and, for the first time in the history of that celebrated building, the floor . . . was *washed*, at a lavish expenditure of some fifty pails of water, the using up of one entire broom, and the melting away of sundry bars of the best yellow soap; . . .

At nine o'clock in the evening, they had an oyster and champagne supper in the Humboldt, which was very gay with toasts, songs, speeches, etc. I believe that the company danced all night; at any rate, they were dancing when I went to sleep, and they were dancing when I woke the next morning. The revel was kept up in this mad way for three days, growing wilder every hour. Some never slept at all during that time. On the fourth day, they got past dancing, and, lying in drunken heaps about the bar-room,

commenced a most unearthly howling;—some barked like dogs, some roared like bulls, and others hissed like serpents and geese. Many were too far gone to imitate anything but their own animalized selves. . . . Some of these bacchanals were among the most respectable and respected men upon the river. Many of them had resided here for more than a year, and had never been seen intoxicated before. It seemed as if they were seized with a reckless mania for pouring down liquor. . . .

Of course, there were some who kept themselves aloof from these excesses; but they were few, and were not allowed to enjoy their sobriety in peace. The revelers formed themselves into a mock vigilance committee, and when one of these unfortunates appeared outside, a constable, followed by those who were able to keep their legs, brought him before the Court, where he was tried on some amusing charge, and *invariably* sentenced to "treat the crowd." The prisoners had generally the good sense to submit cheerfully to their fate.

Towards the latter part of the week, people were compelled to be a little more quiet from sheer exhaustion. . . .

Now, however, the Saturnalia is about over. "Ned" and "Choch," have nearly fiddled themselves into their respective graves,—the claret (a favorite wine with miners,) and oysters are exhausted,—brandied fruits are rarely seen, and even port wine is beginning to look scarce. Old callers occasionally drop in, looking dreadfully sheepish and subdued, and *so* sorry—and people are evidently arousing themselves from the bacchanal madness, into which they were so suddenly and so strangely drawn. . . .

I am bound, Molly, by my promise, to give you a true picture (as much as in me lies,) of mining life and its peculiar temptations. . . . But with all their failings, believe me, the miners, as a class, possess many truly admirable characteristics.[48]

1851–1864

A Chance to Test Santa Claus's Generosity
Drawing by Thomas Nast

1851

Something New

In her diary, Mahala Eggleston Roach,
of Vicksburg, Mississippi,
described how she decorated
her first Christmas tree.

hristmas, 1851. . . . The children had such a number of gifts that I made a Christmas tree for them; Mother, Aunt and Liz came down to see it; all said it was something new to them. I never saw one but learned from some of the German stories I had been reading.[1]

1851

Much Firing of Crackers

This item appeared in the Wilmington, North Carolina,
Daily Journal on December 23, 1851.

ohn Barleycorn retained his usual spirit . . . and our town authorities on Christmas generally let the boys have their way so far as mere noise is concerned. There was therefore much firing of crackers, rockets, sarpients, etc. and a good deal of cheering and shouting, but nothing worse, and as the night wore on even these ceased and the town slept.[2]

1850s

Roman Candles and Sky Rockets

In this letter, John Steger Hardaway, who was born in 1852,
told his little grandsons about Georgia Christmases.

Crawford, Ga.
Dec. 22, 1922

 y Dear Dick Jr. and Theodore,

As we are drawing near to Christmas, Grandfather will tell you about Xmas
when he was a little boy. On Xmas Eve night, they said that Santa Claus came
and gave good little boys and girls nice presents. They said he came in a sleigh
over the snow and that he went up on top of the house, and came down the
chimney—but if he did that he would get full of soot and blackness and he
would sometimes fall into the fire. We little boys and girls would hang up our
stockings for Santa Claus to fill, and you may be sure we would get a great big
one that would hold a heap. So when I was a little boy I would hang my stocking by the chimney piece or at the bureau, and I would lie down to dream
about what Santa Claus would bring me.

Almost always Santa would bring every one of us a nice orange, and a fine
apple, and a bunch of raisins, and all sorts of nuts. . . . He would also bring a
big lot of candy. So we would have lots to eat. One Xmas he brought me a
pretty book called "Reading without Tears." and it was full of pretty pictures,
and very soon I learned how to read. I think I was just six years old then. Once
he brought me a pair of Redtop boots, and I was the proudest little boy you

ever saw. How I did strut around in those fine boots. Often he brought us pop crackers, and Roman Candles, and Skyrockets and Wheels of fire, and torpedoes—but he does not bring little boys fire works, because they might burn themselves, and might put out an eye and hurt some one in some way. So these fire works are brought to boys when they get to be big. Sometimes Santa would bring a tin horn, and some whistles to make a noise with, and we surely did create a din at Xmas. Just as soon as it began to be light in the morning we would get up, and get our stockings, and look to see what we had gotten. And such a hubbub you never heard, as when we pulled out the presents from the stockings. It was a great time. Perhaps there is no greater pleasure in life than that which comes to a little boy unpacking his Xmas stocking. So I am wishing that you and Theodore may have a big time this Xmas, and that Santa Claus may bring you a great many things. But then you must be good little boys.

Now let us ask why it is that we are so glad at Xmas, and why we ought to be kind, and happy. . . . Sometimes while you are playing with your Xmas toys you must think about Jesus whose birthday Xmas is. And as Jesus was good to all, and tried to make us good and gave us many precious gifts, so we ought to be good to others, and try to help them to be good, and to give to others good gifts as we are able.

Your loving
Grandfather,
J. S. Hardaway

It is not surprising that sixty-some years later Mr. Hardaway still remembered the book he received when he was six years old. Reading Without Tears; or A Pleasant Mode of Learning to Read, by Favell Lee Mortimer, was first published in 1857. It was a real page-turner. Here is a sample from Mrs. Mortimer's thrilling and gruesome lessons: "Jack will clamber up high trees. Jack got to the top of the fir tree. But he was dizzy, and he fell and snapped his neck. So he was killed on the spot." [3]

1853

Celebrated with Considerable Éclat

*In 1853, Lieutenant Amiel W. Whipple led an expedition into Arizona,
scouting routes for a potential transcontinental railroad. Over Christmas, he and his
men settled in for a three-day rest at Camp 89, Cosnino Caves, in north central Arizona.
At sunrise on December 24, the temperature registered three degrees below zero.
That evening, the party put together a Southwest Indian-Mexican-French
Christmas Eve celebration to warm hearts and spirits. Below are descriptions of the
festivities from three members of the expedition.*

Lieutenant Whipple:

Christmas eve has been celebrated with considerable éclat. The fireworks were
decidedly magnificent. Tall, isolated pines surrounding the camp were set on fire. The
flames leaped to the treetops, and then, dying away, sent up innumerable brilliant sparks.
An Indian dance, by some *ci-devant [former]* Navajo prisoners, was succeeded by songs from
the teamsters, and a pastoral enacted by the Mexicans, after their usual custom at this festival. Leroux's servant, a tamed Crow Indian, and a herder, then performed a duet improvisated,
in which they took the liberty of saying what they pleased of the company present—an
amusement common in New Mexico and California, where this troubadour singing is
much in vogue at fandangos. These last entertainments are interesting to a stranger
from their singularity. The plaintive tones of the singers, and the strange simplicity of
the people, lead one's fancy back to the middle ages. In this state of society, so free from
ambition for wealth or power, where the realities of life are in a great measure subject to
the ideal, there is a tinge of romance that would well repay the researches of a literary
explorer. Their impromptu ballads alone would make an interesting collection.

Balduin Möllhausen, a German artist with the group:

As night came on, our company was seated in picturesque groups round the fires, which glowed larger and brighter in the darkness. The cooks were running about busily with their hissing frying-pans and bubbling coffee-pots, some were singing, some cheerfully gossiping, some only wrapped in their blankets and calmly smoking their pipes. . . .

Christmas Day   Various dainties that had been hitherto carried in closed cases were brought forth to be eaten up at once, partly with the view of lightening the load of the wagons, but at the same time with an eye to the glorification of our Christmas dinner in the wilderness. When we left Albuquerque, some of the party had bethought themselves of the festive season, and procured a chest of eggs, which, carefully packed, had traveled in safety thus far. Others had brought a stock of rum and wine, and all these luxuries were now produced to do honour to the Christmas banquet.

The marvelous combination of wood and mountain and valley must have tended to remind every one of their Great Creator, and awaken feelings of devout gratitude. This feeling is closely allied to those of love to one's neighbour, and compassion for the brute creation; and there was no one, I imagine, in our whole expedition who did not at this time sincerely grieve for the hardship suffered by our poor beasts, who for their Christmas cheer had to scrape away snow a foot deep to get at the scanty grass and moss beneath.

A toast proposed by Lieutenant Johns, who invited all the officers to his tent for steaming punch:

Let us now forget for a few hours our hardships and privations, the object of our journey, and the labours still before us; and here, under a roof of boughs, and on the spotless white carpet that God Almighty has spread for us, far as we are from our homes, let us think of our friends, who, very likely, are thinking of us as they sit round their firesides; and drowning our cares in a social glass of toddy, drink to their health, and to our own happy return.[4]

1855

They Do Not Accept the Day

Two hundred and fifty years after the Pilgrims landed,
this remark in the New York Daily Times on December 26, 1855,
indicated that some Americans still resisted Christmas.

The churches of the Presbyterians, Baptists and Methodists were not open on Dec. 25 except where some Mission Schools had a celebration. They do not accept the day as a Holy One, but the Episcopalian, Catholic and German Churches were all open. Inside they were decked with evergreens.[5]

1855

The Hall Looked Like A Fairy Place

Another entry from Mahala Eggleston Roach's journal
described flowers in the snow in Vicksburg, Mississippi.

Christmas, 1855. Tuesday; bitter cold; ground covered with snow. Real old-fashioned Christmas weather . . . snow which fell yesterday and last night. Day before yesterday it was quite warm, and there has been no weather sufficiently cold to injure the flowers. So soon as I felt the weather changing, husband and I gathered all the flowers, so as to keep them for the Presbyterian Ladies who had a supper last night. Every one in town did the same, and I am told the hall looked like a fairy place, with its profusion of flowers and sweet odors; while outside the sleet and snows were falling.[6]

1856

Longing to Talk to You

*In 1856, Caja Munch was a homesick young Norwegian woman living
in Wiota, Wisconsin, where her husband Johan served as minister to a
Lutheran congregation. In the three letters that follow, Caja wrote to her parents in
Norway about her first three Christmases in America.*

Christmas 1856:

*B*eloved Parents!

The day, indeed, has drawn to a close, but such a strong longing came over me to talk to you although I am so far, far away from you;

It has been a strange Christmas for me. On Christmas Eve we all had rice porridge, roast beef, and Christmas cookies together with Even and a man and his wife and a little child, who are staying here in the house. Afterwards we said our prayers and sang a hymn and thought of our dear ones at home, who already by that time were sound asleep. You will recall that you are six hours ahead of us in time, which is hard on us sometimes, especially on such holidays when I wish so much for our thoughts to meet, but then it has to be worked out by calculation. Oh, how often have I not taken the watch and figured out what you were doing during the joyful Christmas time.

On the First Day of Christmas, I was with my dear Munch. He gave a beautiful sermon in his main church, but it was so cold that both words and thoughts were almost frozen away, although we lit a fire in the stove in the church. On the way home I wanted to run to keep myself from freezing but tripped in my black silk dress and tore it, but not too much—uh! You will have to be informed about everything, dear Mother, good and bad. . . .

For the winter Munch has rented an old bearskin coat from a man here, and I put on him everything I possibly can, but it certainly takes a lot to protect yourself from the cold here. Only those who have traveled in these parts can have any idea about the cold wind that blows over the prairie.

Christmas 1857:

Our Yuletide entertainments are soon recounted. They consisted of reading and hearing the Word of God, all possible peace and comfort at home, thinking of Norway and all our beloved friends there, besides singing Norwegian patriotic songs, our wedding song, and other snatches that we would think of. . . .

[Despite terrible weather, shortly before Christmas, Caja's husband sent two boys in a borrowed sleigh to announce a New Year's service to a neighboring town.]

They were to return the next day, the day before Christmas Eve, but they did not arrive. Christmas Eve went by, and still they did not come. By this time we were almost certain they had frozen to death on the prairies, and we had a very dismal Christmas Eve. Munch and all three of our servants went to church Christmas Day, I stayed at home alone with the baby. Munch was not very happy and could not at all get into the proper solemn mood because he was thinking of the boys; one of them was one of his confirmants and had twice before gone with him the same road. Their parents came here and were very downhearted. But just as I was sitting down, in came not only the boys but also Madam Holmen with her two children. Her husband was unable to come until a few days later as he could not leave the store, which was kept open both Christmas Day and Boxing Day; there you see how the Americans observe the great Christmas Holidays. They had had much trouble on the way and had to stay overnight because of impassable roads, but God be praised that they returned safely, and you can imagine here was joy.

Indeed, we have a hard winter again this year, a lot of snow, storms, and freezing weather, and under such conditions it is almost impossible to go anywhere. Boxing Day, as Munch was going to one of his annex parishes, his horses went off the road and waded in snow to their ears. Snowplows are unheard of in this country, and to get into a blizzard on the prairies is attended with danger of life. The roads are then drifted over so completely that there is no trace of them, and it may happen that one drives around a circle without knowing where he will arrive. It is not uncommon that people freeze to death in their sleigh, and the horses arrive in town with dead bodies sitting frozen stiff in the sleigh, holding the reins. Last year it happened that a carriage stopped outside an inn, where the horses regularly used to rest, but as nobody came inside, the innkeeper went out, and lo! There were five persons sitting inside the carriage, and the driver in his box holding the reins, completely frozen and dead. However, this is due to their own carelessness, and I don't feel nearly as sorry for them as for the poor cows, pigs, sheep, and other small animals; what these poor creatures suffer when the weather is that cold cannot be described, for they seldom have as much as a bush under which to seek shelter. Although we have a stable to put them in, they still suffer from cold because it is so open that the snow drifts right in at them. On the Sixth Day of Christmas, the Holmens left, and the following day Munch went away, so now I am alone with the baby.

Christmas 1858:

I had a lot of butchering done for Christmas, which I enjoyed doing—I seemed to live over again the old days in my home. Everything turned out well. I made almost all the things you prepare, dear Mother, although I did make some kind of meat sausage which I marvel that we never thought of cooking at home. I had to make black pudding for Munch, he likes it so well, and I had the pleasure of treating my dear Emil and Munch to delicious things for a long time. My baking for Christmas consisted of wort-cake, Christmas bread, flead-cakes, hartshorn pastry, and apple pie. I finished everything early, and we had a quiet, peaceful, wonderful Christmas Eve and Holiday Season. . . .

I find that this letter has a strange, brief style, but for the moment I am not capable of doing any better. The reason for it may be that for so long now I have been staying within these four walls, without seeing or hearing another well-bred person. A couple of days ago, Munch and Emil drove down to Dietrichson's, but I could not come along as the roads were very bad.

We are having a strange winter this year, no snow, no frost—may God bring us a healthy summer![7]

1858

I Have Been Pretty Busy

In 1858, Carrie Williams lived in Gold Flat, California,
a Sierra Nevada mining town. She was a homebody, caring for her first child,
"Walla," and living in warm companionship with her mother-in-law.
The women were often annoyed with their husbands, Wallace and his father,
because they were so seldom at home. The men's days were spent panning
for gold and their nights were passed "tuting" horns in a band. Carrie
described her Christmas in her diary.

ednesday 22nd. The sun shone bright and warm all day. I washed and pressed out my plaid dress, and it looks very much like a new one. Wallace's mother commenced washing today. . . . The children of [the Methodist] Sunday school and Mr. Straton's day school are to have a Christmas tree, and Mr. S. is to make a present to each of the scholars that attend his school. The youngsters anticipate a fine time. The children of the Presbyterian school are invited to attend and help sing.

Thursday 23d. It began snowing about 1 oclock and kept steadily on till dark. Therefore we now have another deep snow to wade through. Tis a heavy, wet snow. Bobtail was here to day, and all I bought was a pair of mittens to put in Walla's stocking Christmas, they just fit the little toad, 25cts was the price; a braid for the skirt of my cashmere, 12½cts. Wallace is in town tonight practicing. He said the teacher would be with them tonight for the last time. Mr. Chittenden's school closed this evening. Mary is delighted that it is so. . . . Before I go to bed I will have finished a dark calico apron for Walla. His grandma finished her washing about dark and has been taking care of him since. I fried onions for supper at the request of his grandpa. I was so affected that I cried all the time during the getting of supper. I cleaned the dining and kitchen.

Friday 24th. I have been pretty busy this day. I cleaned the dining room, kitchen, my room and part of the hall, made starch and starched 4 sh[ir]ts, ironed one. Walla's grandma is now busy baking cake for Christmas. Wallace brought home last night two primers for Walla. One is the history of Jack Horner and his Christmas pie, with which Walla is very much delighted. The other is a primer printed on linen with the alphabet in great large letters. . . . Mr. Chittenden was here today, and he allowed that my geranium was looking fine, and really I think he is sensible on that subject, for as I look up at it sitting so gracefully in its vase on the table I think so too. There is a grand ball at the National tonight, but none of the Williams from Gold Flat will be there. Well I will dry my pen and put up, as Walla would say. There is to be 6 chickens killed tonight, and I have volunteered to dress the fowls.

Saturday the 25th   Well Christmas has come round again, but I cannot say that I enjoyed it much.

The traveling is so bad that tis hard to get around. Therefore we have had to stay within doors. I cleaned the dining room and kitchen this morning, then about 4 dressed up a little myself. Walla has been very fretful all day and [we] have seen but very little peace with the youngster this day. Wallace and his father both condescended to be home to supper. His mother had roasted a turkey and chicken. She also had a bread pudding that was capital and plum cake not to be beat. You see, she baked 10 loaves of cake last night. Now about Sant Clauses pranks, I found a bundle of candy tied on the door knob of my room and on opening a drawer in the beaureau found one of my old ragged stockings containing a beautiful embroidered hand kerchief. That was the amount of Christmas gifts that fell to my share. George had his Christmas tree full, and little Walla's stocking was filled to overflowing. The little toad was very much delighted when he saw the varieties of candy that it contained. Strange to say, he did not know enough about candy to know that it was to eat, never having had any before.[8]

1858

I Shall Be Pleased to See You

*Sylvanus Lines, who was a Connecticut-born printer, and
Amelia Jane "Jennie" Akehurst, who was a New York schoolteacher, both moved South
in search of better jobs. The first two letters below, which were written in 1858,
show the beginnings of a tentative courtship, which got off to an unlucky start
their first Christmas. The 1859 entry, which follows, came from Jennie's diary.
By that time, the newlyweds were living in an Atlanta boardinghouse.*

tlanta, Dec 23

Friend Jennie—

As I intend to leave this place the coming week and as it is impossible to visit

you in the mean time, I shall be pleased to see you in Atlanta on Christmas day if it is convenient. Mrs. Welton says she should like to see you and will make arrangements for a Christmas dinner, as I told her that I thought you would come. As the time is too short for me to hear from you unless you should receive this in time for the mail tomorrow night, I shall be at the train on Saturday morning and shall be happy to meet you if it is your pleasure.

Very truly yours
S. De F. Lines

Covington December 25th/58
Mr. Lines

Allow me to wish you a "merry Christmas" I should be most happy to spend it with you were it possible. Your note has just been handed to me; the train has gone two hours ago. Had I received it a few hours earlier I should have given myself the pleasure of accepting the kind invitation of Mrs. Welton and yourself: but I hope my not being able to do so will not interfere with your merriment at all. I am going to have a few days rest, and expect to spend them very quietly in my room. Last evening I attended a party at the Masonic Hall; and enjoyed myself just about as I always do in a gay crowd. . . .

Please give my love to Mrs. Welton, tell her I regret *exceedingly* that I can not dine with her to-day.

Commence to savin' nuts and apples, fixin' up party clothes, snitchin' lace an' beads fum de big house. General celebratin' time, you see, 'cause husbands is comin' home an' families is gittin' united agin. Husbands hurry on home to see dey new babies. Ev'ybody happy. Marse always send a keg of whiskey down to de quarters by ole Uncle Silas, de house man. Ole Joe would drink all he kin long de way, but dey's plenty fo' all. Ef dat don' las' olde marse Shelton gonna bring some mo' down hisself.[10]

De Debbil Got in Me Good

Mary Wyatt, who claimed to be ninety-nine years old when she was interviewed, told about a dress she couldn't resist.

Ole Missus had one dress dat she wore only in de spring time. Lawdy, I used to take dat dress when she warn't nowhere round an' hole it up against me an' 'magine myself wearin' it. One Christmas de debbil got in me good. Got dat gown out de house 'neath my petticoat tied rounst me an' wore it to de dance. Was scared to death dat Missus gonna come in but she didn't. Marsa come, but I knowed he warn't able to tell one dress from 'nother. Sho was glad when I slipped dat dress back in place de nex' day. Never did dat no mo'.[11]

Chile, I Done Had Plenty Clothes

Nancy Williams, who was ninety years old when interviewed, told how she profited by her talent and her wits.

Clothes, chile, I done had plenty clothes in slavery days. Christmas time used to wear sometimes three or four different dresses de same day. How I git money to buy clothes? Used to quilt de purtiest quilts you ever see. My father made me some shelves an' a closet to keep dose quilts in. Used to sell 'em to de white folks; de best ones Missus herse'f would buy. Sold one quilt for $4.00, sold another for $3.00. Den I would make 'spinders, socks an' ev'ything you could think of. Knit all de summer an' all de fall gittin' ready fo' Christmas.

Wouldn't wear Missus' hand-me-downs, no sir. Wear store-bought clothes. Lord, I 'member one Christmas I wore dat Junie bug silk dress. Dis dress had three ruffles, an' de wais' was all puffed up all round. Den I had other dresses all different colors. How I git 'em? Jes change dey color. Git tired of my white dress I'd dye it red with poke berries. Always paint my shoes to match my dress. Paint 'em wid barn paint fum de stable. Lordy chile, couldn't none o' dem other gals dress lak me.[12]

Sech Dancin' You Never Did See

Louise Jones, a 95-year-old ex-slave from Emporia, Virginia, told the W.P.A. interviewer how her master enjoyed watching his slaves have a good time at Christmas.

Seem like he got as much fun out of it as us did. Let de men go in de saw mill an' put together a great platform an' bring it to de barn fo' us to dance on. Den come de music, de fiddles an' de banjos, de Jews harp, an' all dem other things. Sech dancin' you never did see befo'. Slaves would set de flo in turns, an' do de cake-walk mos' all night.

Ole Marsa stan' off in de corner wid his arms folded jus' a-puffin' on his corn-cob pipe. . . .

An' we sho' used to have a good time. Yes, sir. We was walkin' an' talkin' wid de devil both day an' night. Settin' all 'round was dem big demi-jonahs of whisky what Marsa done give us. An' de smell of roast pigs an' chicken comin' fum de quarters made ev'ybody feel good. Was't nothin' we ain' had Christmas-time.[13]

Harper's New Monthly Magazine, December 1885

He Could Play the Fiddle

Adeline Jackson, who was born about 1849,
was interviewed in Winnsboro, South Carolina, when she was eighty-eight.

arster Edward bought a slave in Tennessee just 'cause he could play the fiddle. Named him Tennessee Ike, and he played along with Ben Murray, another fiddler. Sometime all of us would be called up into the front yard to play and dance and sing for Miss Marion, the chillun, and visitors. Everything lively at Christmas time, dances with fiddles, patting, and stick rattling.[14]

My Beloved Violin

Solomon Northup, a free black man living in New York,
was kidnapped in 1841 and sold into slavery. His northern friends rescued
him from a cotton plantation near the Red River in Louisiana in 1853.
As he revealed in his later memoirs, it was fortunate
that Northup was a good fiddler.

las! had it not been for my beloved violin, I scarcely can conceive how I could have endured the long years of bondage. It introduced me to great houses—relieved me of many days' labor in the field—supplied me with conveniences for my cabin—with pipes and tobacco, and extra pairs of shoes. . . . It heralded my name round the country—made me friends, who, otherwise would not have noticed me—gave me an honored seat at the yearly feasts, and secured the loudest and heartiest welcome of them all at the Christmas dance.[15]

The Fiddler Rules

In his 1856 book of poems, The Hireling and the Slave,
South Carolina poet William John Grayson vividly pictured
plantation slaves at a Christmastime dance.

hen clear the barn, the ample area fill,
In the gay jig display their vigorous skill;
No dainty steps, no mincing measures here—

But hearts of joy and nerves of living steel,
On floors that spring beneath the bounding reel;
Proud on his chair, with magisterial glance
And stamping foot, the fiddler rules the dance.[16]

1 8 5 9

Gas Lights

*Up North, the New York English Lutheran Church of St. James
came up with a tree-lighting innovation for a Sunday school Christmas festival.
The new idea was reported a few weeks later in the January 5, 1859,
issue of the Pittsburgh Missionary.*

The great feature of the occasion . . . was the tree—the Christmas tree! It was a
perfect gem in its way; and I verily believe it would have made your eyes dance with
delight, connoisseur as you are in matters of this kind. The tree presented a new feature
of this kind—a feature which, so far as I know—has never before been introduced into
the Christmas tree. Instead of the usual tapers, it was lighted with gas. Nearly two hundred jets sparkled and glimmered through the branches upon which were suspended
upwards of *six hundred* articles of various size and value, designed as presents for the
children.[17]

1859

The Sound of Merry Bells

This account came from the Chicago Tribune on December 24, 1859.

The streets were alive and astir all day with sleighs and sleighing parties, and far into the night the sound of merry bells and cheerful voices rang on the cold clear air. How we envied them, in our sanctum, "the bells and the belles," the happy fellows who were sleighing last evening.[18]

1860

The Rainiest Season Since '49

Out West, William Henry Brewer, working as a botanist with the California State Geological Survey, experienced an unusually wet December in 1860. He later wrote this account in his book,
Up and Down California in 1860-1864.

Los Angeles
December 26

Rain interfered with Christmas festivities, but it was still quite lively. I stepped in a *fandango* a little while in the evening and looked on to see the dancing, which did not come up to my expectations. In the next room they were playing *monte* for large piles of silver—the stakes not large, but the silver accumulated.

The rain has been the severest for eleven years. Probably as much as six or seven inches fell in about forty hours. You can imagine the effect. It is very hard on these *adobe* houses. Several have fallen, one row of stores, among the rest, involving a loss of many thousand dollars. It has been the rainiest season since '49—lucky we were not in camp during this siege, it is decidedly better at the hotel. As a sample of how damp the air is, when I am writing, fine as my writing is, the first line of the page is not yet dry when the last is written.[19]

1860

Charleston in a Blaze of Excitement

*George Christy's Minstrels, from Broadway, New York, opened in Charleston,
South Carolina, in mid-December 1860. The group's business
agent sent this letter to the New York Clipper months later on March 16, 1861,
explaining why the minstrel show remained neutral when Federal troops
withdrew to Fort Sumter on the night after Christmas.*

e were in Charleston on the night of the evacuation of Fort Moultrie by Major Anderson, and notwithstanding the city was in a blaze of excitement, George Christy's Minstrels performed to a good house. . . . It was reported in Charleston that we had paraded in New York City with the [Republican] "Wide Awakes," the information having been furnished by some anonymous FRIEND of ours from New York. The people were satisfied it was a falsehood, and done for the purpose of injuring us. We informed them that we had never engaged in any political demonstration; that we depended as much upon the people of the North as those of the South for our living, and for that reason we had no right to meddle with politics. In every city we have visited, we have advertised "George Christy's Minstrels, from Broadway, New York," not being ashamed or afraid to own we were Northern men, and for that very reason the people of the Southern country have treated us in the kindest manner.[20]

1 8 6 1

It Would Have Ruined the Christmas Parties

In Gone with the Wind, *Scarlett O'Hara*
expressed her relief about Georgia's date of secession.

'm mighty glad Georgia waited till after Christmas before it seceded or it would have ruined the Christmas parties, too.[21]

1 8 6 1

Very Little Laughing in Our Ranks

Josiah Patterson, a member of the 14th Regiment,
Georgia Volunteers, wrote this letter to his family back home in Georgia.

anassas, Virginia: December 13, 1861

My dear little Sons:

I do not know what my little boys and my angel Anna will do for a Santa Claus this Christmas. It would be fine if the little fel[lows] could get up in the morning and find th[eir] little stockings full of goodies [and] cry out, "Sure, it was Pa! Pa is old Santa Claus!" But I don't think we will have such a happy Christmas morning. But it will be hard if the old fellow did not come just because Pa is not at home. I am sure he need not be afraid. Ma would neither kiss or whip him if she found him in the house filling your little socks with delicacies. I must try and get the old fellow to call and see you, if I am so fortunate as to see him before that time. But he may be afraid of soldiers and keep out of my way. Pa expects to be home before a great while, and I anticipate a very jolly time with my darling Sons and little Daughter. . . . When I come you must call your little [student] company out to drill, so that I can show you how an officer of the army musters men. I expect you all laugh and talk while you are mustering and have a merry time generally. But we have very little to say and very little laughing in our ranks, I assure you. . . .

I must close. May God bless and protect you, my little Sons. Be good little boys. Do not quarrel, kiss little Anna four times apiece for me.

Your Father.[22]

Christmas Furlough
Drawn by Thomas Nast

1861

Our Bereaved Hearts

Jennie and Sylvanus Lines courted in 1858 and married in 1859. By 1861, the couple had lost their baby girl. These passages from Jennie Lines's diary told of the sad Christmas without their Lillie.

Thurs. 24   Have been doing just what I done one year ago to-day. Baking for Christmas. My hands have been employed the same but my thoughts are in sad contrast. Then my little Lillie was with me and I was constantly talking to her, telling her what mama was making for sweet pet. I filled her little stocking that night, although she was only eleven months old and could not understand and enjoy Santa Claus presents. If she was with us now I think to-morrow would be the happiest Christmas of my life. I have been thinking all day what I would make and buy for my darling if she was here, and with how much eagerness and delight she would examine the contents of her little stocking—how sweetly she would prattle and how she would love and caress papa and mama for the toys and candies. O I can imagine it all, and as I think of the happiness I feel the sad weary look pass away from my face and a happy mothers smile lights it up for a moment, but then comes back the crushing reality and again my face is sad and my spirit bowed.

Frid. 25   Christmas day. Sylvanus and I remembered each other last night and slipped a small token of our great love in each others stocking. But O! how inexpressibly sad have been our bereaved hearts to-day. Our thoughts have been with our sweet child. Sylvanus intended to take help and go to the grave yard to-day and have our lot improved. We want to set out choice flowers and make the ground where our sweet one sleeps look as cheerful as possible. The day was very cold and Sylvanus could get no one to go with him, so was obliged to give it up. Hope it need not be neglected much longer. . . . We had a very nice dinner. Sylvanus invited a wounded soldier to dine with us. Hope he enjoyed it.[23]

1 8 6 2

I Did Not Sleep Good Last Night

This letter to his family from Oliver P. Kibbe, a forty-one-year-old captain in the 30th New Jersey Volunteers, was reprinted in the New Brunswick (N.J.) Daily News.

Aquia Creek, Va. December 25, 1862

My dear children—I wish you a Merry Christmas. I hope it is truly a merry one to you, though your father is away down in "Dixie" sick and shut up in a little dirty tent. You can be merry over thinking about Old Santa Claus for I presume he was round last night and left you something. If I was only with you I would care little whether he gave you anything or not. But I hope that you will enjoy yourselves and be merry and happy, and try to make others so, too. I did not sleep good last night, and while I lay awake thinking about Christmas, I did not know [how] I could spend the day most pleasantly. Finally I concluded to write to my children, but I had to get my own breakfast this morning. Isaac is sick. He is going home tomorrow morning. I don't know what I shall do when he goes away, but God will provide some way for me. I hope that my papers will come soon, then I can come home too; but that is uncertain.

We have a goose for Christmas dinner today. We can't bake it, so we cut it up and boil it in a camp kettle. It is fat, but I do not suppose it will be very good. Our sutler [peddlar who sells provisions] appeared yesterday and I had a change in my food. I got some sweet potatoes, some mince pie, apples and cider. If I could get some bread I could live well enough under the circumstances. I have not tasted bread in a long time.

I suppose your exhibition came off last evening. I hope it was a good one. How I would liked to have been there to see and hear you. I have not seen a child of any description in many weeks. There are no children about here except a few colored ones that pass along now and then. Lieutenant Lanning saw a colored woman a few days ago with three girls, one in her arms, the other two on foot, and hardly any clothes enough to cover their nakedness, and barefoot. It was a very cold day and snowing, but they did not seem to mind it at all.

There are no houses for several miles around, they have all been destroyed. It is a hilly and disolate country, though before the war it was pleasant around here. Where the army has been every thing is destroyed or laid waste.

Now dear children, you must think of the many good things you have to enjoy, and thank God when you kneel down to pray that He is so good and kind to you. I know you are not rich, and do not have everything that some children do, but you do not know what it is to suffer for want of food and clothing. Thank God that you can be happy and comfortable. Remember from whence all your blessings come. Be kind to your mother who watches over you with so much care and solicitude. She labors, toils and cares for you even when you are asleep on your soft beds. Be kind to each other. Love each other. Help each other, and strive to be good little children. No matter if other children are bad, don't do as they do. Now I want you all to remember what I say to you, and kiss your Mother for me, and I hope next Thursday you will be able to say it is a Happy New Year.

Good-bye

From your Father[24]

1862

The Fault Lies with the Post Office Department

William White, a soldier with the 18th Regiment,
Georgia Volunteers, wrote this letter to Sophie Buchanan.

Fredericksburg, Virginia, December 24, 1862

Dear Mit:

I spent yesterday with Warren. We had a lively time talking over old times. He told me that you had not received a letter from me in several weeks and that you were very anxious to know what had become of me. Now, my little dear, I must say that it is not my fault that you do not hear from me. The fault lies with the post office department, for I have written to you once every week since I have been in service, which would make 72 letters that I have written to you. But be that as it may, I shall continue to write every week and oftener, if I can. You must do the same. . . .

The weather is very cold here this evening. The clouds are thick and foretell a shower of snow as a Christmas treat. Captain O'Neill is just in from Richmond with plenty of cakes and apples, so we are enjoying ourselves finely. I wish I could be in

Oxford to take breakfast with you in the morning. I know you will think of me often. Answer immediately and direct your letters as before. Tell Aunt M. to kiss you as a Christmas gift from me. I wish you a long and merry Christmas. . . .

My respects to the family and three bushels of love for yourself. I must close. Farewell for the present.

Your devoted lover.[25]

1862

Roses Bloom Abundantly

In his book, Up and Down California in 1860-1864,
*William Henry Brewer, spending his second Christmas in California,
expressed a New Englander's longing for the
white Christmases of his childhood.*

San Francisco

December 27

Christmas Eve I went to midnight Mass in one of the Catholic churches. Christmas was a most lovely day, the city seemed alive, all seemed happy. I took dinner with Mr. Putnam, and in the evening attended a large concert. . . .

Sunday, December 28

It is one of the most lovely days of the season. The sky is bright, and the air of matchless purity, the mountains fifty or sixty miles distant seem as clear as if but half a dozen miles away. . . .

I was at church this morning, an Episcopal church, all decorated with evergreens, and this afternoon it seems as if all the city was on the street.

The customs of Europe and of the East are transplanted here—churches are decked with evergreens, Christmas trees are the fashion—yet to me, as a *botanist*, it looks exotic. . . . Churches are decked with *redwood*, which has foliage very like our hemlock—it is called evergreen, but it is hard for the people to remember that nearly *all* California trees are *evergreen*. While at Christmas time at home the oaks and other trees stretch leafless branches to the wintry winds, *here* the oaks of the hills are as green as they were in August—the laurel, the madroño, the manzanita, the toyon, are rich in their dense green foliage; roses bloom abundantly in the gardens, the yards are gaudy with geraniums, callas, asters, violets, and other flowers; and there is no snow visible, even on the distant mountains. Christmas here, to me represents a *date*, a *festival*, but not a season. It is not the Christmas of my childhood, not the Christmas of Santa Claus with "his tiny reindeer," the Christmas around which clings some of the richest poetry and prose of the English language. I cannot divest my mind and memory of the association of this season with snowy landscapes, and tinkling sleigh bells, and leafless forests, and more than all, the bright and cheerful winter fireside, the warmth within contrasting with the cold without. So do not wonder if at such times I find a feeling of sadness akin to homesickness creeping over me, that my fireside seems more desolate than ever, and my path in life a lonelier one.[26]

1862

They Deserve a Good Turn Out

This plea to support the annual fundraising event held by the Bloomington, Illinois, volunteer fire department appeared in the Bloomington Pantagraph *on December 22, 1862.*

he Prairie Birds are busy making all due arrangements for their Annual Ball, and will soon have them completed. So they will open the holidays by a great affair. The boys are a first rate lot of fellows always on hand when there is a fire. They deserve a good turn out and will be sure to get one.[27]

1862

Rally 'Round the Flag, Boys!

Patriotic songs in the War Between the States sometimes caused hard feelings, as evidenced by this article from the Norristown, Pennsylvania, Herald and Free Press on December 30, 1862.

On Christmas night the Episcopal Church featured a festival at the Odd Fellows' Hall. In the centre of the room a cedar tree was planted reaching the ceiling. From every branch presents for the children were suspended, and from the top to the bottom, it was illuminated by scores of colored lanterns. Around the tree the tables were spread, laden with the good things that were to be devoured. The children entered the room by classes and marched round the tree joining in the chorus of the "Christmas Tree." During the evening they sang several hymns and songs . . . and among them we were pleased to hear the stirring songs of "Rally round the Flag, boys!" notwithstanding the superintendent of the School objected to the song on the ground that it was not right to *mix politics with religion!* After the children had been feasted to their full, the Rector of the Church, Mr. Woart extended an invitation to all other children in the room to partake, and generous supplies of the fragments were handed around the Hall among the spectators. When the feast was over the work of disrobing the tree commenced. Each article bore the name of the scholar for whom it was intended, and as each name was announced, the eagerness and delight of the "little folks" was unbounded.[28]

1862

The Christmas Turkey

When the Civil War broke out, Cornelia Peake McDonald was a middle-class mother of nine children. The oldest of these children was only fourteen. They lived in a medium-sized two-story house in Winchester, Virginia, a town of constant troop movement throughout the war, with both armies sweeping in and out of town. "My Diary was begun at the request of my husband," she wrote, "who was on the eve of leaving Winchester with the Stonewall Brigade, and in the expectation that the town would be immediately occupied by the enemy, he wished to be informed of each day's events as they took place during his absence."

ecember 15th— . . . Christmas is but ten days off, the blessed time that used to be so joyous. It shall have something bright and cheery in it for the children. They shall hang up their stockings, poor little things, even if I have to manufacture the things to put in them.

[On the 18th she read an account of the battle of Fredericksburg.] . . . Twenty-five hundred of our men wounded, and five hundred killed. Some of those very ill-clad, eager faced fellows that I saw pass through the streets.

23rd—Every day an alarm that the Yankees are coming. Yesterday it was said that they were a few miles from town. . . . The day wore away and no Yankees. But this morning as I was dressing I heard a clatter as of cavalry on the march, and looking out beheld the blue coats, five hundred strong.

They posted pickets at our gate and rode on through the town. All was soon quiet as ever. . . .

My two boys have set out for their Christmas visit to their Uncle Fayette which they expect to enjoy greatly. Poor little fellows, they have been for weeks cutting and hauling a supply of wood for our use during the winter. There was no other way to get it, and fortunately we had old Kit left of all our horses. I hated to see them go out to such rough hard work, but they liked it, and have already brought in ten cords.

24th—In the kitchen all day making cakes for the children's Christmas, labour by no means light with only a young servant to assist, but as Aunt Winnie was there to direct and retrieve errors, all went on right smoothly.

In the afternoon I saw from the door a cavalry regiment ride in and take possession of Mr. Wood's yard and beautiful grounds, attracted no doubt by the grass which is still green in many places. I was pitying them from my heart as Mr. Wood and his sisters are such old people and have always been accustomed to quiet and comfort; but my pity for them was suddenly displaced by anxiety for myself, for I beheld two cavalry men on their way through the yard stop and take the Christmas turkey that had been dressed and hung on a low branch of a tree for cooking on the morrow.

He had walked with it a few steps before I realized what had taken place, and with the consciousness of the loss came the remembrance of the straits to which I was reduced before that turkey could be obtained; how I had spent six dollars, and sent a man miles on horseback to get it rather than have nothing good and pleasant for our Christmas dinner. With the recollection of all that, came the inspiration to try and re-cover it, so I flew after him, and in a commanding tone demanded the restoration of my property.

The man laughed derisively and told me I had no right to it, being "secesh" as he expressed it, and that it was confiscated to the United States. "Very well," said I, "go on to the camp with it, and I will go with you to the commanding officer." He gave it up then and I returned triumphantly to the kitchen with it. Just as I got back I looked and saw a regiment of infantry, "foot people," as old Aunt Winnie calls them, filing into our orchard. In five minutes the garden fence had disappeared and the boarding from the carriage house and other buildings was being torn off. Some were carrying off the wood that my poor little boys had cut and hauled. It made me almost weep to see the labour of their poor little hands appropriated by those thieves. How thankful I was that they were far away. . . .

While I was trying to arrest the work of destruction, someone told me the robbers were in the kitchen, carrying off the things. In I went, and found it full of men. One took up a tray of cakes, and as I turned to rescue them, Mary, the servant, pulled my sleeve to show something else they were carrying off, and when I turned to him another seized something else till I was nearly wild. At last Mary said, "Miss Cornelia he's got your rusks." (Those rusks that I had made myself and worked till my wrists ached, the first I ever made.)

A man had opened the stove and taken out the pan of nice light brown rusks, and was running out with them. A fit of heroism seized me and I darted after him, and just as he reached the porch steps, I caught him by the collar of his great coat, and held him tight till the hot pan burnt his hands and he was forced to drop it. An officer was riding by, and beholding the scene stopped and asked the meaning of it. Explaining, I lost my gravity, and so did he, and there we laughed long and loud over it. It was so perfectly

Christmas Eve 1862
Drawn by Thomas Nast

ridiculous that I forgot for the time all the havoc that was going on. The officer went away, and soon a guard came and quiet was restored, at least near the house, but all night long the work of demolition of buildings went on. . . .

25—The day has been too restless to enjoy, or even to realize that it was Christmas. All day reports of the advance of the Confederates, and our consequent excitement. Just as were sitting down to dinner, we heard repeated reports of cannon. We hurried from the table and found the troops all hastily marching off. They expected a fight, I was told by one, as the Confederates were near town. We could eat no more dinner, the girls and myself, so it was carefully put away till we could enjoy it.

In the evening I went over to Mr. Woods' to see how the old people were bearing their burden, and to take them something nice from the dessert we could not eat. . . . As I returned home I saw the troops marching back again, like the King of France. The guard was withdrawn at night, which was rather singular, but all is quiet, and so "I will lay me down to sleep and take my rest, for it is Thou, Lord, who makest me to dwell in safety."

[The day after Christmas, Union soldiers smashed in the windows with their fists, broke into the house, and she found them] . . . jumping out of the window, one with a cut glass decanter full of wine, prints of butter and everything that could be carried off, including the remains of the Christmas dinner.[29]

1862

A Gloomy One

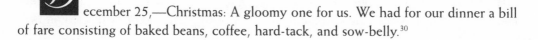

William Bircher of Minnesota, who was fifteen years old and small for his age, talked his parents into signing consent papers so he could join the Union Army as a drummer boy with the Second Regiment Minnesota Veteran Volunteers. In his diary, he wrote of his first Christmas as a soldier.

December 25,—Christmas: A gloomy one for us. We had for our dinner a bill of fare consisting of baked beans, coffee, hard-tack, and sow-belly.[30]

 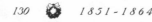

<h1 align="center">*1862*</h1>

<h1 align="center">Who Shall Answer For It?</h1>

Soldiers, acting as battlefield reporters, often sent letters from the front to
their hometown newspapers. The following letter to the Rutland *(*Vermont*)*
Herald *was written by a correspondent camped with the 12th Vermont*
Brigade near Fairfax Court House, Virginia.

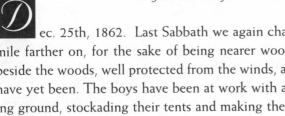

Dec. 25th, 1862. Last Sabbath we again changed our camp, moving about a half mile farther on, for the sake of being nearer wood and water. We are now encamped beside the woods, well protected from the winds, and altogether better situated than we have yet been. The boys have been at work with a hearty good will clearing the camping ground, stockading their tents and making themselves comfortable in various ways. If we are not moved soon, we shall be [so] pleasantly situated that we shall be very happy in seeing any of our Vermont friends here. . . .

A party of us have just returned from the battle ground of Chantilly where our Christmas has been passed. A sad though interesting manner of spending it, amidst so much reminding us both of life and death. Our object in revisiting it was two-fold: partly to gratify our curiosity, and partly for the humane purpose of caring for the still unburied dead. Having partaken of a hasty breakfast, we started out under the guidance of one of our party who had already visited the ground. The weather was foggy, and, as often happens in such cases, we lost our way. To lose one's way, however, on such occasions, only serves to enliven the party, and give zest to the walk; so we quietly retraced our steps, and started anew. It is only three miles from camp, but the sun pointed almost noon before we found ourselves entering the woods, which skirt the eastern side of the open field where the battle was principally fought. A solitary grave, with its small wooden head-board, marked "J. Fellows, Louisiana Tigers, killed September 4th 1862," was the first indication that death had been there.

As we walked on, the trees on every side showed abundant proof that the bullets flew thick as hail on their death dealing errands. Emerging from the woods, the battle ground lay before us. A pleasant field of 20 or 30 acres, of gently swelling ground, skirted on the east and north by woods, with its pleasant farm house on the south. It did not seem, to look over it, as though death and destruction had so recently been there in such horrid forms. We were not long in discovering the traces of the conflict. Only a short distance from the woods in a narrow gully, a number of bodies had been rudely thrown, with nothing but a scant covering of earth which the rains had already washed away, leaving their bleached skeletons partially exposed. We gave such burial as our means afforded and passed quickly on. A little further on in the edge of the woods, we found the skeleton of some poor fellow lying at the roots of an old oak tree, wholly unburied. His accouterments were beside him, even to his shelter tent. His musket stock had been shot away, and lay beside him. It furnished the only identification, being marked "J.B.H." Alone and unhonored he died; who shall answer for it? A bountiful supply of mother earth was all we could give him, and we passed on.

A line of rail fence runs through the center of the field, and here was where our line of battle was formed. The ground was thickly carpeted with the bitten ends of cartridges, showing how bravely our men stood their ground. Further on, in a long row of cedars, the rebels formed their line, and scattered fragments of their accouterments are thickly strewn around.

We wandered over the field for an hour or two, picking up here and there a memento of the battle ground, and doing what kindly services we could for the unburied dead. We turned homeward with more thoughtful countenances, feeling sick at heart with the sight of such war's horrors. Whoever, hereafter, visits the battle ground of Chantilly, will not be shocked by such sights as we saw, I trust, but can view the ground with more pleasant feelings, and carry away with them more pleasant thoughts.

Very truly,

B.[31]

1862

There is a Day of Retribution

*Nurse Kate Cumming of Mobile, Alabama, worked with the Confederate
Army of Tennessee's medical service. The two entries below are from the journal she kept
during the war. The first entry was written in 1862 while she served as matron
(executive nurse) in a Chattanooga hospital. The second was written in 1863 in
Newnan, Georgia, south of Atlanta, as Kate's hospital moved
ahead of retreating Southern troops.*

*D*ecember 30—Have just recovered from a severe spell of sickness. I received much kindness from one and all, for which I am sincerely grateful. I suffered much, and thought often about the sick men, and my admiration rose more and more for their fortitude and patience.

Have received a number of letters from home, telling me about Christmas, and how unlike what it was before the war; but my folks say that all in Mobile are very thankful they are permitted to remain in peace, for they fully expected that by this time the enemy would be thundering at their ports. They also say that many there are making fortunes, and living as if there was no war. I am told it is the same in all large cities. There is no use worrying about these things. I expect all will come out right, and that there are enough self-sacrificing people in the land to save it.

The haughty foe has had another "On to Richmond," and been repulsed; Virginia has been again drenched with the blood of martyrs—Fredericksburg, another of her fair cities, laid in ruins. North Carolina has also suffered. Williamston and Hamilton have been completely sacked. Women and children are driven out without shelter, while their homes are laid in ruins. Well, these things will not always last. There is a day of retribution for the northern people.

1863

Wondering If the Girls
Will Marry Them Now

*C*hristmas-day, December 25—We have had quite a pleasant one. Miss W. [Womack] and myself were up hours before daylight making eggnog. We wished to give some to all in the hospital, but could not procure eggs enough; so we gave it to the wounded who are convalescent, the cooks, and the nurses.

Just at peep of dawn the little gallery in front of our house was crowded with the wounded. The scene was worthy of a picture; many of them without a leg or an arm, and they were as cheerful and contented as if no harm had ever happened them. I constantly hear the unmarried ones wondering if the girls will marry them now. Dr. Hughes did his best to have a nice dinner for the convalescents and nurses. Turkeys, chickens, vegetables, and pies. I only wish the men in the army could have fared as well.

In the afternoon we had a call from all of our surgeons, and from one or two from the other hospitals. I had hard work to get Mrs. W. to spare a few hours from working for "her dear boys," and have a kind of holiday for once, as nearly all of our wounded are doing well. . . .

We have only lost one or two from gangrene. I am confident that nothing but the care and watchfulness bestowed on them by the surgeons has been the means of saving the lives of many. Their recovery has taken me by surprise, as I could not see how it was possible for such bad wounds to heal.

Many of the wounded are still in tents, with chimneys which smoke badly, and the whole tent has rather an uncomfortable appearance; still I like tents for wounded, as they seem to improve much more rapidly in them than in rooms.

The nurses, on windy nights, are compelled to sit up and hold on to the tent-poles to prevent their being blown down. . . .

Dr. W. [Wellford] is a perfect Virginia gentleman. He is one of the gentlest and most attentive surgeons that I have ever met. I think we owe the recovery of many of the wounded mainly to his great care. I have known him many a time work from daylight till dark attending to the wounds. Dr. Burks of Kentucky has been here but a short time; so I can say little about him. The men all like him very much, and they are generally good judges. . . .

Dr. W. has a nurse from Arkansas. He came here with the wounded after the battle of Chickamauga. We called him "rough diamond," as he is so rough-looking, and seems to have such a kind heart. He thinks nothing a trouble which he has to do for the wounded. . . .

We are using a great deal of charcoal on the wounds, and the nurses have it to pulverize, which gives them constant work, besides the dirt which it causes in the wards. . . .

General Bragg has resigned. For his own sake and ours, I am heartily glad.[32]

1863

Christmas Bells

On December 1, Henry Wadsworth Longfellow's
seventeen-year-old son, Charles,
who was a second lieutenant with the First Massachusetts Cavalry,
was seriously wounded at New Hope Church, Virginia.
During long hours at the boy's bedside while he recuperated,
Longfellow wrote this sorrowful poem.

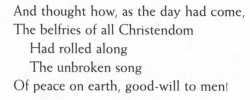

I heard the bells on Christmas Day
  Their old, familiar carols play,
    And wild and sweet
    The words repeat
Of Peace on earth, good-will to men!

And thought how, as the day had come,
The belfries of all Christendom
    Had rolled along
    The unbroken song
Of peace on earth, good-will to men!

Till, ringing, swinging on its way,
The world revolved from night to day
    A voice, a chime,
    A chant sublime
Of peace on earth, good-will to men!

Then from each black, accursed mouth
The cannon thundered in the South
    And with the sound
    The carols drowned
Of peace on earth, good-will to men!

It was as if an earthquake rent
The hearth-stones of a continent,
    And made forlorn
    The households born
Of peace on earth, good-will to men!

And in despair I bowed my head;
"There is no peace on earth," I said;
    "For hate is strong
    And mocks the song
Of peace on earth, good-will to men!"

Then pealed the bells more loud and deep,
"God is not dead; nor doth He sleep!
    The Wrong shall fail,
    The Right prevail,
Of peace on earth, good-will to men!"[33]

 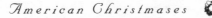

<h1 style="text-align:center">1863</h1>

<h1 style="text-align:center">He Says I Am a Magnet</h1>

*In December 1863, Pauline DeCaradeuc Heyward,
who was twenty years old, lived on Montmorenci plantation,
near Aiken, South Carolina. In her journal, she wrote about the romance
that bloomed while a soldier was on Christmas furlough.*

 ec. 29th, 1863   Well, since last I wrote here a good deal has happened, some of which I feel now like telling you, dear old Journal, so stop & listen. . . .

On Christmas day we went to walk and met Father coming home with Mr. John H. Cochran, Mrs. McChesney's eldest son, he is on the coast with Wise's Brig, and Mother by . . . writing to his General, obtained a five day furlough to spend with us. He is quite handsome, nicely educated, and with very easy pleasant manner, and when he left this morning we all felt sorry to part, and all like him so much.

Cousin Maxine & Julia came over and stayed with us too, and we played all sorts of games, & had music, the first time I had touched the piano since the death of my darling Brothers. Oh! How strange it seemed to have a young man staying here who was not *their* guest & how I more than ever missed them.

Yesterday John Cochran & I walked together a very long walk, he made me tell him *all* about our boys & spoke *so* kindly to me. He says I am a magnet & draw him more closely to him every moment he spends with me, that he felt as tho he has known & loved me all his life, and wants me to correspond with him until he comes again, . . . He told me of all his annoyances & troubles in camp, and I do feel the greatest interest in him. I made him a beautiful scarf, he said he valued it too highly to take it to Camp and sent it on to Virginia to his mother to keep for him. He says he never met with so congenial a mind as mine, and in truth we are alike; . . . he told me again of his love, &

I told him the same thing I did before, that I knew him too short a time for my heart to have been touched, but old Journal, there's that about him, which, I feel sure, time & acquaintance will put into my heart.[34]

Santa Claus in Camp
Drawn by Thomas Nast

1863

How Cold,
How Dark and Dreary

Union drummer-boy William Bircher spent his second Christmas in the army. As these diary entries show, he was struggling with the hard question of whether to re-enlist or to go back home and finish his schooling.

December 24: All quiet in camp. The re-enlisting continued. The camp reminded one of an old-fashioned political caucus, the way the boys stood around in knots trying to convince others that it was all for the best for them to re-enlist; and some of them, to prove their argument, re-enlisted themselves.

December 25: Christmas: but how dark, how cold and dreary. How dismal every-thing was in camp. The band boys had all re-enlisted except Wagner and I, and we now made up our minds not to remain out; the others had used every endeavor to coax us in, so we at last consented, and were mustered in for another three years.[35]

1863

23 Holes In My Blanket

In his diary, Confederate orderly Sergeant Robert Watson of Key West, Florida, recorded his third wartime Christmas (this one at Dalton, Georgia), which followed a close call at Chickamauga.

ecember 25: . . . a bullet struck my knapsack at the right shoulder and came out at the left shoulder, making 23 holes in my blanket.

Christmas day and a very dull one but I find a tolerable good dinner. I had one drink of whiskey in the morning. There was some serenading last night but I took no part in it for I did not feel merry as my thoughts were of home.[36]

1863

Yells, Curses, and Coughing

In November, Union soldier Robert Knox Sneden, a mapmaker and skillful artist, landed in Libby Prison, Richmond, Virginia. The building housing

the prison was a converted tobacco warehouse at the James River docks.
All through his imprisonment, Sneden managed to find enough loose pages and pencil
stubs to compile an illustrated wartime journal. He later supplemented these scraps
with a partially used notebook and a New Testament, in the margins of
which he made shorthand notations.

ecember 25, 1863   Fine clear and cold. As our "grub" did not come in to us until 3:30 p.m. we thought the delay was caused by getting a good Christmas dinner of some kind. Turkey or beef could not be expected of course, but when it did come in we were not served until 4:30 p.m. It consisted of six or eight ounces of heavy corn bread and half boiled rice in a big pine box with a pint of the old strong smelling goober bean soup. We were ravenously hungry and the small ration was swallowed in a minute, when we were as hungry as ever. The Rebel cooks were all drunk, and the vile food was kept from us purposely by [prison commandant Major "Dick"] Turner's orders, as we learned afterwards.

The sailors had brought in yesterday some coffee, sugar, and beef tea. They had these within our mess only. I got some of the beef tea, however, which was a luxury. It comes in thick cakes, and looks much like glue in color and appearance. Hot water soon dissolves it, when we can get at the stove to heat it. We have lots of tin tomato cans as the sailors bring them in from the empty lot near us, where they are thrown by the Rebels after they have devoured the contents. This canned vegetables, etc., were sent to us prisoners but the Rebels are not so gullible as to give it to us. So the U.S. Sanitary Commission at home are actually feeding the Rebel officers with hams and all kinds of good things. Jeff Davis no doubt has his share. . . .

All the guards and their officers were more or less drunk all day. Many fell down helplessly drunk while on post, when another fellow was put in his place. Several fired their muskets right into the upper stories of Libby. I watched one fellow aim a dozen times before he fired. Some of our officers put [an] old hat out on a stick when three of the guards fired at it thinking that there might be a head behind it.

It got to be very cold in the afternoon, while a thin skim of ice was seen in the river close in shore and in the canal back of Libby. Several of us tried to make a fire in the big stove, and succeeded after a while, but here the stove having no pipe, sent the smoke out in the room in thick volumes choking us, and making it impossible to see twenty feet. All the windows were thrown open on our floor amid yells, curses, and coughing. The Rebels seeing the smoke pouring out of the windows thought the building was on fire. The officer of the guard with twenty or more came rushing upstairs, but did not stay any longer than was necessary to see the cause, and went down again cursing us for "ignorant blue bellied Yankees." Water had to be used to put the fire out and we sat on the floor all night in the cold.[37]

1863

A Little Warm Bundle Beside Me

*During Christmas 1863, a very pregnant Sara Rice Pryor
was camped in an overseer's empty cabin in the "quarters" of her brother-in-law's
place, near Petersburg, Virginia. Her husband was off serving as a
special courier with General Fitzhugh Lee's cavalry. She wrote of that time in*
My Day, Reminiscences of a Long Life.

great snow-storm overtook us a day or two before Christmas. My little boys kindled a roaring fire in the cold, open kitchen, roasted chestnuts, and set traps for the rabbits and "snowbirds" which never entered them. They made no murmur at the bare Christmas; they were loyal little fellows to their mother. My day had been spent in mending their garments,—making them was a privilege denied me, for I had no materials. I was not "all unhappy!" The rosy cheeks at my fireside consoled me for my privations, and something within me proudly rebelled against weakness or complaining.

The flakes were falling thickly at midnight, when I suddenly became very ill. I sent out for Mary's husband and bade him gallop in to Petersburg, three miles distant, and fetch me Dr. Withers. I was dreadfully ill when he arrived—and as he stood at the foot of my bed I said to him: "It doesn't matter much for me, Doctor! But my husband will be grateful if you keep me alive."

When I awoke from a long sleep, he was still standing at the foot of my bed where I had left him—it seemed to me ages ago! I put out my hand and it touched a little warm bundle beside me. God had given me a dear child!

The doctor spoke to me gravely and most kindly. "I must leave you now," he said, "and, alas! I cannot come again. There are so many, so many sick. Call all your courage to your aid. Remember the pioneer women, and all they were able to survive. This woman," indicating Anarchy, "is a field-hand, but she is a mother, and she has agreed to help you during the Christmas holidays—her own time. And now, God Bless you, and goodby!" . . .

I soon slept again—and when I awoke the very Angel of Strength and Peace had descended and abode with me. I resolved to prove to myself that if I was called to be a great woman, I *could* be a great woman. Looking at me from my bedside were my two little boys. They had been taken the night before across the snow-laden fields to my brother's house, but had risen at daybreak and had "come home to take care" of me!

My little maid Julia left me Christmas morning. She said it was too lonesome, and her "mistis" always let her choose her own places. I engaged "Anarchy" at twenty-five dollars a week for all her nights. But her hands, knotted by work in the fields, were too rough to touch my babe.[38]

1863

Charleston Still Holds Her Head High

Four days after the recruiting office opened in New Bedford, Massachusetts,
Corporal James Henry Gooding, who had been a sailor on a whaling ship,
enlisted in the Fifty-fourth Massachusetts Volunteer Infantry. In July, his
African-American regiment proved its unflinching valor spearheading an
assault on Fort Wagner, a Confederate earthwork protecting the entrance to
Charleston Harbor. Gooding also acted as a war correspondent to the
New Bedford, Massachusetts, Mercury, *where this letter*
appeared on January 7, 1864.

orris Island, [South Carolina], Dec. 26, 1863

Messrs. Editors:—Christmas has come and gone, but Charleston still holds her head high, as the leading city in the van of the rebellion. But then, Secretary [of the Navy] Welles, in his annual report, considers it to be no great matter whether the Union army occupies the city or not, as it is not, he says, any strategic point of value or commercial importance to the Confederate guerrillas. All that is very fine, as a defence of the miserable operation of the naval arm during the recent operations against that stronghold; but it will not possibly make the nation see why having it in our possession is not better than to leave it in the hands of the insurgents. Strategy or not, almost every one knows that the rebels depend upon Charleston for a very large amount of ammunition, which is manufactured there on account of its central position and being connected by all the interior lines of railway with different parts of the Confederacy. But the worthy old gentleman does not think that it would be any object to somewhat curtail these facilities, and it has not struck him as an idea, that in sealing Charleston up as a commercial help to the rebels, the most effective way is to take it, . . . But do, good Mr. Secretary,

let us have the 4th of July in Charleston, and we will not regret not having spent a merry Christmas therein so much.

Yesterday (Christmas) morning, we gave the rebels in Charleston a Merry (or dismal) Christmas greeting, by throwing a few shell in among them. The shell thrown evidently set fire to some part of the city, as there was a grand illumination visible in a few minutes after the shell were thrown. The wind being then from the northwest, and the air very clear, the sound of the church bells could be distinctly heard at Fort Strong, but whether it was the regular ringing of Christmas bells by the Catholic and established churches, or merely the alarm bells on account of fire, is difficult to determine. From the hour (3 o'clock) it may have been both circumstances that occasioned the loud ringing of bells in the Palmetto City; one set of bells ringing to commemorate a glorious event, bringing joy and mirth to the rising generation, and reflection and thankfulness to those of mature age,—and the other, to warn the guilty conspirators of the avenging flame thrown in their midst, ready to leave them houseless, unless they make efforts to extinguish it.

Soon after, the rebel batteries on James and Sullivan's Islands were opened, but with the same effect as heretofore—a waste of powder and shell; but about daylight we could hear very rapid and heavy firing on James Island in the neighborhood where our gunboats are stationed in Stone river. I have not found out anything as yet in regard to it, but I suspect the rebels were retaliating on the gunboats for our firing on the city, and the gunboats of course must have given them as good as they sent. I don't think it was anything more than for annoying each other in that quarter. . . .

Christmas was rather a dull day with us, the 54th. . . . Apple dumplings, equalling a young mortar shell in weight, with rye whiskey sauce, was the principal item on the bill of fare. So far as my observation went, apple dumplings formed the first and last course, but the boys enjoyed them notwithstanding the seeming lack of talent in the pastry cooks. The dinner to the boys shows a warm attachment between the shoulder straps and the rank and file, for the expense was borne by the officers.[39]

Gooding was wounded and taken prisoner at Olustee, Florida.
For five months he suffered the horrors of Andersonville Prison, until he finally died there.
Generations later, his regiment was honored in the powerful film, Glory.

1863

Santa Claus Had Done His Best

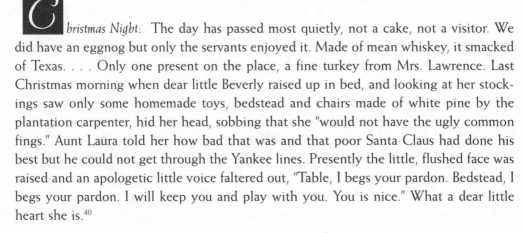

When the Civil War began, Sarah Katherine Stone was twenty
and living at Brokenburn, a large cotton plantation in northeast Louisiana.
By 1863, Kate and her widowed mother and family had abandoned the
plantation and fled to Tyler, Texas. This passage came from the journal she kept.

Christmas Night: The day has passed most quietly, not a cake, not a visitor. We did have an eggnog but only the servants enjoyed it. Made of mean whiskey, it smacked of Texas. . . . Only one present on the place, a fine turkey from Mrs. Lawrence. Last Christmas morning when dear little Beverly raised up in bed, and looking at her stockings saw only some homemade toys, bedstead and chairs made of white pine by the plantation carpenter, hid her head, sobbing that she "would not have the ugly common fings." Aunt Laura told her how bad that was and that poor Santa Claus had done his best but he could not get through the Yankee lines. Presently the little, flushed face was raised and an apologetic little voice faltered out, "Table, I begs your pardon. Bedstead, I begs your pardon. I will keep you and play with you. You is nice." What a dear little heart she is.[40]

A Visit from St. Nicholas
Drawn by Thomas Nast

1 8 6 3

Endless Variety of Toys

In this article from the Cincinnati Daily Enquirer
on December 25, 1863, a newspaperman covering the shopping district assured
his readers that Santa would have no trouble finding his way to
Cincinnati, Ohio, where the stores overflowed with merchandise.

The catalogue includes books splendidly bound in morocco and gold, jewelry costlier than ever before witnessed in this city, furs from the polar regions, silks, velvets, and . . . the endless variety of toys that everywhere meet the eye. . . . If young America does not rejoice this year as never before, it will not be the fault of our storekeepers.[41]

1863

A Carnival of Pleasure

Judging from this article in Frank Leslie's Illustrated Newspaper *on January 9, 1864, Christmas seemed merry as ever in New York, too.*

Everything is twice as dear as it was last year, and as twice as much of everything is bought, some idea may be formed of the abundance of money. . . . For a war-ridden people, for a tax-burdened people, for a calamity-stricken people, we are the lightest-hearted, the most thoughtless, reckless people in the world. . . . These holiday times have proved a perfect carnival of pleasure.[42]

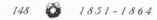

1863

Gayety Has Become Epidemic

From Washington, D.C., Frederick Seward, the son of the secretary of state, reported that Christmas 1863 was noticeably brighter than in recent years.

Gayety has become as epidemic this winter as gloom was last winter. A year ago [father] was 'heartless' or 'un patriotic' because he gave dinners; now the only complaint of him is that he don't have dancing.[43]

1864

Darkest of All Decembers

*Mary Boykin Chesnut was the wife of James Chestnut, former
U.S. senator from South Carolina, who resigned at the start of the
Civil War to become aide to Jefferson Davis. In 1854, she was
living in Richmond, Virginia, when she wrote this mournful poem.*

Darkest of all Decembers
Ever my life has known,
Sitting here by the embers
Stunned, helpless, alone.[44]

1864

A Christmas Gift

*On December 22, two days after Savannah fell to Union forces,
General William T. Sherman telegraphed his famous message
to Lincoln, following the suggestion of a U.S. Treasury agent who
had said, "The President particularly enjoys such pleasantry."*

To his Excellency President Lincoln,
Washington, D.C.
I BEG TO PRESENT YOU AS A CHRISTMAS GIFT, THE CITY OF SAVANNAH,

WITH ONE HUNDRED AND FIFTY HEAVY GUNS AND PLENTY OF AMMUNITION. ALSO ABOUT TWENTY-FIVE THOUSAND BALES OF COTTON.
W. T. SHERMAN
Major General

To which momentous news the president responded:

December 26:
My dear General Sherman:
Many, many thanks for your Christmas gift, the capture of Savannah.

When you were about leaving Atlanta for the Atlantic coast, I was anxious, if not fearful; but feeling that you were the better judge, and remembering that "nothing risked, nothing gained," I did not interfere. Now, the undertaking being a success, the honor is all yours; for I believe none of us went further than to acquiesce. . . .

Please make my grateful acknowledgments to your whole army—officers and men.[45]

1864

A Blazing Good Fire

*When drummer-boy William Bircher wrote these passages
in his diary, he was camped within a mile of Savannah with his
Minnesota regiment, living on rice with no salt.*

December 21: Warm. Hardee evacuated Savannah, leaving all his artillery, amounting to one hundred and twenty pieces, and seventeen hundred bales of cotton.

[On December 23, some of the New England boys went over to see captured Savannah. Bircher was surprised at how beautiful the city was, with its parks and wide streets.]

December 24: Rather warmer. As rations were yet very scarce, we were informed that a short distance below Savannah were several large oyster-beds. A detail of two men and two teams went down to see if it was possible to procure enough for a Christmas dinner in the regiment.

On their return we found they had succeeded in filling one wagon-box; but they were of a very inferior quality. The natives called them the "cluster oyster." There were two to five in one bunch, and hard to get out. So our Christmas dinner did not consist of turkey with oyster filling and cranberry sauce.

What a glorious camp fire we had that Christmas Eve of 1864! It makes me rub my hands together to think of it. The nights were getting cold and frosty, so that it was impossible to sleep under our little shelter-tents with comfort; and so, half the night was spent around the blazing fires in front of our tents.

I always took care that there should be a blazing good fire for our little squad, anyhow. My duties were light and left me time, which I found I could spend with pleasure in swinging an axe. Hickory and white-oak saplings were my favorites, and I had them piled up as high as my head on wooden fire-dogs. What a glorious crackle we had by midnight!

We could go out to the fire at any time of night we pleased (and we were pretty sure to go out three or four times a night, for it was too cold to sleep in the tent more than an hour at a stretch), and we would always find half a dozen of the boys sitting about the fire logs, smoking their pipes, telling yarns, or singing snatches of old songs. . . .

It was hard to be homeless at this merry season of the year, when folks up North were having such happy times, wasn't it? But it was wonderful how elastic the spirits of our soldiers were, and how jolly they could be under the most adverse circumstances. . . .

December 25: Cold and windy. Snow still on the ground; but in the afternoon it warmed up.[46]

1864

Our End Cannot Be Far

As this troubled entry from her journal shows,
Pauline DeCaradeuc Heyward no longer dreamed
of romantic Christmas furloughs,
as she had during Christmas 1863.

Dec. 26th, 1864   Christmas came and went, not much thought of, the fact is things are rushing along at so terrible a rate, to some fearful climax, that we feel all the time as tho we hadn't time to stop to *think* or *feel*, I *cannot make* myself feel anything, 'twould be hypocrasy to say I am sorrowful, (though I should be, I have cause to be, *every way*, surrounded by death & misfortunes) but I don't stop to think of them, I feel as tho sympathy, sensibility, *all* were suspended during the whirl & rushing of everything, & I put off *everything*, *all*, until after the result—of what, I know not—

Savannah is taken by Sherman and it can't be long now ere our state is overrun by the enemy. Already in this neighborhood have bands of wicked deserters commenced their work of pillage & destruction. I do not go out unless armed. We are in most fearful times & the end is not yet, tho as thing go, our end cannot be far. God may yet help us & I rely on Him and feel nearer to Him than in my life before. I wish

I could feel frightened, anxious—anything, but this *waiting*. I am perfectly astonished at myself. I am the life of the house, & I feel lively & cheerful *all* the time, I do not disguise my feelings, for I cannot affect what I don't feel, neither can I describe what I do feel, unless one word can do it, and that word is—nothing.[47]

1864

We Talked Of Old Times

On December 25, 1864, John Buckly Bacon, a Union soldier from Wisconsin, was far from home, camped in Mississippi. That evening he wrote in his diary. He described that Christmas and the old times it brought to mind.

Our Christmas dinner consisted of a few Irish potatoes and a little fresh beef. After dinner we sat around a campfire which was in front of our tent and talked of old times, each one telling where he was and what he was doing in years gone by on this day. Midnight and all is quiet. Thus ends Christmas day in the army at Pascagoula, Mississippi.[48]

1864

The Band Played "Home Sweet Home"

Private George Peck, who served with the Fourth
Wisconsin Cavalry, wrote this description of a Christmas
spent in the southern piney woods.

The young pines, growing among the larger ones, were just such little trees as were used at home for Christmas trees, and within an hour after getting the camp made, every man thought of Christmas at home.

The boys went off in the woods and got holly and mistletoe, and every pup tent in the whole regiment was decorated, and they hung nose bags, grain sacks, army socks and pants on the trees. Around the fires, stakes had been driven to hang clothes on to dry; and as night came and the pitch pine fires blazed up to the tops of the great pines, it actually looked like Christmas, though there was not a Christmas present anywhere.

After supper the Brigade band began to play patriotic airs, with occasionally an old fashioned tune, like "Old Hundred," and the woods rang with music from the boys who could sing, and everybody was as happy as I ever saw a crowd of people, and when it came time to retire the band played "Home, Sweet Home," and three thousand rough soldiers went to bed with tears in their eyes, and every man dreamed of the dear ones at home, and many prayed that the home ones might be happy, and in the morning they all got up, stripped the empty stockings off the evergreen trees, put them on, and went on down the road.[49]

Private Peck made it through the war and became a successful and popular
politician, publisher, and the author of Peck's Bad Boy *stories.*

 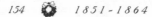

1864

Masquerading and Deviltry

According to this article from the Philadelphia
Sunday Dispatch of December 25, 1864, celebrants far from
the battlefields "carried on" in a strange manner.

Last evening was a carnival of tin trumpets, penny whistles and deviltry generally. Crowds of roystering blades passed through the principal street, blowing tin horns and penny whistles, and making night hideous with their descordant music. In some cases the bands of Calathumpians were clad in fantastic dresses, and with smutted faces, wigs, false beards, and ridiculous costumes, generally, they cut a queer figure. Eighth street from Walnut street to Race, was the grand centre to which the tin-horn carnival tended, and the scene there beggared description. The street was jammed with legitimate shoppers and sight-seers; but in addition to them there were crowds of masqueraders who marched in procession, making, meanwhile, all sorts of diabolical noises . . . and the racket which prevailed was ear-splitting and distracting. . . .

As usual, there was a good deal of rowdyish pushing and pulling in the crowd, and several young men who were engaged in this work were overhauled by the police and afforded the opportunity of spending the remainder of the night in the station house. Such events as that of last evening tend to damage the business of the streets that are the scenes of them. Decent females dare not venture into the streets for fear of insult, and quiet persons of the sterner sex have no taste for such scenes of confusion. The masquerading and deviltry are fine fun for those who indulge in them, but the game is death to the storekeepers, whose business is ruined by such rough "carryings on."[50]

1864

Cold and Cheerless

*Charles Humphreys, who served as a Unitarian chaplain with
the Second Massachusetts Cavalry assigned to General Grant's army in
Virginia, recorded his recollections of Christmas 1864 in his book,*
Field, Camp, Hospital and Prison in the Civil War, 1864-65.

Friday, December 23, reveille sounded at five again, and with a breakfast of coffee alone, we started. Our rations and forage were now exhausted, and for the rest of our journey we must live on the country. In the course of the day our headquarters forager brought in two hams, a spare-rib, and enough flour for several days. We marched until eleven o'clock that night, and encamped under the cold light of stars on a side hill so steep that we had to crawl on our hands and knees to keep from falling. The top of the snow was frozen into a hard crust which the horses' hoofs scarcely broke. However, we made ourselves comfortable with a log fire, a supper of coffee, ham, and griddle cakes, and a bed of boughs, and after five hours we started again.

Our regimental position this day was in the rear of the column, a very uncomfortable place to be in when the column is long and the roads are bad. There were many places where an obstruction or break in the road made it impossible for more than two horses to pass abreast; and as we generally marched by fours, the column at such places would be drawn out to twice its normal length; and if the advance moved steadily it would get away eight or ten miles from the rear at such an obstruction, and then the rear companies, after having waited to let the others pass the obstacle, would have to gallop to close up the column. Generally, however, at such a place, the advance waits for the rear to catch up, as a caterpillar when it meets an obstruction huddles up, fixes its tail, then lengthens out over the obstacle, fixes its head and, drawing in its length-

ened body, huddles up again and then creeps on as before with equal length. Besides this unevenness of motion, a position in the rear is also unpleasant from the sights one has to witness. On this day we passed hundreds of horses worn out by the toilsome march and left dead by the side of the road; and we kept passing dismounted men who could not keep up with the column, some of them with boots worn through and a few barefoot and leaving tracks of blood in the frozen crust. That night we got into camp at nine o'clock, cold, tired, and hungry; still we brightened up a little to think it was Christmas Eve, and that our friends at home were enjoying it in quiet comfort and happy meetings, even though we could not enjoy it, but must spread our cold and cheerless tables in the presence of those enemies who otherwise would make our home firesides cold and cheerless as our own. Next day was Sunday, December 25th, and as we woke, the "Merry Christmas" wishes went around, but always with the added wish for a merrier Christmas next year.

We forded this day the two branches of the Rappahannock, having first to cut a passage through the ice that covered the river. In our march we often had to dismount and lead our horses down the steep hills, sliding with them most of the way. Their shoes were now so smooth that they with difficulty kept from falling even on level ground. Our sufferings this day from the cold were very severe. Our feet were almost frozen, encased as they were in wet and frozen boots, and dangling in the frosty air. There is not sufficient exercise in the slow motion of a cavalry column to send the warm blood away down to the feet. Our only relief was a partial one when the column halted— in stamping upon the ground.[51]

1864

Try And Get Off And Come Home

A desperate wife from Nansemond County, Virginia, wrote this letter to her husband, who was on duty with General Pickett.

Dec. 17, 1864

My Dear B——: Christmus is most hear again, and things is worse and worse. I have got my last kalica frock on, and that's patched. Everything me and children's got is patched. Both of them is in bed now covered up with comforters and old pieces of karpet to keep them warm, while I went 'long out to try and get some wood, for their feet's on the ground and they have got no clothes, neither: and I am not able to cut the wood, and me and the children have broke up all the rails 'round the yard and picked up all the chips there is. We haven't got nothing in the house to eat but a little bit o' meal. The last pound of meet you got from Mr. G—— is all eat up, and so is the chickens we raised. I don't want you to stop fighten them yankees till you kill the last one of them, but try and get off and come home and fix us all up some and then you can go back and fight them a heep harder than you ever fought them before. We can't none of us hold out much longer down here. One of General Mahone's scouts promise me on his word to carry this letter through the lines to you, but, my dear, if you put off a-comin' 'twon't be no use to come, for we'll all hands of us be out there in the garden in the old graveyard with your ma and mine.[52]

After he received this letter, the husband went home without a furlough. On his return to camp he was arrested as a deserter and found guilty. He appealed to Mrs. Pickett, who in turn appealed to her husband. General Pickett ordered the execution postponed. Three days later, an order came from Richmond, reprieving all deserters.

1864

Anything But Merry

*Kate Cumming wrote this entry in her journal while resting up
from her nursing service, back home in Mobile, Alabama.*

December 25,—Christmas day—the nativity of our Lord and Savior; the day he left his throne on high, and came in his humility to dwell on earth, and on which was sung in heaven

"Gloria in excelsis! peace! to man
   Good will!. . ."

"Good will to man!" Many of our enemies profess to believe these precious words, and yet how little of it they manifest for us.

What visions of cheer does not the sound of "Merry Christmas" bring in review—happiness, plenty, and a forgetting for a few short hours the cares of this weary world! This one has been any thing but merry to us; a gloom has hung over all, that, do what we will, we can not dispel. Our thoughts, whether we will or no, wander to where our armies are struggling to maintain our rights against fearful odds. Alas! when will this strife and bloodshed cease? When will we have peace? "Sweet peace is in her grave!"

The weather is very inclement; too much so for us to attend the services of the sanctuary. Last evening I visited St. John's Church. It was very beautifully dressed with evergreens, I thought more so than I had ever seen it before. I am told that all the Episcopal Churches in the city are decorated the same.[53]

In 1866, when preparing her journal for the printer, Kate Cumming said of the Civil War:

The vivid recollections of what I have witnessed during years of horror have been so shocking, that I have almost doubted whether the past was not all a fevered dream, and, if real, how I ever lived through it.

1 8 6 4

Long Given Up For Dead

In December, Union soldier Robert Knox Sneden was released from Libby Prison. In his journal, he described his journey home.

December 20, 1864: Fine and clear. I, with others was paid off today [ration money accumulated during imprisonment] and after investing heavily at the sutler's in boots, hat, satchel, and a few luxuries, took the cars for Washington by the evening train on thirty days' leave of absence. Last night, the Raiders made an attempt to rob those in the next building adjoining where I was, when they were set upon and clubbed unmercifully by the inmates. Some will die. Others are arrested, and perhaps this will break up the gang. At the sinks, which are a long way from the barracks, many men were "mugged" and robbed. The thieves got over $1,000 from the different men who had to go there, and who had been paid off in the morning. I have searched all through the barracks and

 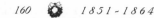

elsewhere without success to find those who were captured with me at Brandy Station, Virginia. Walsh, Colviun, Halley, etc. They must still be at Andersonville, or on their way home. . . .

December 21, 1864: I arrived at Washington at 7 a.m. and after putting up at "the National" ordered a uniform suit of clothes. I then went to our old headquarters corner 15½ Street and Pennsylvania Avenue, where I was received by my old friends still here on duty as one risen from the dead. . . . The officers attached were all strangers to me. Several of the old clerks were here still, and with them I had a grand time in the evening.

My object in coming here is to investigate and secure my pay, as I had not drawn any in the field before I was captured. . . .

December 24: Snow and rain. For the past three days I have been searching through piles of paymasters' books to find my last payment. And finally today found my name against which was written "missing or killed" to which I added "found alive," in pencil. I had not drawn pay since September 1st, 1863, when I had left headquarters here for my first absence from the army since 1861. After this, I was furnished with proper documents and transportation home. I went to the theatres and capitol, seeing sights, and meeting old friends, very few of whom could believe the horrors of Rebel prisons as set forth by my experiences.

After making calls on friends at headquarters, and investing heavily in "steamed oysters," I took the train for Baltimore, where I arrived in due time and put up at the Eutaw House. Provost guards came on board the train at every place, in search of soldiers who were trying to desert, or go north without passes. Everyone had to show passes who wore military clothing, but there were numbers of soldiers among us who were in citizen's clothes who escaped.

December 25: Snow two inches. I went over the principal streets of the city this forenoon, visited the battle monument and Barnum's large hotel. Baltimore Street was crowded with people and many handsome women could be seen there shopping. I met some army officers at the Eutaw House bar and had a very enjoyable time "swapping stories."

December 26: Three inches of snow on streets but fine and clear. I took the evening train for New York, and arrived about midnight. Put up at [the] Mansion House [in] Brooklyn and next day about 2 p.m. found my family who had long given me up for dead.[54]

1865 - 1899

1865

Liquor And Fire-crackers

This item from the December 27, 1865, issue of the
Richmond (*Virginia*) Daily Whig *reflected the city's public mood
the first Christmas after the War Between the States.*

Christmas was celebrated in this city with unprecedented hilarity. . . . It was more a street than a home celebration. "King Alcohol" asserted his sway and held possession of the town from Christmas eve until yesterday morning. Liquor and fire-crackers had everything their own way. A disposition was manifested to make up for lost time. This was the first real old-fashioned Christmas frolic that has been enjoyed in the South for four years. The pent up dissipations and festivities of four Christmas days were crowded into this one day.[1]

1865

A Grand Display on Christmas Day

*The next two reports of Midwestern winter entertainments
appeared in the* Galena Weekly Gazette *on December 26, 1865.*

Freeport is putting on metropolitan airs. A skating park has recently been instituted there at a heavy expense, which will be opened with a grand display on Christmas Day. It is the intention to have the band present every evening during the skating season to add zest to the enjoyment.

Skaters
Harper's New Monthly Magazine, December 1857

1865

Gliding The Mazy Dance

Forty ladies and gentlemen and several cans of oysters started from this city at about six o'clock Friday evening for a sleigh ride out to the Tyler House. Two sleighs with four horses each and two with two horses were well packed with human freight, and the sleighing being good and weather pleasant nothing was wanting which could contribute to the happiness of the participants. At about eight o'clock the party arrived at Tyler's and a few minutes later Ostrander brought out his "fiddle and bow" and a portion of the party were soon gliding the mazy dance. As none of the party had taken tea before leaving the city, the ringing of the supper bell which was heard at about eleven o'clock was not an unwelcome sound, and the party were by no means tardy in paying a practical compliment to the well spread table. At two o'clock all were on board and homeward bound.

The evening was the pleasantest of the winter so far and nothing occurred to mar the occasion.[2]

1 8 6 6

The Ice Was Elegant

Ice-skating was a fashionable and popular new winter sport in Milwaukee, Wisconsin, as readers learned from the December 26, 1866, issue of the Milwaukee Sentinel.

At this new and fashionable resort everything went favorably for the highest development of fun. The ice was "elegant" (we heard a very handsome young lady pronounce it so), the weather was just right, not windy, the attendance large and fashionable, the music stimulating, the park spacious, and—it was Christmas! Under all these circumstances it is no wonder that several thousand persons visited the park. There was also fancy skating by Mr. Sterling and a game of curling. The fun kept up in the park until ten o'clock in the evening.[3]

1 8 6 6

Strung and Hung in Profusion

The January 18, 1866, issue of the Western Missionary *in Dayton, Ohio, described the latest idea in Christmas-tree decoration at a Sunday school festival at the Dayton German Reformed Church.*

The first object claiming his attention was a large Christmas tree. Wonderful how that tree was carried into the church! It was beautifully ornamented. Pop corn was strung and hung in profusion over the far reaching branches; this is a new feature to him in ornamenting Christmas trees, but a good one.[4]

1 8 6 7

Hemlock And Holly By The Yard

This article printed in the December 23, 1867, issue of the Philadelphia North American *commended New Jersey farmers for developing a new Christmas industry—greens all ready for hanging.*

Now is the time that people decorate the churches, halls and saloons with spruce, holly and pine. The barrens of New Jersey now yield their only crop. Raids upon them are made at this season, and many an "honest penny" is turned from a soil whose only other productions are huckleberries and garter snakes. The ravages upon these barrens for Christmas trees are by no means inconsiderable, and whole tracts are denuded every

Christmas Greens
Drawn by Thomas Nast

winter to supply the demand for Philadelphia customers. In their thrift and industry the farmers along these barrens engage in another enterprise that a few years ago was never thought of. They gather the fronds of the hemlock and the holly, and making them into continuous strands, sell them by the yard for wreaths and festoons, as if the material were ribbon or tape. A congregation therefore who wish to decorate a church can buy from these Jersey people ready prepared for hanging, all the material they require.[5]

1 8 6 8

Nothing But *Pop, Pop, Bang*

Several entries from the correspondence and journals of
Sylvanus and Jennie Lines appeared in the 1851-1864 section.
Here Sylvanus wrote to Jennie.

acon, Ga., Dec. 27th, 1868

My Dear One,—

The Post Office being closed on Friday [Christmas day] I failed to receive your letter, which would have been the most acceptable Christmas present that I could have received, but however it reached me on Saturday morning, and I assure you found a welcome reception. Christmas has come and gone, and never had I witnessed such a celebration; it commenced on Thursday night at dark and every body seemed determined to see which could make the most noise. You know in this country it is like the 4th of July at the North. Everything that would hold powder was brought into requisition, from a cannon down to a fire-cracker, and it was nothing but *pop, pop, bang*, until 11 o'clock last night when a copious rain dispersed the crowds and cooled their excitement....

With much love and affection I am Yours Devotedly
Sylvanus[6]

1869

No Improper Characters Admitted

On December 22, 1869, the Denver Daily Rocky Mountain News
announced an upcoming high-class affair.

M. Sigi will give a grand ball at Colorado brewery hall Christmas eve, to which a general invitation is extended. Everything will be in the best style. Carriages will be in attendance free and may be ordered at the hall, or at Stockdorff's restaurant, Blake Street. No improper characters will be admitted. Tickets, including supper, $4, for sale at the door.[7]

1869

Viewing the Tree

*The January 1, 1870, issue of the Pottsville, Pennsylvania, Miners' Journal
described a Christmas treat for the "slate pickers." Slate pickers were ragged boys
who labored all day in a dusty, noisy room in the coal mine,
snatching slate from troughs of black coal as it slid past.*

At 10 A. M. all the "Slate Pickers" of the Honeybrook Coal Co. were formed in line by the screen boss of each breaker, and marched to the residence of our Superintendent, who had fitted up a very handsome Christmas tree in the vestibule of his residence, and after viewing the tree each one as he left was presented with a new 25 cent note, as a Christmas present.[8]

1871
Rise Up, Shepherd

Fisk University, in Nashville, Tennessee, was established in 1866
to educate former slaves. Five years later, on concert tours through the United States,
England, Scotland, and Germany, the Fisk Jubilee Singers raised
over $150,000 for the university. Along the way, they introduced black spirituals,
which were created during slavery times. More than 1,000 spirituals by unknown
musicians have been collected, including the following songs that celebrate the Nativity.

Go Tell It on the Mountain

Go tell it on the mountain,
Over the hills and everywhere;
Go tell it on the mountain,
That Jesus Christ is born.

Rise Up, Shepherd, and Follow

There's a star in the east on Christmas morn,
Rise up, shepherd, and follow;
It'll lead to the place where the Savior's born,
Rise up, shepherd, and follow.

Leave your flocks and leave your lambs,
Rise up shepherd and follow,
Leave your ewes and leave your rams,
Rise up shepherd and follow.

If you take good heed to the Angel's word,
Rise up, shepherd, and follow;
You'll forget your flock, you'll forget your herd;
Rise up shepherd, and follow.
Follow, follow, rise up shepherd and follow, follow,
Follow the star of Bethlehem,
Rise up, shepherd, and follow.

What You Gonna Name That Pretty Little Baby?

Oh, Mary, what you gonna name
That pretty little baby?
Glory, glory, glory
To the new born King!
Some will call Him one thing,
But I think I'll call Him Jesus.
Glory, glory, glory
To the new born King!
Some will call Him one thing,
But I think I'll say Emanuel.
Glory, glory, glory
To the new born King![9]

1872

Our Christmas Feast

*Captain Jack Elgin and his party of West Texas surveyors
left this account of dining like kings beside the Upper Brazos River in 1872.*

We had buffalo, antelope, deer, bear, rabbit, prairie-dog, possum and possibly other animals that I do not recall; turkey, goose, brant, ducks, prairie-chicken, curlew, quail and other birds. The most expensive meat which we had upon the table was bacon, which we had had to haul 500 miles. Of course I had a small supply of bacon to use in a contingency and we took a little of it to fill up the menu. . . . Two of my men had killed a young bear on Christmas Eve. The bear had climbed a tree, and after the man killed him, he discovered it was a bee tree, so for our Christmas feast we also had honey.[10]

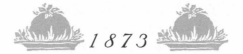

1873

Cakes Piled Upon Cakes

The Ottawa (Illinois) Free Trader *published this mouth-watering
description of bakery-shop sweets on December 20, 1873.*

If you want to witness a sight that will delight you, go to the confectionery and bakery, near the post office, and see the Christmas goods, such as sugar toys of all descriptions, fancy candies in a thousand new and beautiful shapes, and cakes piled upon cakes. Among the latter we observed pound cake, fruit cake, nut cake, sponge

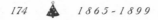

cake, macaronni, and every manner of sweet cake, besides mammoth frosted beauties, as sweet and palatable as they are ornamental. Besides these there are here all sorts of fruits in season, and plenty of nuts. Here is the place to get your Christmas goods.[11]

1 8 7 4

Christmas Is A Foreign Day

The December 26, 1874, issue of the Pittsburgh Gazette
*printed these remarks about Christmas by Henry Ward Beecher
(Harriet Beecher Stowe's brother). Because of his New England Puritan heritage,
he explained, Christmas would always be like any other day to him.*

To me Christmas is a foreign day, and I shall die so. When I was a boy I wondered what Christmas was. I knew there was such a time, because we had an Episcopal church in our town, and I saw them dressing it with evergreens, and wondered what they were taking the woods in church for; but I got no satisfactory explanation. A little later I understood it was a Romish institution, kept up by the Romish Church. Brought up in the strictest State of New England, brought up in the most literal style of worship, brought up where they would not read the Bible in church because the Episcopalians read it so much, I passed all my youth without any knowledge of Christmas, and so I have no associations with the day. Where the Christmas revel ought to be, I have nothing. It is Christmas day, that is all.[12]

1874

Thrills Of Delight

This item appeared in the Daily Rocky Mountain News *in 1874.*

Miss Figg, the philanthropic president of the Ladies Relief Society, presented gifts to the poor children of Denver at her home, 447 Lawrence Street.

Little toys, books, puzzles, candles, fruits and clothes, sent thrills of delight to the hearts of the fifty-six waifs assembled at Miss Figg's rooms.[13]

1876

A Very Beautiful Tree

*The Lancaster, Pennsylvania, Examiner and Express
on December 28, 1876, praised a local doctor for his novel,
handmade Christmas tree ornaments.*

Dr. M. I. Herr has a very large and very beautiful tree, upon which are over 60 eggs, of a variety of bright colors, all painted by the Doctor. They are the first ornaments of the kind we have seen, and we give this hint for the benefit of others. They are real egg shells. A small opening is made in one end of the egg, the contents are abstracted, and the shell is then dried and painted and hung up with a string. It makes a beautiful ornament.[14]

1877

A Gala Night

This announcement in The Miner *on December 22, 1877,*
promoted the upcoming first annual Fireman's Ball
in Georgetown, Colorado.

Of course everybody is getting ready for Christmas night. There will be music and gaiety in Cushman's Opera House. "The Beauty and Chivalry" of Georgetown and the region round about will be gathered there. It will be a gala night for all who accept the invitation of Georgetown Fire and Hose Co. No. I and attend their first annual ball. Let everybody prepare to give the boys a fine send off and a big benefit. Tickets including carriages only $2.50. Orders for carriages to be left at Kinney's. Gorton's will furnish the music.[15]

1879

I Will Tell You What I Study

*Eight-year-old Ella E. Oblinger was a baby when she and her mother
left friends and family behind in Indiana to homestead
in a new sod house that her father had prepared for them in Nebraska.
She wrote this nice letter to distant grandparents she hardly knew.*

From your Grand child
Ella "E" Oblinger.
Jan 12th 1880

Dear Grand Pa and Grand Ma as Ma was writing I thought I would write you a few lines to let you know we are all well there was the sweetest little baby here last night Mr. Johnson staid here all night Mr Johnson preaches here evry two weeks Maggie & Stella are in bed asleep & I must tell you how I spent Christmas eve we all went to a Christmas tree on Christmas eve I got a new red oil calico dress I will send you a piece of them each one of us girls got a doll and uncle Giles put a book on for Sabra and me & each one of us girls a string with cady and raisins on it. Christmas day we all went to uncle Gileses & Newyears we were invited to a Newyears dinner up to Mr Bumgardners. I eat till I nearly bursted eating oysters & good things. I will tell you what I study Reading and Arithmatic & Spelling & Geography & Writing Christmas night I got pair of stockings & a nice new book called the three white kittens & Sabra & Maggie both got a new pair of stockings & primer books & Newyears all of us girls got a candy apple apeice & a paper sack of mixed cand & a paper sach of raisins.[16]

 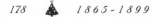

1880

The Children's Joy Will Be Complete

The December 20, 1880, issue of the Milwaukee Sentinel
offered this thrifty idea for a dollar's worth of Christmas.

irst the tree, fifteen cents secures a splendid one. Somewhere in the shed or cellar is an old box, just the thing to set it in. Ten cents buys eight good candles that can be cut in two pieces. A pin stuck stoutly wherever a light is wanted, will hold the taper well in place. Five cents gets a pound of corn for popping. Then purchase twenty cents worth of stick candy with a quarter pound of raisins (five cents) to sprinkle with it. Gauze to make little bags in which the candy could hang on the tree takes another five cents. Now forty cents still remains, and with it can be purchased a whittling knife with two blades (fifteen cents) for a boy and a set of toy dishes (twenty cents) for a girl. The remaining nickel can be used to buy a brightly colored Christmas card, and the children's joy will be complete.[17]

1880

"I Don't Believe They Would Sell"

In his unfinished autobiography, Frank W. Woolworth
admitted that he guessed wrong about the popularity of newfangled
Christmas tree ornaments from Germany in his original five-and-ten-cent
store in Lancaster, Pennsylvania.

n the fall of 1880 I went to an importing firm on Strawberry Street, Philadelphia,

Meyer & Schoenaman, to buy some toys and about the first thing they did was drag out a lot of colored glass ornaments the like of which I had never seen.

"What are those things?" I asked.

They explained that these goods were, oh, such fine sellers, but I laughed.

"You can't sell me any foolish thing like that," I said. "I don't believe they would sell and most of them would be smashed anyway before there was a chance to sell them."

They explained that the profit was big enough to offset the breakage, but I was incredulous. It was hard to understand what the people would want of those colored glass things.

We argued back and forth a long time and finally the house made me the proposition that it would guarantee the sale, at retail, of twenty-five dollars worth of Christmas tree ornaments.

"All right," I agreed. "You can send them to me wholly at your own risk."

The goods arrived a few days before Christmas and, with a great deal of indifference, I put them on my counters. In two days they were gone, and I woke up. But it was too late to order any more, and I had to turn away a big demand. The next Christmas season I was on hand early with what I considered a large order, but it was not large enough. They proved to be the best sellers in my store for the holidays.[18]

In February 1890, Woolworth, who by then had thirteen stores,
went on his first European buying trip. In Germany that year he
bought more than 200,000 ornaments.

1881

It Was Pathetic

Booker T. Washington, who was born a Virginia slave
about 1856, wrote in his autobiography about settling in as the founding
president of a new college for African-Americans at Tuskegee, Alabama.

T he coming of Christmas, that first year of our residence in Alabama, gave us an opportunity to get a farther insight into the real life of the people. The first thing that reminded us that Christmas had arrived was the "foreday" visits of scores of children rapping at our doors, asking for "Chris'mus gifts! Chris'mus gifts!" Between the hours of two o'clock and five o'clock in the morning I presume that we must have had a half-hundred such calls. . . .

During the days of slavery it was a custom quite generally observed throughout all the Southern states to give the coloured people a week of holiday at Christmas, or to allow the holiday to continue as long as the "yule log" lasted. The male members of the race, and often the female members, were expected to get drunk. We found that for a whole week the coloured people in and around Tuskegee dropped work the day before Christmas, and that it was difficult to get any one to perform any service from the time they stopped work until after the New Year. Persons who at other times did not use strong drink thought it quite the proper thing to indulge in it rather freely during the Christmas week. There was a widespread hilarity, and a free use of guns, pistols, and gunpowder generally. The sacredness of the season seemed to have been almost wholly lost sight of.

During this first Christmas vacation I went some distance from the town to visit the people on one of the large plantations. In their poverty and ignorance it was pathetic to see their attempts to get joy out of the season that in most parts of the country is so sacred and so dear to the heart. In one cabin I noticed that all that the five children had to remind them of the coming of Christ was a single bunch of firecrackers, which they had divided among them. In another cabin, where there were at least a half-dozen persons, they had only ten cents' worth of ginger-cakes, which had been bought in the store the day before. In another family they had only a few pieces of sugarcane. In still another cabin I found nothing but a new jug of cheap, mean whiskey, which the husband and wife were making free use of, notwithstanding the fact that the husband was one of the local ministers. In a few instances I found that the people had gotten hold of some bright-coloured cards that had been designed for advertising purposes, and were making the most of those. In other homes some member of the family had bought a new pistol. In the majority of cases there was nothing to be seen in the cabin to remind one of the coming of the Saviour, except that the people had ceased work in the fields and were lounging about their homes. At night, during Christmas week, they usually had what they called a "frolic," in some cabin on the plantation. This meant a kind of rough dance, where there was likely to be a good deal of whiskey used, and where there might be some shooting or cutting with razors.

While I was making this Christmas visit I met an old coloured man who was one of the numerous local preachers, who tried to convince me, from the experience Adam had in the Garden of Eden, that God had cursed all labour, and that, therefore, it was a sin for any man to work. For that reason this man sought to do as little work as possible. He seemed at that time to be supremely happy, because he was living, as he expressed it, through one week that was free from sin.[19]

c. 1881

If They Had The Money

Carrie Mason was born right after Emancipation.
When she was interviewed by a W.P.A. worker at her home
in Milledgeville, Georgia, in 1937, she told about Christmases
during slavery and afterward.

ammy was a religious woman, and the first day of Christmas she always fasted half a day, and then she would pray. After that, everybody would have eggnog and barbecue and cake, if they had the money to buy it. Mammy said that when they was still slaves, Marster always gived 'em Christmas, but after they had Freedom then they had to buy they own rations.[20]

1881

What I Got For Christmas

Maud Rittenhouse lived with her brothers in a fifteen-room
brick house in Cairo, Illinois, where the mile-wide Ohio River joined the Mississippi.
Her father was a well-to-do grain merchant. In the first entry below,
sixteen-year-old Maud listed in her diary what she got for Christmas from her
family and from Elmer, her beau. The second entry was a similar list made a year later.

ew Year's Day Jan 1, 1882
But I've not even told you what I got for Christmas.

From Mama .... that opera-cap and a basket of flowers.
Papa .... (in five volumes, bound in sheepskin) McCauley's Histories of
    England.
Wood .... 3 oz. of Lundborg's perfume.
Harry .... a geological specimen and crochet needle.
Aunt Amarala .... Tennyson in blue and gold.
Edith .... A bottle of white-rose.
Corrine .... Satin whisk-broom-holder with broom.
Aunt Mattie .... Linen cambric emb. handkerchief.
Aunt Belle .... "   " bordered   "
Elmer .... Large sized rose-wood writing desk, pearl inlaid, name "Maud"
    cut in silver plate on top containing Christmas cards, ruler, ink-bottles and gold pen.
    Silly youth! Lovely desk!

1882

My Christmas Presents

ew Years, 1883

Another unrecorded week has flown. . . .

I have not told you about my Christmas presents.

Mama . . . . Lemon colored dress and nearly 6 yards satin, to go with it

Papa . . . . Morocco music-case and embroidered hdk [handkerchief]

Elmer . . . . Daintily exquisite book of paintings and poems entitled
    "Heart's Ease and Happy Days." Also a pretty table with a drawer in it on
    which was a costly and sweet-toned telegraph instrument—a beauty. Also four

or five beautiful fringed Christmas cards. (P.S. I'd made him promise to get something simple.)

Aunt Amarala . . . Wine-colored plush hand-bag.

Aunt Mattie . . . . Green ink-stand.

Papa gave Mama a set of garnets. I gave her a banjo covered with pale pink satin, hand-painted rose and lilacs, morning glories under silver strings on handle, pale blue velvet round the bowl. Its nearly eight, must dress.[21]

Christmas Flirtation
Drawn by Thomas Nast

1882

The Hurt I Felt

In her autobiography, Anne Ellis wrote of her hardscrabble
Rocky Mountain childhood in the silver-mining town of Bonanza, Colorado.
She was about six years old when the following disappointing events took place.

This winter was the first time I had ever heard of Santa Claus. . . . I, with neighbor children, plan on all the things we are to have. It seems Santa brings toys and candy, so I decided on a doll for myself, and a wagon for Ed, leaving it to his judgment what to bring the baby. Christmas night our stockings are hung up, and we go to bed with high hopes; but morning finds these stockings as lank and raggy-looking as the night before. We were so disappointed, and after this I pretended there was a Santa Claus for the other children, and through all the years managed to fix something for each one of them, using old cigar boxes, pieces of tin foil, scraps of silk, and tissue paper, cutting the pictures from fruit cans, using them to decorate the work box, pencil box, cornucopia, or whatever I happened to be fixing. The hurt I felt when I saw those empty stockings has been with me always, and after my own children came, never did they find an empty stocking, although the stuffing was ofttimes pitiful. Mama saw how hurt we were and said, "Never mind, he will come to our house New Year's." It seems we did not have a payday till the first, and then Santa Claus did come, and leave shoes and stockings, but the thrill was gone; and also my belief in Santa Claus.[22]

1882

A Twinkling Of Dancing Colors

Thomas Edison invented the first practical light bulb in 1879.
Three years later, New York journalist William Augustus Croffut published this article
in the Detroit Post and Tribune, describing the spectacular way
that one of Edison's business associates decorated his Christmas tree
with electric lights.

Last evening I walked over beyond Fifth Avenue and called at the residence of
Edward H. Johnson, vice-president of Edison's electric company. There, at the rear of
the beautiful parlors, was a large Christmas tree presenting a most picturesque and un-
canny aspect. It was brilliantly lighted with many colored globes about as large as an
English walnut and was turning some six times a minute on a little pine box. There were
80 lights in all encased in these dainty glass eggs, and about equally divided between
white, red and blue. As the tree turned, the colors alternated, all the lamps going out
and being relit at every revolution. The rest was a continuous twinkling of dancing
colors, red, white, blue, white, red, blue—all evening.

I need not tell you that the scintillating evergreen was a pretty sight—one can hardly
imagine anything prettier. The ceiling was crossed obliquely with two wires on which
hung 28 more of the tiny lights; and all the lights and the fantastic tree itself with its
starry fruit were kept going by the slight electric current brought from the main office
on a filmy wire. The tree was kept revolving by a little hidden crank below the floor
which was turned by electricity. It was a superb exhibition.[23]

1883

When A Pleasure Becomes A Burden

In the December issue of The Century Magazine,
Susan Anna Brown offered some well-meaning and likely-to-be-ignored advice.

A Word About Christmas

When what was designed to be a pleasure becomes a burden, it is time to stop and examine it carefully, and see if it is the thing itself which has grown to be such a weight, or whether it is simply an awkward manner of carrying it. During the first three months of the year, nothing is more commonly given as a reason for ill health than an overstrain during the holidays. "She got so worn out at Christmas," or "She worked too hard in finishing her Christmas presents," or "The week before Christmas she was tired out with shopping," are excuses which appear as surely as January and February come. The question must occur sometimes to every one, whether all this worry and wear of heart and hand and brain are really worth while. Is there not some better way of celebrating this day of days than for women to wear themselves out in making or buying pretty trifles for people who already have more than they can find room for? Setting aside all effort of eyes and fingers, the mental strain is intense. Merely to devise presents for a dozen or more people, which must be appropriate and acceptable, and which they do not already possess, and which no one else is likely to hit upon, is enough to wear upon the strongest brain; and when one's means are not unlimited, and the question of economy must come in, the matter is still more complicated. The agony of indecision, the weighing of rival merits in this and that, the distress when the article which is finally decided upon does not seem as fascinating as one had hoped, the endless round of shopping, the packing to send to distant friends, the frantic effort to finish at the last moments something which ought to have been done long ago, result in a relapse when all is over into a complete weariness of mind and body which unfits one for either giving or receiving pleasure. Now, when all this is looked at soberly, does it pay? It is a remarkable fact that, although Christmas has been kept on the twenty-fifth of December for more than a thousand years, its arrival seems as unexpected as if it had been appointed by the President. No one is ready for it, although last year every one resolved to be so, and about the middle of December there begins a rush and hurry which is really more wearing than a May moving.

It seems to be a part of the fierce activity of our time and country that even our pleasures must be enjoyed at high pressure. While it is almost impossible, in matters of business, to act upon the kindly suggestions of intelligent critics that we should take things more leisurely, surely, in matters of enjoyment, we might make an effort to be less overworked. Cannot the keeping of Christmas, for example, be made to consist in other things than gifts? Let the giving be for the children and those to whom our gifts are real necessities.[24]

1883

Happiness on Every Bough

This article in the December 23, 1883, issue of the
Milwaukee Sentinel *showed that Christmas trees had not*
yet caught on generally.

In this city the custom of decorating a Christmas tree for the enjoyment of the little ones seems to be confined largely to the German element of the population, and the trade in trees during the past week on the South Side and in the Northwest part of the city is extensive. The sidewalk on Third Street above Chestnut resembles a miniature forest, the bushes being erected on every inch of spare space. . . . For fifty cents a very fair-sized Christmas tree can be secured and when it occupies the position of honor in the parlor, decked with its gay-colored trappings and bearing its load of toys and candies it becomes a beautiful object to the happy youngsters. The giant trees of California would be nothing in the estimation of the children when compared to this stunted little bush that bears happiness on every bough.[25]

1 8 8 5

The Room Was Togged Out Gorgeous

*In 1885, a lively frontier dance at the Star Hotel in Anson, Texas,
so delighted William Lawrence Chittenden that he composed this rollicking ballad.*

The Cowboys' Christmas Ball

Way out in Western Texas, where the Clear Fork's waters flow,
Where the cattle are a-browsin', and the Spanish ponies grow; . . .
Where the antelope is grazin' and the lonely plovers call—
It was there that I attended The Cowboys' Christmas Ball.

The town was Anson City, old Jones' county seat,
Where they raised Polled Angus cattle, and waving whiskered wheat; . . .
'Twas there, I say, at Anson, with the lively Widder Wall
That I went to that reception, The Cowboys' Christmas Ball.

 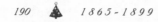

"That Lively Gaited Sworray" flyer from Pioneer Hall in Anson, Texas

The boys had left the ranches and come to town in piles;
The ladies—kinder scatterin', had gathered in for miles.
And yet the place was crowded, as I remember well,
'Twas got for the occasion, at The Morning Star Hotel.
The music was fiddle an' a lively tambourine,
And a viol come imported, by the stage from Abilene.
The room was togged out gorgeous—with mistletoe and shawls,
And candles flickered frescoes, around the airy walls,
And wimmin folks looked lovely—the boys looked kinder treed,
Till their leader commenced: "Woah! Fellers, let's stampeed."

And the music singin', and a-wailin' through the hall,
As a kind of introduction to The Cowboys' Christmas Ball.

The leader was a feller that came from Swenson's Ranch,
They called him Windy Billy, from little Deadman's Branch.
His rig was kinder keerless, big spurs and high-heeled boots;
He had the reputation that comes when fellers shoots,
His voice was like a bugle upon the mountain's heights;
His feet were animated, a mighty moving sight,
When he commenced to holler, "Neow, fellers, stake her pen!
Lock horns ter all them heifers, an' russel 'em like men.
Saloot yer lovely critters; neow swing an' let 'em go,
Climb the grape vine 'round 'em—all hands do-ce-do!
You Mavericks, jine the round-up—jest skip her waterfall."
Huh. Hit was gittin' happy, The Cowboys' Christmas Ball.

The boys were tolerable skittish, the ladies powerful neat,
The old bass viol's music just got there with both feet!
That wailin', frisky fiddle, I never shall forget;
And Windy kept a-singin'—I think I hear him yet— . . .

The dust riz fast an' furious, we all just galloped 'round,
Till the scenery got so giddy that Z Bar Dick was downed;
We buckled on our partners, an' tole 'em to hold on,
Then shook our hoofs like lightning, until the early dawn.
Don't tell me 'bout cotillions, or germans. No sir'ree!
That whirl at Anson City just takes the cake with me.
I'm sick of lazy shufflin's, of them I've had my fill,

Give me a frontier break-down, backed up by Windy Bill.
McAllister ain't nowhar! when Windy leads the show,
I've seen 'em both in harness, and so I sorter know—
Oh, Bill, I shan't forget yer, and I'll oftentimes recall
That lively gaited sworray—The Cowboys' Christmas Ball.[26]

*The Star Hotel burned down years ago, but the Cowboys' Christmas Ball
is re-enacted each December in the frontier atmosphere of Anson's Pioneer Hall.
("Dresses required for ladies on the dance floor. No hats allowed on the dance floor.")*

1886

A Baby On Christmas Day!

*Writing of her life in Bonanza, Colorado, Anne Ellis
recalled one Christmas day when she tested an old wives' tale,
only to find it did not work.*

The Christmas following my tenth birthday, a miner who had eaten at our house left town, and sent, as a bread-and-butter gift, a huge box of candy, all in fancy shapes; I remember one in the shape of a cross with dents in it as though pressed with a waffle iron; there was also a tiny straw box filled with gum. All this seemed to inspire Henry to fix us a tree, and he did, making tiny candles by dipping string in hot grease, letting it cool and dipping again, till a dear little candle was the result. Then these and our candy were hung on the tree, how filled the cabin was with light and gladness! Not a shadow, except one—and I tried so hard to avoid this, too! I had been told it was a sure sign that some one was coming into the family if a dog lay with his head in the door; if he lay with his head out of the door, some one was going out of the family. So I didn't take any chances, but kicked and pulled him away every time he lay near the door. But, in spite of all my trouble, didn't we up and have another baby on Christmas Day! Mama attended to the baby herself, then had the chicken which we were to have for dinner brought to the side of the bed and showed us how to stuff it.[27]

1887

I Did Have Fun

Helen Keller lost her sight and hearing to a mysterious illness when she was eighteen months old. She was a wild and uncontrollable seven-year-old the spring Anne Sullivan came to live with the Keller family in Alabama. By Christmas time, "Teacher" had opened a brilliant new world to Helen's touch, and transformed her into the cheerful child who wrote the first entry in the group that follows—a letter to a Perkins schoolmate. In it, Helen tells of her holiday fun. In the second entry, a grown-up Helen Keller remembered that same Christmas in her autobiography. Sullivan, who had severe visual problems of her own, came to Helen Keller from the Perkins Institution for the Blind in Boston. In the final account, Sullivan described this same joyful Christmas to Mrs. Sophia C. Hopkins, a Perkins school matron.

Tuscumbia, Ala. Jan. 2nd 1888

Dear Sarah

I am happy to write to you this morning. . . . I saw Miss Betty and her scholars. They had a pretty Christmas tree, and there were many pretty presents on it for little children. I had a mug, and little bird and candy. I had many lovely things for Christmas. Aunt gave me a trunk for Nancy and clothes. I went to party with teacher and mother.

We did dance and play and eat nuts and candy and cakes and oranges and I did have fun with little boys and girls. Mrs. Hopkins did send me lovely ring. I do love her and little blind girls. . . .

Good-by

From Helen Keller in The Story of My Life:
The first Christmas after Miss Sullivan came to Tuscumbia was a great event. Every one in the family prepared surprises for me, but what pleased me most, Miss Sullivan and I prepared surprises for everyone else. The mystery that surrounded the gifts was my greatest delight and amusement. . . . Miss Sullivan and I kept up a game of guessing which taught me more about the use of language than any set lessons could have done. Every evening, seated round a glowing wood fire, we played our guessing game, which grew more and more exciting as Christmas approached. . . .

That night [Christmas Eve], after I had hung my stocking, I lay awake a long time, pretending to be asleep and keeping alert to see what Santa Claus would do when he came. At last I fell asleep with a new doll and a white bear in my arms. Next morning it was I who waked the whole family with my first "Merry Christmas!" I found surprises, not in the stocking only, but on the table, on all the chairs, at the door, on the very window-sill; indeed, I could hardly walk without stumbling on a bit of Christmas wrapped up in tissue paper. But when my teacher presented me with a canary, my cup of happiness overflowed.

From Anne Sullivan:
Christmas week was a very busy one here, too. Helen is invited to all the children's entertainments, and I take her to as many as I can. I want her to know children and to be with them as much as possible. . . .

Saturday the school-children had their tree, and I took Helen. It was the first Christmas tree she had ever seen, and she was puzzled, and asked many questions. "Who made tree grow in house? Why? Who put many things on tree?" She objected to its miscellaneous fruits and began to remove them, evidently thinking they were all meant for her. It was not difficult, however, to make her understand that there was a present for each child, and to her great delight she was permitted to hand the gifts to the children. There were several presents for herself. She placed them in a chair, resisting all temptation to look at them until every child had received his gifts. One little girl had fewer presents than the rest, and Helen insisted on sharing her gifts with her. . . . The exercises began at nine, and it was one o'clock before we could leave. My fingers and head ached; but Helen was as fresh and full of spirit as when we left home. . . .

It was touching and beautiful to see Helen enjoy her first Christmas. Of course, she hung her stocking—two of them lest Santa Claus should forget one, and she lay awake for a long time and got up two or three times to see if anything had happened. When I told her that Santa Claus would not come until she was asleep, she shut her eyes and said, "He will think girl is asleep." She was awake the first thing in the morning, and ran to the fireplace for her stocking; and when she found that Santa Claus had filled both stockings, she danced about for a minute, then grew very quiet, and came to ask me if I thought Santa Claus had made a mistake, and thought there were two little girls, and would come back for the gifts when he discovered his mistake. The ring you sent her was in the toe of the stocking, and when I told her you gave it to Santa Claus for her, she said, "I do love Mrs. Hopkins." She had a trunk and clothes for Nancy, and her comment was, "Now Nancy will go to party." When she saw the braille slate and paper, she said, "I will write many letters, and I will thank Santa Claus very much." It was evident that every one, especially Captain and Mrs. Keller, was deeply moved at the thought of the difference between this bright Christmas and the last, when their little girl had no conscious part in the Christmas festivities. As we came downstairs, Mrs. Keller said to me with tears in her eyes, "Miss Annie, I thank God every day of my life for sending you to us; but I never realized until this morning what a blessing you have been to us." Captain Keller took my hand, but could not speak. But his silence was more eloquent than words. My heart, too, was full of gratitude and solemn joy.[28]

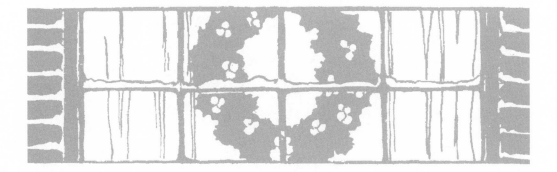

1 8 9 1

This Is Our Harvest Time

*In his autobiography, F. W. Woolworth recalled how he rallied
his store managers for the holiday trade, beginning in early December.*

ive your store a holiday appearance. Hang up Christmas ornaments. Perhaps have a tree in the window. Make the store look different. This is our harvest time. Make it pay. This is also a good time to work off 'stickers' or unsalable goods, for they will sell during the excitement when you could not give them away other times. Mend all broken toys and dolls every day. Also, watch your clerks and customers to see they do not steal. When the store is crowded, don't allow any boys or girls in the store at all, unless they are with their parents, as most of them come in on purpose to steal. The cashier also needs your watchful eye, as it has been the experience of at least one store every year to lose large amounts through the cashier's dishonesty. Remember, the cashier has the best chance of all to steal.[29]

1890s

A Regular Stampede

*One of Lizzie Miles's favorite memories was of all the commotion
Santa caused when he dropped in on a party in the
gold-mining town of Superior, Montana.*

I remember a Christmas tree we had once at the Thomas Hotel. Johnston had fixed up as Santa Claus, rigged out with a cotton beard. He came in by a ladder, on the third floor. In those days we didn't have electric lights, only coal-oil lamps and the colored candles on the tree. Johnston got too close to the candles, and his whiskers caught fire. Grandma Riefflin grabbed her plaid shawl, one she had brought from Berlin, Germany, and smothered the blaze with it. By that time, there was a regular stampede, everybody hitting for the stairs. A bunch of big men held them back, or some would have been trampled to death.[30]

1 8 9 2

May My Work Your Hearts Rejoice

This flyer was dispensed by the Alford Brothers Steam Laundry in Madison, Wisconsin.

Christmas Greeting

This is fair greeting to my friends,
To those who come and those who go,
From one who to your linen lends
The whiteness of the driven snow.

Greeting to the ones who find
Their chiefest joy in linen fair,
Smooth as a grape's rich bloom outlined,
And laundered with the best of care.

And when my wagon standing waits
Beside the homes that know me best,
Greeting to those who ope the gates,
On north or south or east or west.

Fair greeting then with cheerful voice,
Long life and mirth and music's cheer,
And may my work your hearts rejoice
All through the onward coming year.

And as these pictures you admire,
And while these lines you lightly scan
Remember at the Christmas fire
This greeting from your laundryman.[31]

1892

To Trim A Tree

Christmas tree hooks, patented in the United States,
were announced in a wholesaler's 1892 catalogue.

*I*t is a well known fact, that heretofore it has taken the best part of Christmas Eve to trim a tree by tying strings or threads to the trinkets, and then tying these to the tree, thus taking about 2 to 3 hours of one person's time and labor to trim a tree with 100 articles. With these hooks, the same number can be applied in less than half an hour.[32]

1893

Tickled The Big Folks

In her diary, Miss Maud Rittenhouse recorded how the
Cairo, Illinois, Sunday school class that she taught charmed the entire
congregation at the Episcopalian Christmas program.

*C*hristmas Eve—93—

We had our S.S. festivities last night, as today is Sunday. My children were the sweetest things there; twenty six of them bore the 26 letters of the alphabet, and each baby said a text beginning with the letter. Curly-headed little Donald in his kilts held his A aloft and repeated boldly "A soft answer turneth away wrath." Then baby Edna, her little cheeks pink with excitement mounted the platform with her "B" and sung out in her soft, clear little voice, *"Be* not overcome of evil but overcome evil with good." Birdie Donaldson, aged three, came next. Her long white gown was too much for her going up the high step of the platform, so she gathered it into her arms, which made everybody laugh. That done, she put one little arm to my shoulder and whispered, "Cleanse thou me from secret faults."

"But you must say it to the people, dearie," I said, "out loud, and turn around." So she did. It was all too cunning for anything. Each tot had some funny little trick or lisp or inflection that tickled the big folks nearly to death.[33]

1893
Santa, Covered With Spangles

From the Champaign County Gazette, *on December 27, 1893, came notice of a sparkling St. Nick.*

In accordance with the usual custom, the First Methodist church had a Christmas tree; not a small ordinary affair, but a monster tree, its huge branches nearly covering the large platform, and capable of supporting a multitude of gifts; . . . from the base to summit it was beautifully set with long strings of popcorn, mingled in good taste with colored balls and sparkling ornaments of various kinds; and, to add to the general pleasing effect, it was brilliantly lighted with small wax tapers. Then there was Santa Claus—a real live St. Nick,—who was dressed in a loose shift of white clothes, covered with spangles from head to foot, and whose huge beard almost hid his smiling face.[34]

1895

The Ways And Means Committee

*This article in the New York Times, on December 26, 1895,
disclosed that everyone in Washington, D.C., (except for members
of the Ways and Means Committee of the House of
Representatives) had enjoyed the holiday.*

ashington, D.C.

The President and Mrs. Cleveland spent the day at home quietly with their little family, and the building has been closed to visitors.

The weather during the afternoon was delightful, if unseasonable, the sun shining with the warmth almost of a June day. The streets and street cars were crowded with holiday makers, and the beautiful country roads, of which Washington has so many in its vicinity, were thronged with vehicles and cyclers. Only in the Ways and Means Committee room of the carefully guarded Capitol was a semblance of labor preserved, but even that hard-pressed committee shortly after 1 P.M. "adjourned from labor to refreshment" on the completion of its tariff and bond bills.[35]

1895

Never-Ending, Beautiful Surprises

*The following two accounts feature a family Christmas party
hosted by George Washington Vanderbilt at his mammoth new estate
in the North Carolina mountains. The first story appeared in*

the New York Times *on December 26, 1895; the second was*
in the Asheville *(N.C.)* Citizen, *datelined December 25.*

iltmore Thrown Open
George W. Vanderbilt Entertains at
His Country Estate.
Special trains carry the guests
Fox Chasing to be Part of the Holiday Diversion
Asheville, N.C., Dec. 25—George W. Vanderbilt formally opened his country
home near Asheville to-day.

All immediate members of the Vanderbilt family now in this country are
guests at Biltmore House. [*A diagram in Gertrude Vanderbilt's* Dinner Book *showed
twenty-seven seated at the Christmas table*] . . . All of these persons have come here in
their own private cars, and brought with them an army of servants.

G. W. Vanderbilt has for two weeks past personally directed a corps of carv-
ers, joiners, decorators, and florists in giving the finishing touches to the great
mansion [*for example, electricians wired more than five hundred of the newly fashionable electric tree lights onto the thirty-four-foot tree that towered, with room to spare, in the 72' x 42' x
70' Banquet Hall*], and it doubtless stands to-day, in connection with its surrounding park and outlying hunting and fishing preserves, the most valuable as well
as the most extensive private property in America. The house tract contains
8,040 acres, upon which seventy-five miles of driveways have already been constructed, while the hunting preserves embrace 87,000 acres in which is included
Mount Pisgah, one of the most prominent peaks on the Asheville plateau, which
boasts the highest point east of the Rocky Mountains.

"Biltmore House" stands upon a splendid terrace overlooking the French
Broad and Swananoa Valleys, and from its turrets are to be seen not fewer than

fifty mountain peaks, having an altitude of 5,000 feet and over. Every conceivable modern adornment and convenience is found within its walls. Driveways have been constructed at an enormous expense, and wind over rustic bridges, besides artificial lakes and natural water courses, while on either hand mountain sides, so attractive in their native ruggedness, have been aided by the art of landscape artists, and enriched in foliage from the arboretum until they form never-ending, beautiful surprises.

A Christmas tree donation was given at 11 o'clock to-day to all the employees on the estate, numbering between three and five hundred. Barrels of mistletoe and wagonloads of holly and cartloads of packages were distributed. A dinner was later served to the employees.

The company now at Biltmore is made up exclusively of members of the Vanderbilt family, but the festivities will broaden toward the close of the week, when a large company of Mr. Vanderbilt's New York friends will be his guests for, perhaps, ten days. The time will be spent in coaching parties, hunting, fox chasing, quail shooting and fishing.[36]

The hearth fires on Biltmore House cracked a cheery Christmas warming to members of George W. Vanderbilt's family who came from the North to honor the occasion. Apart from the pleasures of a family gathering on the day of the great festival of the year, the event of absorbing interest on the estate was the welcome given in the great house to the resident workman, wives and children. . . . The hour of the festivities was put on at ll o'clock and upward of 200 persons were promptly present in the Banquet Hall when Mr. Vanderbilt in a short speech wished the company a merry Christmas. . . . A beautiful tree that stood in the Banquet Hall causing the liveliest anticipation of the little folks, was then stripped of its heavy trimmings of gifts. Each of the guests was remembered.[37]

After these festivities, George's young niece, Gertrude Vanderbilt, told her best friend that the Biltmore get-together was so delightful that she hated to go home. "I tried to make the family leave me," she said, "but it was in vain."

Modern-day visitors can share in the delights of Christmas at Biltmore Estate each November and December, when the grand old place is lavishly decorated and rich with music.

1 8 9 5

In America It Might Be Different

Hinda Satt, whose name was changed to Hilda in America, moved with her Jewish family from Poland to Chicago when she was ten. Three years later, she apprehensively attended her first Christmas party at Jane Addams' Hull House—a welcoming oasis to Hilda, as it was to a multitude of other immigrants. In later years, Hilda Satt Polacheck wrote this account of that visit.

 everal days before Christmas . . . one of my Irish playmates suggested that I go with her to a Christmas party at Hull-House. I told her that I never went to Christmas parties.

"Why not?" she asked.

"I do not go anywhere on Christmas Day," I said.

"But this party will not be on Christmas Day. It will be the Sunday before Christmas Day," she said.

I repeated that I could not go and she persisted in wanting to know why. Before I could think, I blurted out the words: "I might get killed."

"Get killed!" She stared at me. "I go to Hull-House Christmas parties every year, and no one was ever killed."

I then asked her if there would be any Jewish children at the party. She assured me that there had been Jewish children at the parties every year and that no one was ever hurt.

The thought began to percolate through my head that things might be different in America. In Poland it had not been safe for Jewish children to be on the streets on Christmas. I struggled with my conscience and finally decided to accompany my friend to the Hull-House Christmas party. This was the second time that I was doing something without telling Mother.

My friend and I arrived at Hull-House and went to the coffee shop where the party was being held. There were many children and their parents seated when we arrived. It was the first time that I had sat in a room where there was a Christmas tree. In fact, there were two trees in the room: one on each side of the high brick fireplace. The trees looked as if they had just been brought in from a heavy snowstorm. The glistening glass icicles and asbestos snow looked very real. The trees were lighted with white candles and on each side stood a man with a pail of water and a mop, ready to put out any accidental fire.

People called to each other across the room. Then I noticed that I could not understand what they were saying. It dawned on me that the people in this room had come from other countries. Yet there was no tension. Everybody seemed to be having a good time. There were children and parents at this party from Russia, Poland, Italy, Germany, Ireland, England, and many other lands, but no one seemed to care where they had come from, or what religion they professed, or what clothes they wore, or what they thought. As I sat there, I am sure I felt myself being freed from a variety of century-old superstitions and inhibitions. There seemed to be nothing to be afraid of.

Then Jane Addams came into the room! It was the first time that I looked into those kind, understanding eyes. There was a gleam of welcome in them that made me feel I was wanted. She told us that she was glad we had come. Her voice was warm and I knew she meant what she said. She was the second person who made me glad that I had come to America. Mrs. Torrance [*Hilda's first grade teacher*] was the first.

The children of the Hull-House Music School then sang some songs, that I later found out were called "Christmas carols." I shall never forget the caressing sweetness of those childish voices. All feelings of religious intolerance and bigotry faded. I could not connect this beautiful party with any hatred or superstition that existed among the people of Poland.

As I look back, I know that I became a staunch American at this party. I was with children who had been brought here from all over the world. The fathers and mothers, like my father and mother, had come in search of a free and happy life. And we were all having a good time at a party, as the guests of an American, Jane Addams.

We were all poor. Some of us were underfed. Some of us had holes in our shoes. But we were not afraid of each other. What greater service can a human being give to her country than to banish fear from the heart of a child? Jane Addams did that for me at that party.

While I felt that I had done nothing wrong or sinful by going to the Christmas party, I still hesitated telling Mother where I had been. I was glad that she did not ask me.[38]

1897

A Little Too Strong?

This untested recipe for Alaskan Gold Rush Christmas Punch
came from Jack London's story, "To the Man on Trail."

Dump it in."

"But I say, Kid, isn't that going it a little too strong? Whiskey and alcohol's bad enough; but when it comes to brandy and pepper-sauce and"—

"Dump it in. Who's making this punch, anyway?" And Malemute Kid smiled benignantly through the clouds of steam. "By the time you've been in this country as long as I have, my son, and lived on rabbit-tracks and salmon-belly, you'll learn that Christmas comes only once per annum. And a Christmas without punch is sinking a hole to bedrock with nary a pay-streak." . . .

Malemute Kid's frightful concoction did its work; the men of the camps and trails unbent in its genial glow, and jest and song and tales of past adventure went round the board. Aliens from a dozen lands, they toasted each and all. It was the Englishman, Prince, who pledged "Uncle Sam, the precocious infant of the New World;" the Yankee, Bettles, who drank to "The Queen, God bless her;" and together, Savoy and Meyers, the German trader, clanged their cups to Alsace and Lorraine.

Then Malemute Kid arose, cup in hand, and glanced at the greased-paper window, where the frost stood full three inches thick. "A health to the man on trail this night; may his grub hold out; may his dogs keep their legs; may his matches never miss fire."[39]

Stepping High and Handsome

*This excerpt from Anne Ellis's autobiography finds her beginning
married life in a raw, new Rocky Mountain town called Chance—
home of The Last Chance mine.*

That Christmas we decide to have a community tree, followed by a dance and supper. We all bake for the supper, and take it with us, putting it on tables and benches. The coffee is made in a wash boiler of the big box stove which heats the room. One man makes fine lemon pies and this is his donation, but this wasn't his lucky day, as he used pans with removable bottoms and started a kid with one in each hand, who had tin bracelets and no pie, before he learned how to carry them. Pete Peterson had a new girl and was spreading himself for her benefit. He brought her in, helped her off with her things, came back stepping high and handsome, and sat down, but felt at once that all was not well, and arose with all the frosting off Jenks's pie on the back of his pants.

The Iris people are invited over for the dance, and now we hear the sleigh coming. A sound of laughter, the door is thrown open, and people and snow drift in. They all stamp their feet and wish every one a Merry Christmas. By now some of our people who took more than their share of apples (Tom and Jerry, too, I expect), have begun to throw them at each other. As a big miner from Iris steps in, one takes him in the temple. I am not going to stand for any roughhouse, as I had set out to have a ladylike, refined affair, so I jump up on a chair and yell—"Here, you two stiffs, cut out the apple throwing!" At this, George drags me down and takes me home, but I guess it was just as well, as the dance ended up in a free-for-all.[40]

1899

300 Pairs of Shoes Flying in the Air

Herbert Hoover graduated with Stanford University's first class in 1895.
After graduation, he began his career as a mining expert in the western states and
Australia. In 1899 he returned to California to marry Stanford classmate Lou Henry, class of '99.
Immediately after the wedding, the couple sailed to China, where Hoover headed the new
Department of Mines at Peiping. Because of events beyond his control, as Hoover explained
in his memoir, the newly-weds missed spending their first Christmas together.

*O*n a return journey from Hen Si I came into Kalgan a gate to the Great Wall of China on Christmas Eve with snow and temperatures below zero. The caravan was tired out from my pushing to arrive home to be with Mrs. Hoover for Christmas—but it was impossible and the caravan must have rest. . . .

[The next day] I called upon the Mission. Here I found some twelve American men, women and children under the direction of a beautiful old gentleman Dr. Williamson. It was a large compound of schoolrooms, living quarters and medical clinic. The good doctor asked me to stay to Christmas dinner and promised turkey. It was a good dinner but the fine American faces were a better tonic. . . . I found that among the Christmas gifts from the states for the Mission Chinese children were four regulation footballs. Dr. Williamson's daughter seemed stumped on what to do with them.

I suggested I was experienced in that game and if they would produce the players I would instruct. She produced three hundred alert youngsters in usual Chinese dress and loose shoes with snow on the ground. I divided them into two equal squads, put all four balls into play, and signaled for them to go in opposite directions. In a minute, 300 pairs of shoes were flying in the air but not even the stocking feet in the snow checked the vitality of the kids.

These missionaries were good folks of whose devotion Americans can be proud.[41]

1900 – 1940

1900
Christmas Dinner, 35 Cents

German House

George A. Dumont, Proprietor

Christmas Menu, 1900

Dinner at 12:30.   Price, 35 cents.

Middle Park Trout   Baked Halibut

Consomme of Calcutta   Chicken a la Creole

Olives   Celery   Green Onions

Sugar Cured Boiled Ham
with Champagne Sauce

Boiled Salmon with Egg Sauce

Smothered Spring Chicken with Cream Sauce
Banana Fritters with Wine Sauce
Barbecued Belgian Hare with Pomme de Terre
Compote of Rice

Roast Turkey with Cranberry Sauce
Prime Rib Roast of Beef with Sweet Potatoes
Mashed and Browned Potatoes
Sweet Potatoes   French Peas
Sugar Corn

Boiled English Plum Pudding
with Brandy Sauce

Mince Pie   Green Apple Pie

Chocolate Cake   Cocoanut Cake

Fruit Cake   Pound Cake

Lemon Ice Cream   Assorted Fruits

This menu came from a restaurant in Idaho Springs, Colorado, in 1900.[1]

c. 1900

If You Wanted a Whole Pie You Was Welcome

Otis W. Terpening, a lumberjack from the Wisconsin north woods,
remembered the men's Paul Bunyan–sized appetites, especially at Christmas.

or two weeks before the great day, things took on a brighter hue, at least they seemed to. The lads were better natured than usual. And why shouldn't they be. Some had left their families and kiddies early in the fall, with the understanding that at Christmas they would all be united again, while others thought of the sweetheart back in the settlement. Then we had a kind with us that I can't describe in this up to date language. But us Jacks called them lushers: a class that was shunned by the better class of lumberjacks. For the only thing they seemly thought of getting out of life was a big drunk and a feed of ham and eggs. As there was no drinking allowed in camp, it was real hard on them.

And they all seemed to hail Christmas as a time of getting out of their bondage. As the day drew near the real Christmas Spirit seemed to prevail. And in the snatches of song that we would hear in the woodland during the day there was a real ring of joy in them. And in the voice of the Jacks on Christmas morning as they wished one another

 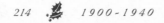

Merry Christmas. And to hear one Jack say, "Thanks, Pal, I hope you live forever and I live to see you die." We seldom ever worked on Christmas, but the day was spent in visiting, darning our socks and mittens. While some spent their time in playing cards and listening for the cheerie sound of the dinner horn, saying come and eat, eat. The cook would always have something extra, and plenty of it.

There was roast beef, brown gravy, good home-made bread, potatoes, shiny tins heaped with golden rings called fried cakes, and close to them a pumpkin pie baked in a ten-inch tin, about one-and-a-half-inch deep, and cut in four pieces. Any other day to a Jack it was one piece, but today it was Christmas. It only came once a year and help yourself, if you wanted a whole pie you was welcome. And rice pudding black with raisins, dried prunes, or the old-fashioned dried apples for sauce. Black coffee sweetened with brown sugar. And tins full of sweet cookies. They were white and had a raisin in the center of them. Did we eat, I will say we did! . . .

After Christmas dinner—which was served at noon—the loggers relaxed until it was time for supper, which was almost a repeat of the main repast. Some would get out the old greasy deck of cards and climb into some pal's top bunk for a quiet game of poker, while others took to the old-time square dances. The "ladies" had a grain sack tied around their waist so we could tell them from the gents. And woe to the one that stepped on a lady's toe, and did not apologize. And do it quick. Or it would be one quick blow and a Jack would measure his length on the floor. Then it was the first two gents cross over and by the lady stand. The second two cross and all join hands. And we had to have a jig every set.[2]

1900

In Its Way, Wonderful To Behold

 On December 22, 1900, a reporter for the Philadelphia North American *wrote of a Christmas tree only a biology professor could truly appreciate.*

In accordance with an old custom, the students in the University of Pennsylvania's Biological School presented a Christmas tree yesterday to their instructors. In its way, it was wonderful to behold. Long strings of vertebrae, arranged from an evolutionary stand-point, formed part of the decorations. Then on the branches were worms, crabs, bugs and beetles, while various kinds of fish hung near worms, to illustrate the inclination of one for the other. Twining in and out among the branches were specimens of reptiles, and near them birds' nests, full of eggs, and with the mother birds guarding them. The mammals were chiefly represented by stuffed monkeys.

Around the base of the tree were jawbones, old teeth, skulls and a pile of carpal and tarsal bones. Animal specimens in alcohol were so placed as to form a background for a collection of chickens, pigs and cats. Eggs of various ages filled in the interstices, and in addition there were various forms of fungi, while green mould, blue mould and slime appeared everywhere on old boots, green cheese and pieces of rotten logs.[3]

 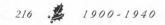

1902

There Was A Surprise For Me

*President Theodore Roosevelt was upset to learn that people were cutting
Christmas trees from national forests. To set a good example of conservation,
Roosevelt declared there would be no tree in the White House. In this letter
to President Garfield's grandson, Roosevelt explained how his son
Archie did not go along with the idea.*

White House, December 26, 1902

Jimmikins:

Yesterday morning at a quarter of seven all the children were up and dressed and
began to hammer at the door of their mother's and my room, in which their six stockings, all bulging out with queer angles and rotundities, were hanging from the fireplace.
So their mother and I got up, shut the window, lit the fire (taking down the stockings,
of course), put on our wrappers and prepared to admit the children. But first there was a
surprise for me, also for their good mother, for Archie had a little Christmas tree of his
own, which he had rigged up with the help of one of the carpenters in a big closet; and
we all had to look at the tree and each of us got a present off of it. There was also one
present each for Jack, the dog, Tom Quartz, the kitten, and Algonquin, the pony, whom
our Archie would no more think of neglecting than I would neglect his brothers and
sisters. Then all the children came into our bed and there they opened their stockings.
Afterward we got dressed and took breakfast, and then all went into the library, where
each child had a table set for his bigger presents. Quentin had a perfectly delightful
electric railroad, which had been rigged up for him by one of his friends, the White
House electrician, who has been very good to all the children. Then Ted and I, with
General Wood and Mr. Bob Ferguson, who was a lieutenant in my regiment, went for a

three-hour ride; and all of us, including all the children, took lunch at the house with the children's aunt, Mrs. Captain Cowles—Archie and Quentin having their lunch at a little table with their cousin Sheffield. Late in the afternoon I played games of single stick with General Wood and also Mr. Ferguson. I am going to get your father to come on and try it soon. We have to try to hit as light as possible, but sometimes we hit hard, and today I have a bump over one eye and a swollen wrist. Then all our family and kinsfolk and the Senator and Mrs. Lodge's family and kinsfolk had our Christmas dinner at the White House, and afterward danced in the East Room, closing up with the Virginia reel.[4]

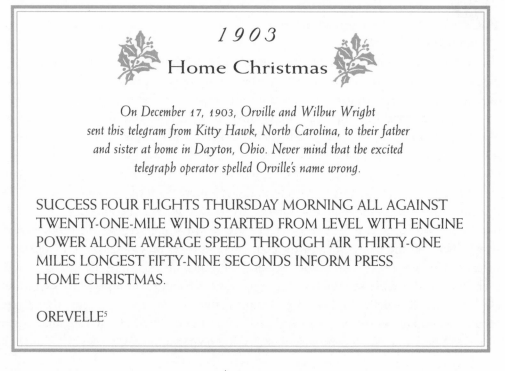

1903

Home Christmas

*On December 17, 1903, Orville and Wilbur Wright
sent this telegram from Kitty Hawk, North Carolina, to their father
and sister at home in Dayton, Ohio. Never mind that the excited
telegraph operator spelled Orville's name wrong.*

SUCCESS FOUR FLIGHTS THURSDAY MORNING ALL AGAINST TWENTY-ONE-MILE WIND STARTED FROM LEVEL WITH ENGINE POWER ALONE AVERAGE SPEED THROUGH AIR THIRTY-ONE MILES LONGEST FIFTY-NINE SECONDS INFORM PRESS HOME CHRISTMAS.

OREVELLE[5]

 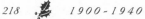

"*A Happy & Blessed Christmas to You All, Ralph,*" *was written in a personal note on the bottom corner of this embossed card, postmarked Atchison, Kansas—December 21, 1905. It had a one-cent stamp, "good for delivery to any place in the U.S.*"

Courtesy of Nannette Rod

1905

A Tree 30 Feet High

*Author Edith Wharton wrote this letter
to her friend, Sarah Norton, describing the joys
of a Biltmore Christmas in North Carolina.*

iltmore House
December 26 [1905]

Dear Sally

The journey here was frightfully fatiguing, but this divine landscape, "under a roof of blue Ionian weather," makes up for all the hardship, & prolongs for me a little the sweet illusion of autumn, which must soon be lost in the horrors of the thrice-loathsome New York.—Yesterday we had a big Xmas fete for the 350 people on the estate—a tree 30 ft high, Punch & Judy, conjuror, presents & "refreshments." It would have interested you, it was done so well & sympathetically, each person's wants being thought of, from mother to last baby.—In this matchless weather the walks thro' the park are a joy. I should like to share with you—great sheets of fruited ivy pouring over terrace walls, yellow stars still shining on the bare branches of the nudiflora, jasmine, & masses of juniper, heath, honeysuckle, rhododendron & laurel making an evergreen covert so different from our denuded New England lanes.—Alas, that it is so far from everything.

Affly yrs
E. W.[6]

c. *1908*

Star of Bethlehem

*Writing of an early period in her life, Katharine Ball Ripley said that even
when she was broke, she managed to find enough money to buy Christmas rockets
to shoot off for her young son. To a Southerner, Christmas
would not be Christmas without fireworks.*

When I was a child in Charleston we always had fireworks at Christmas. Christmas Eve the grown people set them off to amuse us. Flowerpots and skyrockets. Huge Chinese fish with flaming tails floating over the housetops. And last of all the steady burning Star of Bethlehem, brilliant, serene, warm and friendly, floating away in the dark sky.[7]

1910

Never Let The Gas Stove Burn At Night

*Anna C. McDonald grew up in Oil City, Pennsylvania.
By the time she was nineteen, Mrs. McDonald had finished high school and State Normal,
and signed a contract to teach in a one-room school three miles from Fryburg, where she boarded.
At her daughter's insistence, Mrs. McDonald later wrote down
episodes from her life, such as this anxiety-ridden Christmas Eve.*

[The school] was one room, with a big round stove in the center—heated with gas. In 1910 there were many gas and oil pumps on every farm. People could burn all the gas they wanted. Every farmer had big gas jets outside which he burned all night. When

I went there to teach, Dr. Hess, chairman of the school board, told me I must never let the gas stove burn at night. Without any control, gas would come on after people lowered their gas supplies at night. Several schoolhouses had burned down. Now I was from the city, never had had this responsibility. So each evening before starting my 3 mile hike into town, I checked and double-checked the stove. . . .

Two days before the Christmas holiday, we had a terrific snow storm—all day. About two o'clock in the afternoon, people began coming for the smaller children in horse-drawn sleds. They told me I'd have to leave immediately. If I didn't, the narrow road between the mountains would be closed. The farmer close by came to take me to his farm house to spend the night. . . . But I felt I couldn't go the last day before Christmas, because at my boarding house in the village of Fryburg, I had gotten gifts for each child, plus oranges and candy. Since the next day was our Christmas program, tree and gifts, I asked him if he could take me into town. He did. In all the excitement of the hasty departure, I couldn't remember turning off the gas.

I never thought of it until I wakened about 3 a.m. The room and sky was alight from the flames of my school!—Of course I was dreaming—but it was *so* real.

I suffered until 6 a.m. and couldn't wait any longer. I packed up my Christmas loot and started walking—drifts up to my knees. Of course I had high top boots, but I'll never forget that walk—taking one step after another thru snow drifts for 3 miles! And I'll never forget my prayers of thanksgiving when I arrived to find I had turned off the gas. I didn't mind the cold nor the hardships, I was so grateful.[8]

"Good to   build with."

"YOU wrote me for something to build with," said Santa Claus. "So here I've brought you the best thing I have in stock in that line. In fact, it's the best 'building up' stuff you ever heard of.

"You can not only build houses, and churches and steeples with these handsome red-and-white cans, but you can build up health and strength and rosy cheeks and snapping bright eyes, and a lot of other good things with

Campbell's SOUPS

Advertisement in the Saturday Evening Post *on December 24, 1910*

1913

The Celebrated Trombone Choir

This article from the Record *on December 25, 1913,
described how Philadelphia's first community Christmas tree was heralded
with Moravian trombones, played very sweetly.*

High above the crowd came a flash of light from an unexpected place. It was the cupola of the tower of Independence Hall, the place where the Liberty Bell first rang out the news of the signing of the Declaration of Independence. The oldest attendant at the hall could not remember a time when the cupola had been lighted before.

Into the lighted space stepped the six members of the celebrated trombone choir of the Moravian Church at Bethlehem, who welcome Christmas with the sounding of their instruments every year in their home town. They had been brought to Philadelphia for the first time to take part in the city's first municipal celebration. Raising their long instruments to their lips, the trombonists sent forth a blast over the heads of the crowd. First they played "How Brightly Shines the Morning Star," then "From Heaven High to Earth I Come," and finally, very sweetly and in moderated tones, they sounded the notes of "All My Heart This Night Rejoices."[9]

The Cheer Bringer

This Campbell Soup Kid from 1915 shows one of the chubby cherub-faced twins,
first created for a 1904 streetcar advertising campaign.
From *Good Old Days: Christmas Memories*

1914 - 1917

Christmas Was The Event Of The Year

*Harrison Salisbury recorded these memories of growing up
in Minneapolis in the years heading toward World War I.*

hristmas was the event of the year for me. . . .

For weeks we had been building up to it. The anticipation started immediately after my birthday in mid-November. There were not-too-subtle warnings that Santa Claus was observing the conduct of young children with special care. And if one wanted his full attention and kind response, one had best give him no cause for displeasure—that is, eat your meals quietly and leave nothing on the plate, no joking or playing at the table; go to bed swiftly at the appointed hour, no "five minutes more"; do your chores without being told; pick up your boots, don't leave them strewn about the kitchen; see that your toys are in their places in the cupboard or the window seat, and don't leave the building blocks scattered around; and don't complain about errands to the basement and the woodshed.

Well, there were many more admonitions and they changed a bit, year by year, but that was the start of Christmas. Then came the composition of the letter to Santa Claus, a serious occupation which required much thought. . . . The list was usually completed just after Thanksgiving Day. Then the pace began to quicken. There were visits downtown, perhaps to Donaldson's Glass Block, the nearest thing to Brighton which Minneapolis boasted. A sight of Santa Claus with his bell and his chimney (soliciting alms for the Salvation Army or the Volunteers of America). Sometimes—heavens—two Santa Clauses were spotted and that required a bit of explanation. But the climax of the pre-Christmas activity was the visit to Holtzermann's store. I don't know how I managed to square this most wonderful of institutions with my deep-seated germanophobia.

Holtzermann was the most German of German stores. It had been transported direct from the Black Forest. It was crammed from top to bottom with German toys (and there *were* no other toys in the years coming up to World War I). Somehow, . . . likely by prudent advance buying, the stock of German toys, the mechanized animals, the Anchor blocks, the miniature trees, the small chimes which played "Stille Nacht," the *lebkuchen*, the *pfeffernusse*, the gilded angels, the shepherds, the golden stars, and the crimson ornaments with German Christmas mottoes on them did not vanish in 1914. They went on through 1915 and 1916. Only in 1917 did Holtzermann's become more of a ghost than a store, with Japanese trinkets replacing the Black Forest music boxes and cuckoo clocks, but, miracle of miracles, the great basement bins of Dutch wooden shoes were somehow still filled to the brim. But no tin soldiers, no Prussian horsemen with their lances, no small leaden cannons, no banners and flags of grenadier regiments, no flaxen-haired dolls with slow-closing blue eyes, no stuffed animals with genuine leather hides. I did not cry on that wartime visit to Holzermann's. I was too big a boy. But I felt like it. It was a dream vanished. A world that was never to return.[10]

The boy who grew up in the shadow of World War I
went on to receive a Pulitzer Prize for his Moscow reports during World War II.

1915

Ham And Eggs For Two

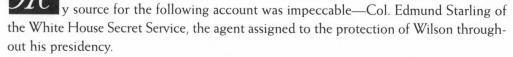

*President Woodrow Wilson, widowed soon after he took office, fell madly
in love with a charming Washington widow, Mrs. Edith Galt. With the help of
Secret Service agent Colonel Edmund Starling, the couple carried on a discreet and
highly secret courtship during the summer of 1915. Years later in a conversation
with a friend, Agent Starling passed on a delightful glimpse of the president's
Christmas honeymoon. Starling's friend, Voit Gilmore, later recorded
that conversation.*

My source for the following account was impeccable—Col. Edmund Starling of
the White House Secret Service, the agent assigned to the protection of Wilson throughout his presidency.

Woodrow Wilson and Edith Bolling Galt were married at her residence at 8 p.m.,
Dec. 18, 1915, by his Presbyterian minister and her Episcopal priest. It was Starling's
job to get them secretly to their honeymoon. . . .

The Colonel explained, "We had to get them out of town without attention—it was
a perfect occasion for cranks and emotionally unstable persons."

Earlier in the day, Starling had two limousines, one for the President and one for
the Secret Service, loaded in the baggage car of a secret presidential train. The two
chauffeurs were told to pack for a two weeks stay at an unknown destination and to
remain out of sight.

"The train crew didn't know the destination either. Suddenly they were ordered to
depart, without the President. The engineer was told to pull into a siding at the edge of
the freight yards in Alexandria.

"The newlyweds left via a back door and were driven to Alexandria, arriving just as their private train pulled in. Only then was the engineer told by officials to proceed to Hot Springs, Virginia."

The Wilsons were ensconced on a private floor of the famed Homestead Hotel . . . for a 14-day honeymoon. Privacy was the word.

Starling's eyes twinkled as he told me the end of the "Wilson Escape" story.

"I saw the newlyweds and their luggage into their suite then took up my station in a chair beside the elevator landing on the private floor. Then, so help me God, two days passed with total silence—not a word from the suite, not a call by phone.

"I grew numb. Here I was, the only person in the world who knew exactly where the President of the United States was, or thought I knew, and even though I was there night and day I began to wonder if he had given me the slip.

"Then, miraculously, on the third morning, the door flew open. Out stepped President Wilson in his pajamas with a huge smile on his face. He said, 'Hi, Ed, how about ham and eggs for two?' " [11]

1920s

The Chain Gang

In her book, Memory of a Large Christmas, *writer Lillian Smith told of the year she and her sister came home to the Georgia mountains and shared the true spirit of Christmas with some extraordinary dinner guests.*

We were not alone in being poor. Times were hard in the South. . . . Our region was deep in a depression long before the rest of the country felt it—indeed, it had never had real prosperity since the Civil War. . . .

The two of us had agreed to skip Christmas. You don't always have to have Christmas, we kept saying to each other. Of course not, the other would answer.

We had forgotten our father.

In that year of austerity, he invited the chain gang to have Christmas dinner with us. The prisoners were working the state roads, staying in two shabby red railroad cars on a siding. Our father visited them as he visited "all his neighbors." That night, after he returned from a three-hour visit with the men, we heard him tell Mother about it. She knew what was coming. "Bad place to be living," he said. "Terrible! Not fit for animals much less—" He sighed. . . . "Mama," he said softly. "How about having them out here for Christmas? Wouldn't that be good?" A long silence. Then Mother quietly agreed. Dad walked to town—we had no car—to tell the foreman he would like to have the prisoners and guards come to Christmas dinner.

"All of them?" asked the chain-gang foreman.

"We couldn't hardly leave any of the boys out, could we?"

Close to noon on Christmas Day we saw them coming down the road: forty-eight men in stripes, with their guards. They came up the hill and headed for the house, a few laughing, talking, others grim and suspicious. All had come, white and Negro. We had helped Mother make two caramel cakes and twelve sweet-potato pies and a wonderful backbone-and-rice dish (which Mother, born on the coast, called pilau); and there were hot rolls and Brunswick stew, and a washtub full of apples which our father had polished in front of the fire on Christmas Eve. It would be a splendid dinner, he told Mother, who looked a bit wan, probably wondering what we would eat in January.

While we pulled out Mother's best china . . . our father went from man to man shaking hands, and soon they were talking freely with him, and everybody was laughing at his funny—and sometimes on the rare side—stories. And then, there was a hush, and we in the kitchen heard Dad's voice lifted up: "And it came to pass in those days—"

Mother stayed with the oven. The two of us eased to the porch. Dad was standing there, reading from St. Luke. The day was warm and sunny and the forty-eight men and their guards were sitting on the grass. Two guards with guns in their hands leaned against trees. Eight of the men were lifers; six of them, in pairs, had their inside legs locked together; ten were killers (one had bashed in his grandma's head); two had robbed banks, three had stolen cars, one had burned down his neighbor's house and barn after an argument, one had raped a girl—all were listening to the old old words.

When my father closed the Bible, he gravely said he hoped their families were having a good Christmas, he hoped all was well "back home." Then he smiled and grew hearty. "Now boys," he said, "eat plenty and have a good time. We're proud to have you today. We would have been a little lonely if you hadn't come. Now let's have a Merry Christmas."

The men laughed. It began with the Negroes, who quickly caught the wonderful absurdity, it spread to the whites and finally all were laughing and muttering Merry Christmas, half deriding, half meaning it, and my father laughed with them, for he was never unaware of the absurd which he seemed deliberately, sometimes, to whistle into his life. . . .

When Mother said she was ready, our father asked "Son," who was one of the killers, to go help "my wife, won't you, with the heavy things." And the young man said he'd be mighty glad to. The one in for raping and another for robbing a bank said they'd be pleased to help, too, and they went in. My sister and I followed, not feeling as casual as we hoped we looked. But when two guards moved toward the door my father peremptorily stopped them with, "The boys will be all right." And "the boys" were. They came back in a few minutes bearing great pots and pans to a serving table we had set up on the porch. My sister and I served the plates. The murderer and his two friends passed them to the men. Afterward, the rapist and the two bank robbers and the arsonist said they'd be real pleased to wash up the dishes. But we told them nobody should wash dishes on Christmas—just have a good time.

That evening, after our guests had gone back to their quarters on the railroad siding, we sat by the fire. The parents looked tired. Dad went out for another hickory log to "keep us through the night," laid it in the deep fireplace, scratched the coals, sat down in his chair by the lamp. . . . "We had a good Christmas, didn't we?" . . .

After a long staring in the fire, we succumbed to a little do-you-remember. And soon we were laughing. . . .

And now the fire in front of us was blurring.

My sister said softly, "It was a large Christmas."

"Which one?"

"All of them," she whispered.[12]

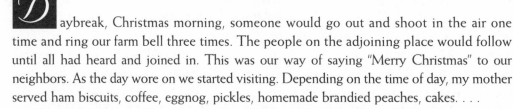

1924

Reindeer Tracks In The Snow

Sarah Watkins Cooke grew up in Brunswick County, Virginia, at Woodlawn—a four-hundred-eighty-seven-acre "home place" that was once part of a thousand-acre 1770 plantation. Mrs. Cooke recorded these memories at age eighty-eight.

Daybreak, Christmas morning, someone would go out and shoot in the air one time and ring our farm bell three times. The people on the adjoining place would follow until all had heard and joined in. This was our way of saying "Merry Christmas" to our neighbors. As the day wore on we started visiting. Depending on the time of day, my mother served ham biscuits, coffee, eggnog, pickles, homemade brandied peaches, cakes. . . .

For many Christmases my parents would fix each of the three families living on the place a Christmas box of goodies, clothes for children, extra food like smoked meat, flour, meal, etc.; line the front hall with orange crate boxes of presents and food. Christmas morning the families would come up, bring our family a gift and receive their family's presents.

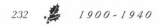

I remember the Christmas when I was 8 years old and was doubting about Santa Claus. Everyone assured me there was a Santa Claus—It snowed on Christmas Eve. I went to bed wondering if Santa would make it through the snow—I was awakened by my family to prove to me that Santa had come—besides the presents there was other proof! Outside there were reindeer tracks in the snow at the bottom of the chimney! (My father had brought our Billy Goat up and walked him around in the snow.) To me at 8 years old, that was surely living proof.

By next Christmas I had crossed over into the real world.[13]

1927

Mistletoe

Countee Cullen, a popular literary figure associated
with the Harlem Renaissance, wrote this holiday poem.

Under the Mistletoe

I did not know she'd take it so,
Or else I'd never dared:
Although the bliss was worth the blow,
I did not know she'd take it so.
She stood beneath the mistletoe
So long I thought she cared;
I did not know she'd take it so,
Or else I'd never dared.[14]

1924

Contact MGM

Lucille LeSueur (who would later be known as Joan Crawford,
thanks to a movie-magazine naming contest) worked as a dancer at Nils Granlund's
New York club. Her big break came when Granlund arranged some
Hollywood screen tests. The tests resulted in Granlund sending this
December 25, 1924, telegram to Lucille on behalf of MGM.

> YOU ARE PUT UNDER A FIVE-YEAR CONTRACT START-
> ING AT SEVENTY-FIVE DOLLARS A WEEK.   LEAVE IM-
> MEDIATELY FOR CULVER CITY, CALIFORNIA. CONTACT
> MGM KANSAS CITY OFFICE FOR TRAVEL EXPENSES.[15]

1927

Christmas Is A State Of Mind

On December 25, 1927, President Calvin Coolidge's
Christmas message was printed in newspapers all over the country.

Christmas is not a time or a season, but a state of mind. To cherish peace and good will, to be plenteous in mercy, is to have the real spirit of Christmas. If we think on these things, there will be born in us a Savior and over us will shine a star sending its gleam of hope to the world.[16]

1930

He Offered Young Herbert a Doll

Putting aside worries over the national Depression, and personal anxiety over their eldest son's health, President Herbert Hoover and his wife Lou planned a festive White House Christmas for their visiting grandchildren, Peggy Anne and Herbert III. The children's mother was in the North Carolina mountains for a Christmas reunion with their father, who was recuperating from tuberculosis.
On Christmas morning, during breakfast in the state dining room, which was the room with the biggest fireplace, who should appear but jolly old Santa himself.
This newspaper article described the festivities.

Washington *Citizen*, December 26, 1930—Do you believe in Santa Claus? President Hoover does, and so do Mrs. Hoover and the children. Santa Claus visited the White House in person yesterday, coming down the great chimney in regular old-fashioned style and stepping forth to the amazement of the adults and the delight of the kiddies. His pack was on his back, he was red faced and bearded, with long white whiskers, a resonant voice and a jolly, rollicking air that captured all and confirmed them in the faith of all good little girls and boys.

Santa proceeded to make friends with Peggy Ann and Herbert 3rd, grandchildren of the President. They were a bit shy at first, but took his offered hands and walked to the other end of the big room, where he opened his pack. The good old Saint came near coming a cropper when he offered young Herbert a doll from the top of his pack. The youngster, quite recovered from his shyness, handed it back, saying critically, "You must have intended that for my sister." Santa won the waning affections of the little lad by replying, "So I did," and handing Herbert a railroad train and other things more suitable to the male sex.

Long after the departure of the children's patron Saint the two youngsters looked curiously up the chimney, whence he had gone, wondering. Then they turned to their toys. The adults were as much surprised and interested as the little ones. It is believed that Mrs. Hoover planned the affair and kept it a dead secret from all except from Santa himself, who was impersonated, it is hinted, by one of the White House secretaries who had assisted her in the arrangements for Christmas.[17]

1933

The Applause Was Brief

*Poet and author Robert Peters came from rural northern Wisconsin.
In his book about growing up in the thirties, he reminisced about a place where
social life was sparse and the highlight of the school year was
the Christmas program.*

For three weeks, on wintry afternoons, huddled near the heating stove, we rehearsed the Christmas Program. Each of us had an individual recitation: Most were short winter or Christmas bits with humorous twists. We recited "'Twas the Night Before Christmas" in unison. Paper snowflakes covered the windows. The tree was decorated with home-made ornaments: flashing tops from condensed milk cans, tiny crosses covered

with gum-wrapper tin foil, Santa Claus heads, feeble attempts at reindeers, crayola renditions of balls, dolls, books. And, of course, the ubiquitous colored paper chains, with string of popcorn.

My assignment was to memorize vast chunks of "Christmas in Other Lands" from an encyclopedia. I started memorizing in November. I copied out the text by hand and carried sheaves of paper, memorizing at odd moments. I recited while pumping water. We made cuts in my piece.

We strung hay wire across the end of the schoolroom and hung white bed sheets. Presents for Miss Crocker, mostly handkerchiefs and cheap perfume, lay beneath the tree. Tiny paper bags, mysterious in their contents, were also there. We were promised a Santa. (The real St. Nick couldn't visit all the schools in the world.) We agreed to spend no more than a quarter on gifts and prayed that the Jollys wouldn't draw our names. They were the poorest family, and whatever they gave would be soiled. I bought jacks for Osmo Makinnen.

The performance started at 7:30. Miss Crocker arrived early. Families walked to school. There was a startling display of the aurora borealis. The air hovered near zero. We dressed warmly, and the walk, which took half an hour, was festive. Excited kids ran back and forth behind their parents, using far more energy than the walk required.

Despite some problems with the bed sheets, the program went well. I appeared halfway through, reciting facts about Christmas in other lands. That I was a bore never entered my head, despite the restlessness of the audience. Most of the men hung to the rear, behind the women. I concluded with Norway. The applause was brief. Holding lighted candles, the school sang "The Night Before Christmas" and "Silent Night."

Jingling bells heralded the entrance of the old soul who was bewhiskered with cotton batting and wore a dime-store suit. He made his way to the front where a couple of kids were sniveling. He inquired of our behavior, gave his ho hos, and presented us with candy canes. My suspicions were confirmed—this was not Santa but my cousin Albert. I recognized his throat, and I recognized his boots—black leather with buckles resembling silver harps.[18]

1930s

The Social Event of the Year

In this entertaining essay about her school days, Dolores Curran agreed with Robert Peters' view that a Wisconsin Christmas program was the best show in town.

For one magic evening each year, our one-room schoolhouse in southern Wisconsin was turned into a theater. The December night might be snowy and cold, but inside our snug schoolroom the furnace roared, pine branches scented the air, and the soft glow of Christmas lights fell on the proud faces of parents, neighbors, and friends. On makeshift benches entire families crowded together, waiting excitedly for the moment when a small hand would part the burlap curtains on the sawhorse-and-plank stage and a small voice would announce, "Uh . . . welcome . . . uh . . . to our Christmas program and here's 'Silent Night'." . . .

To the country kids of yesterday, the Christmas program was the social event of the year, with the county fair and the school picnic running very distant second and third. . . .

On the big day, the schoolroom was gaily decorated. We were dismissed an hour early, the only day of the year this was permitted, and our fathers came to stack the

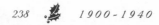

desks in the hall and set up sawhorses and plank benches in the temporary theater. A freshly cut pine was trimmed, and an extra supply of coal and logs for the furnace was brought in.

At home, tension had been running high the last few days before the program. Our teacher had enjoined us to rehearse at home until our parents were sick of us. My sister, an accomplished pianist for her age, was always relentless in practicing her Christmas selection, and I can recall overhearing my dad asking my mother, "Haven't we had enough of that d--- song?". . .

My mother started getting us dressed shortly after the cows were milked, and once each of us was dressed, we sat, without moving, for fear of getting mussed. The boys were packed into white shirts, whose sleeves were usually too short, and bow ties, which were always slanted. Then a liberal quantity of hair oil was applied. For the girls it was sheer heaven. We were able to abandon for one evening those horrible, itchy, long, brown, ribbed, cotton stockings—our town must have been the only place in the country where they were still worn. Instead, we wore knee socks, Christmas dresses, and big striped or polka dot hair bows atop our Shirley Temple curls. . . .

Each program consisted of several dialogs by the older kids and a piece by each of the younger ones. Since our school budget was slim, we used dialog and piece books like *That Good Christmas Book* and *Spice Dialogs and Plays* over and over, so that anyone in the community who had seen his third program had sampled all the dramatic offering available.

The biggest boy in school acted as emcee and some of them were pretty good. I remember one who couldn't find the opening in the curtain to get back on the stage. He finally turned to the audience, shrugged his shoulders, and said, "I guess it healed."

Actually, the evening's worst hurdle came first. Every year the youngest boy—and some were pretty young because we could start first grade at four—recited the piece by Eugene Field titled "Jest 'Fore Christmas." It started like this,

Father calls me William,
Sister calls me Will,
Mother calls me Willie,
But the fellers call me Bill.

and ended like this,

'Most all the time, the whole year round,
There ain't no flies on me,
But jest 'fore Christmas,
I'm as good as I kin be!

The whole school rooted for this youngster because if anyone could ruin the program, he could. Many a family suffered the embarrassment of having their Willie stare in stony-eyed terror at the friendly audience a short six feet in front of him and finally break into tears. At best, Willie stared at a spot on the floor or ceiling, rattled off a roll of syllables ending with "but jesforechrismasimasgoodasicanbe," and disappeared before the applause even began. Everyone—students, teacher, and audience—relaxed when this annual obstacle was overcome, and the program could proceed. . . .

After the hour-long program of dialogs, pieces, and carols, came the real highlight of the evening. While the entire cast and audience sang, a portly farmer was stuffing himself into the district-owned Santa suit. His cue was the song, "Up on the Housetop," and if he missed it, or had beard trouble, we just sang the song over and over until he finally appeared. . . .

Then [Santa] got down to the important business of passing out the presents. Early in December we had all drawn the name of a schoolmate for whom we would purchase a Christmas gift. . . . within our twenty-five-cent limit. . . . The night of the program the packages were piled beneath the tree along with the presents from our teacher. She

always gave something special, not useful. It might be a pretty pin or bracelet for the girls, or a bottle of perfume. For the boys, she chose a real fountain pen, a yo-yo, or something similar.

By the time the presents had been bestowed, the high excitement had spent itself and it was all over for another year.[19]

1930s

You Never Knew You Were Poor

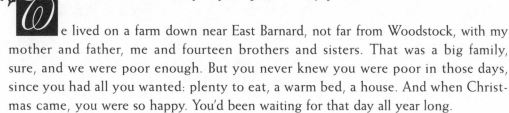

In this account, Rita Bumps told how her big eastern Vermont family brought home the perfect tree.

We lived on a farm down near East Barnard, not far from Woodstock, with my mother and father, me and fourteen brothers and sisters. That was a big family, sure, and we were poor enough. But you never knew you were poor in those days, since you had all you wanted: plenty to eat, a warm bed, a house. And when Christmas came, you were so happy. You'd been waiting for that day all year long.

Maybe a week before the big day my father took us into the woods to get a Christmas tree for the house, the whole gang of us. He was like the Pied Piper with that ax of his, the question always was, which tree was the right tree? With that kind of choice, you always had a nice-looking tree, but it drove you crazy trying to guess which tree was best. Each one had its drawbacks: short limbs, a bare spot here, a brown patch there. The perfect tree, like the perfect anything, didn't exist. And the arguments we would have! With that many kids, somebody always has a separate idea about something. But my father didn't like too much talking, so pretty soon he'd say, "Quiet yourselves!" Then he'd hack down the one he liked, ignoring what we'd all been shouting. After it was down, we'd hitch a rope to the bottom end of it and drag it to the house, a dozen kids like a locomotive, all sticky and smelly with pine tar.[20]

Silhouette
Good Old Days Christmas Memories

1933

Dear Mrs. Roosevelt

*When Franklin Roosevelt took office in 1933, Depression unemployment
had hit a peak. On a daily basis, both the president and the first lady received
an avalanche of mail from desperate Americans, old and young. In her first year
in the White House, Eleanor Roosevelt received more than 300,000 pieces of mail, far
more than any previous first lady. The volume increased as her fame grew.
Most of the letters pleaded for help. Many were from children. The following three
were among those letters.*

Jersey City, New Jersey: December 14, 1933

Our good Friend Mrs. & Mr. Roosevelt:

Hope this reach you & your good husband Mr. Roosevelt in the best of health. Well Mrs. Roosevelt I am a little girl 12 years old. My mother has 7 small children and my father just started on to work in one of those job your good Husband started for the poor people and we were sure glad to see him working as he did not work in year he is only makeing $15 a week. But thank God he is getting that so my Good Friend you see he will recived he first cheack. Just the time our rent is due so my poor mother will not be able to get my little sisters & Brother a little doll or a toy for Christmas so if your little granchildren have any little things from last year I will be thankful to see you send them to us Hope God send you Plenty luck & Health and Hope you have a Happy Christmas & New Year.

C.H.

Keegan, Maine: Dec. 23, 1933

Dear Friend:

Mrs. Roosevelt I am writing you to ask you a little favor. Please if you have some old cloth to send us, we would be very glade. For we are a poor family. I am the oldest one I am 16 years old. The oldest of my sister is 12 years old. We are 14 children in the family. My father works, he earns only $14 a week. With fourteen dollars we can't spear any money to dress ourselves. I tried to have some work but they wouldnt give me some work because there is more married man that they can't employ. If you have some old clothes that you have spear. If you please send a part of it to us. If you send us anything you can spear we'll pray for you. We're in need so much that three of my sisters would go to school, but they're not dress to go. We are six that goes to school. We're trying to have help in town but the people are as poor as we are. We are writing you because every person in town that talks of you say that you're the only woman to look for the poor as much as you. Yesterday we were reading on the newspaper in the first page was written in black, "Mrs. Roosevelt looks for the poor." We read that about you and it says that since last Christmas that you were picing cloths and toys for the poor. I don't ask you any toys but I ask you clothes that you have spear. It makes three years that we didn't see christmas and my little sisters don't know what's christmas. You're the first president's wife that looks for the poor. It's nearly insulting for a poor little boy like me to a person like you. We didn't write to other president's wifes because they only try to owns money, but not you. I am asking you some old clothes that can be remade for my sisters and brothers. If you want information to know if it's true, write to the priest of our church. His name is, Rev. Father St. Martin S.M. Keegan Maine. I'm wishing you a Merry Christmas and a Happy new year.

Your friend,
J.B. Jr.

[address lost]: [received Dec. 27, 1937]

Dear Sir and Madam,
I guess you don't know what this is,
or what's this all about
But I'll tell you in no time
So you can find out.

I'm a girl who's very poor
And in the age of twelve
I never have anything
Not even underwear.

I don't have pretty dresses
Like the rich girls do
I only have ragged ones
That's because I'm poor

I asked my mother
What for Christmas I would get
But she says
I haven't the money yet.

Even if she would have
I wouldn't get nothing
Because my daddy only gets
44 a month.

Then comes a light bill
And the rent
And the grocer bill
And the milk
Oh help me if you will

Ther's five in the whole family
And like "hobos" we all look
Oh help the poor if you could

Thank you
L.C.[21]

c. 1940

What A Hooha

Shirley Schoonover, who grew up in a Finnish family
in Minnesota, wrote about an unforgettable Christmas there.

The Christmas I remember most was when we ate Petrice, our goose. She had come to our farm as a gosling. Thinking she was a gander, we named her Pete. When she laid an egg, we renamed her Petrice. She thought she was human and would have nothing to do with the other fowl. She always followed me around the farm, daffy, crooning to me, and I could never sit down without her getting into my lap and resting her head on my neck. She also wanted to mother puppies, and when our cocker bitch, Flicka, left her babes unattended once, Petrice nestled on them, wings outspread, crazy eyes soft and maternal. What a hooha there was when Flicka discovered Petrice gabbling there. The puppies didn't mind, but Flicka went mad. Foaming at the mouth, she attacked. Petrice did her best to fly, but, weighing twenty pounds, all she could do was lollop away, flapping her wings, while Flicka helped her along by grabbing mouthfuls of rump and feathers. Around and around the house they went, Petrice trundling, lurching, and honking and Flicka snapping and spitting out feathers. At last, poor Petrice ran headlong for the doghouse and stuck fast in the doorway, her fanny exposed, her cries dreadful, as Flicka lay down and promptly began denuding that plump backside. I scolded Flicka away and pityingly hauled Petrice feetfirst out of the doghouse. And when Christmas came and Petrice lay wreathed with parsley on the platter, I could not touch a drumstick or lay a fork on her white meat. I could not eat at all; cranberry sauce sparkled, sweet potatoes swam in golden sauce, apple pie bubbled and crisped, all to no avail, as I sat, pea green, at the table, posed on the edge of my chair, the brittle tears ready to break down my face.

But that was the only sad Christmas. All the other Christmases roll together into a white and woolly ball of remembering how it was to come to the rim of wakefulness on Christmas morning and lie there quilted and snug before flying out of bed to see what magic had happened during the night.[22]

1941 - 2004

1941

No Music, No Lights, No Greetings

On December 7, Pearl Harbor, Oahu, Hawaii, was attacked.
After ten days of confusion and consternation, Army nurse Ruth Marie Straub,
who was stationed in the Philippines at Manila faced the truth that her fiancé,
who was a pilot at Clark Air Field, was killed soon after the attack. In her diary,
she recorded the events leading up to Christmas 1941.

ecember 17. They brought me Glen's personal effects today. Now I know he is dead.

December 24. The Japs continue to bomb the port area. Christmas eve. The girls milling around, no music, no lights, no greetings. Sent a note to Miss MacDonald [chief nurse at Stotsenberg]. Asked her to put some flowers on my darling's grave for Christmas.

Christmas. We hardly realized it. Sent more nurses out today to Bataan and Corregidor. Only 14 left now. Orders say we are all to evacuate by the first.[1]

1941

Fireflies in a Mango Tree

Private Alvin Garrett, who served with the 200th Coast Artillery
Anti-Aircraft (formerly the 111th Cavalry of the New Mexico National Guard),
was inducted into federal service for one year of active duty on January 6, 1941.
In December, one month short of going home, he found himself at
Clark Air Field, on the Philippine Islands, when both Pearl Harbor and
then Clark Field were attacked.

It was Christmas 1941. I was in a little town called Hermosa on Bataan in the Philippine Islands.

The night before we had retreated from Clark Field, and before we left we made sure we had all the trimmings for a real Christmas dinner. The cooks had worked through the night and morning preparing the meal, and just before the meal was ready, a Jap bomber had dropped part of his bombs in a water buffalo wallow right next to the kitchen. No one had been hurt but it sure ruined our Christmas dinner. My Christmas dinner consisted of a handful of prunes and a piece of cheese.

That night I walked back up the road toward Manila, and off to the right was a mango tree with a swarm of millions of fire flies over, under, around, and through with none over two feet from the tree.

I stood for quite awhile and admired the work of God. It sure made a wonderful Christmas tree.

Merry Christmas
Mukden 623[2]

1942

The Only Holiday in All the Year

One of the great qualities Franklin Roosevelt brought to the presidency
was his ability to communicate confidence to a nation gripped in all-out war.
His fireside chats, which drew millions around their radio sets across the country,
became a source of comfort in a time of intense uncertainty.
Here is an excerpt from one of these chats.

This year, my friends, I am speaking on Christmas Eve not to this gathering at the White House only but to all of the citizens of our nation, to the men and women serving in our American armed forces and also to those who wear the uniforms of the other United Nations. I give you a message of cheer. I cannot say "Merry Christmas," for I think constantly of those thousands of soldiers and sailors who are in actual combat throughout the world, but I can express to you my thought that this is a happier Christmas than last year, happier in the sense that the forces of darkness stand against us with less confidence in the success of their evil ways. . . .

It is significant that tomorrow—Christmas Day—our plants and factories will be stilled. That is not true of the other holidays that we have long been accustomed to celebrate. On all other holidays the work goes on, gladly, for the winning of the war.

So Christmas Day becomes the only holiday in all the year.

I like to think that this is so because Christmas is a holy day. May all that it stands for live and grow through all the years.[3]

1942

A Catch in My Throat

*Eleanor Roosevelt's syndicated "My Day" column
made her a familiar and friendly visitor to millions of homes
all over the country. This passage came from one of her columns.*

How completely the character of Christmas has changed this year. I could no more say to you: "A Merry Christmas" without feeling a catch in my throat than I could fly to the moon! We all know that for too many people this will be anything but a Merry Christmas. It can, however, be a Christmas Season of deep meaning to us all. . . .

Whatever our particular religious beliefs may be, we still can feel a share in this Christmas spirit and try to do our part at this Season by making life just a little bit brighter wherever we touch it. . . .

I am going as usual on Christmas morning to a church service and then I hope to have time for a flying visit to Walter Reed Hospital to the wards where some of our returned wounded from Africa are being treated. After that I will stop for a few minutes at the YWCA where they are having a Christmas dinner for Government workers who are strangers in Washington and who have no family connections here. This seems to me a very nice gesture for the YWCA to make, and I am glad to be given the opportunity to stop in for a few minutes to wish them all a pleasant day, before returning to our own family concerns for the rest of the day.[4]

1943

Our Busload of Strangers

Olive Nowak shared her memory of how the spirit of fellowship brightened the trip home for the holidays.

It didn't promise to be the best of Christmas Eves—America was in the midst of World War II.

By the time I arrived at the little bus depot in Albert Lea, Minnesota, a crowd of impatient travelers, many of them servicemen, were waiting for the bus. I was eager to get home to my family. My younger brother was already talking about enlisting in the Marines. This might be the last Christmas we would be together for a long time. My thoughts were also on a certain soldier overseas who was very special to me.

There was a collective sigh of relief as the bus rounded the corner, then dismay when after a few passengers departed, we saw it was still full. The bus driver shook his head sadly as he told us there wasn't any more room.

Suddenly a young sailor called out, "Hey, if there's a cute blonde out there, I'll be glad to hold her on my lap!" Amid the laughter of the crowd, other bus passengers then began calling to the driver, "Put them all on—we'll share our seats so no one has to be

left behind." Within minutes, there were three and four people snuggled into seats for two, some people sitting in others' laps.

As our busload of strangers sped through the night, someone began softly singing "Silent Night." One by one we all joined in, until every passenger was singing—"Joy to the World," "Away in a Manger," "White Christmas," "I'll Be Home for Christmas." We laughed, we sang, we shared candy and cookies. And we watched, misty-eyed, as departing servicemen, who only a few minutes before had been so cool, cried unashamedly as they were embraced by waiting wives, mothers, and fathers. When the bus reached my destination, the remaining passengers shouted out, "Merry Christmas, Happy New Year!" . . .

As I stood there, watching the bus disappear into the night, I was eager to be home but reluctant to break the spell of fellowship. The snow had stopped falling, and the sky was studded with stars. . . . And I understood that even in the midst of war there could still be "Peace on earth, good will to men."[5]

1943

Feeling Sad and Blue

*This verse was on a handmade 1943 Christmas card, treasured by
Inez McDonald of the Army Nurse Corps during her years as a prisoner in a
Bataan internment camp. When she and her fellow nurses were liberated in 1945,
the card traveled home with her to Tupelo, Mississippi.*

It is never Merry Christmas
　　When you're feeling sad and blue

And the one you care the most for
Forgets to think of you.
But when hopes and dreams are fading
And your fondest joys depart
You can still have Merry Christmas
If it's Christmas in your heart.[6]

1944

The European Situation is Certainly Grim

By December, World War II had reached a critical stage. Britain had been at war for five years, the United States had been involved since Pearl Harbor. Allied troops poured into Great Britain, preparing for an expected invasion of the continent. On June 6, combined Allied forces crossed the English Channel, landed in Normandy, and took the Germans by surprise. The Allies' early advances to liberate Paris and reach Germany were challenged by a massive Nazi counterattack in December. Captain First Class Rosemary Langheldt volunteered for overseas duty with the American Red Cross in the spring of 1944. At Christmastime, she and her Clubmobile Unit crew were stationed on the Southampton docks in England. They served coffee, doughnuts, and good cheer to boys who were shipping off across the Channel, toward the Battle of the Bulge. She wrote the following letter to her family. The passage following the letter came from Rosemary's journal that same night.

Saturday, December 30, 1944

Dearest Family,

Christmas is over and it's been a little hectic. We've been stationed here so long we had a cheery one in many ways as we know lots of people to wish a Merry Christmas. We're working day and night—our Christmas celebration was sandwiched in between loadings and hospital ships and emergencies. . . .

We managed to get to mess for a turkey dinner on Christmas Day, but our celebrating consisted mainly of amusing the GIs going through the Port all day and most of the night. . . . [O]ur Clubmobile was bright with holly and greens and mistletoe and the GIs seemed to appreciate our being on hand. . . . One huge bunch of troops had the docks rocking with their "Jingle Bells" rendition before we finished serving them.

The European situation is certainly grim and we're seeing some of the most heartbreaking sights. The results of the German drive have affected us so directly, the stark horror of war impresses itself upon our minds more strongly each day. I wish I could say more as there's so much I'd like to write but it will have to wait until a later date. . . .

All my love,
Roses

From Rosemary Langheldt's journal:

Just sealed my letter home and am feeling frustrated because I can tell the family only light and trivial details of a Christmas week so shadowed it broke our hearts. Hope they read between the lines and know there are more important things going on than those I am permitted to write about.

The day before Christmas Eve we started work at 0400 to feed several shiploads of troops. Just as we finally finished, the boys were suddenly offloaded, and I was informed the ships were to reload that night with infantry replacements. A high-security operation and real rush job because of the German drive in the Bulge. I already had made crew assignments for Christmas week and knew several of us hoped to grab a few free hours to be with friends after finishing work. But when I asked for volunteers (sure to be six extra hours—at least—in the middle of the night on bone-chilling cold, damp, and foggy docks), all I got was the usual "Okay, coach, which piers and how many?" It's no wonder I love my crew.

The division being rushed over was the 66th. On December 23rd, they were yanked out of camp so fast—without any notice—they still wore 66th snarling Black Panther division patches on their uniforms. Usually all division insignia is removed if it's a high-security operation. The cooks had to leave stuffed turkeys and Christmas dinner preparations behind. They'd all had Christmas parties planned and suddenly they were eating K rations and headed for a channel crossing. Always especially tough in winter.

They dragged into the dock area exhausted and it was easy to see they were not in a happy frame of mind. They began arriving early evening and our crews were there to serve units before the Port started loading the two troopships waiting at Pier 38: the British-controlled ship *Leopoldville*, a huge Belgian passenger liner, and the USS *Cheshire*. It was so cold in the dock sheds some of the guys lit little bonfires to try and keep warm during the long wait. There seemed to be more than normal confusion in the loadings and we'd see an occasional "lost" platoon wandering through the piers trying to locate their company. The men seemed so young. Many carried Christmas-wrapped boxes or goodies that wouldn't fit into their packs and told us they were determined to celebrate Christmas wherever they happened to be. . . .

By the time I drove into Pier 38 the troops crowded into that huge cavernous shell were in full-voiced rendition of "White Christmas," the reverberating sound of thousands of voices seeming to swell the shed in a mighty plea. I broke out all over in goosebumps. Eloise and Kari were in charge of our main Clubmobile and I noticed their eyes misted over too.

For hours we served the men, and sang and talked and laughed with them. We did, as usual, a lot of listening and admiring pictures in wallets. We lingered past midnight to stand by the gangplank and wish the last units well and cheer them off as they finally boarded. It was so dark you couldn't see much, but every now and then a GI leaned over to kiss one of us on the cheek or give an awkward one-handed pat on the shoulder.

Most of us sleepwalked our ways through the loading schedule for Christmas Eve as it was just as busy—and just as long. The docks and Hards were full of embarking troops being poured cross-channel. Late on Christmas Eve, Eloise and Kari reported,

 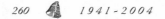

they rushed over to serve a hospital ship that arrived unexpectedly. They spotted it coming in to dock ablaze with lights, white sides gleaming, a huge Red Cross symbol clearly visible on each side because hospital ships sped straight across channel brightly signaling their presence to friend and foe alike. Eloise kept thinking how familiar some of the walking wounded looked as they came down the gangplank and, being Eloise, bubbled out to one hollow-eyed boy in a disheveled uniform, "Gosh, you look familiar, friend!" and the boy said, "You're right. You just served us last night—on the *Leopoldville.*" And that's how they heard that the *Leopoldville* had been sunk just before entering Cherbourg Harbor. Eloise was so shocked that the GI was gone before she could ask him anything else. . . .

Christmas Day was beautiful but freezing cold hoarfrost weather—and devastating as rumors flew around the Port about the *Leopoldville.* While I was checking our work schedules early Christmas morning at the Maritime Chambers, the Port loading head-quarters, Colonel Jim told me the details. The ship was in sight of the harbor when it was torpedoed and they feared at least 800 lives or more had been lost. Since I've been stationed here other ships have hit mines crossing the channel and been lost, but the *Leopoldville* was a large transport with over 2,200 troops aboard. The thought of it going down was horrible.

When Barbara drove into the dock area for her very early Christmas morning Assignment she spotted a British "dockie" holding a soggy life jacket from the *Leopoldville.*

He told her it had just been brought in by one of the channel patrol boats. She sat down on the dock and began sobbing. Told me she couldn't help it as she remembered all the guys she had talked with and all those pictures of wives and girlfriends she'd admired and all the singing during that long night.

So Christmas Day was especially difficult. We served thousands of troops being rushed over to try and stop the German drive. It was obvious they all knew where they were headed. On the Hards, looking up into the clear sky, we could see literally hundreds of contrails from a flight of bombers rendezvousing overhead. The bomber flights had been grounded by fog for days, unable to help out with the German breakthrough. But since Christmas morning dawned clear and bright, they could again fly. When the big flight started to head off toward the channel, first a few GIs, then instantly everyone on the Hards, looked up, waved their arms, and shook their fists skyward as they joined in a shouting mass chant: "Go, Go, Goooo!"

That's why it was so hard to write home. The first chance we had, our crew finally got together to celebrate a late Christmas and share our feelings of the past days. Drew numbers so we each gave one gift. Barbara, our artistic one, decorated the tree in the room she shares with Bettie with gift wrap ribbon tied in bows and sparkling balls of crinkled wrapping paper, retrieved from Christmas packages sent from home. It was wonderful to share true feelings with our family—for that's what our crew has become.[7]

1944

Don't Move. I'll Be Right Back!

In mid-December, the Germans attacked the Allies in the Ardennes Forest of Belgium. American forces stubbornly held the small, vital town of Bastogne.

Hundreds of thousands of troops on both sides spent Christmas engaged
in what would later be called the Battle of the Bulge. In his later memoir,
Private First Class Don Addor described what happened as his battle-weary outfit,
the 10th Armored Division, 20th Armored Infantry Battalion (the spearhead unit
for General Patton's Third Army) began to move.

[In Germany, December 16]

No one had told us why or where we were going, just to get going, but we knew we were heading north.

We knew nothing of Bastogne or about the German "break through." Nor did we have any idea that we were heading into the biggest land battle ever fought. In fact when we saw that the road signs were indicating that we were heading to the rear through towns that we had fought from the enemy not too long ago, we actually thought just maybe we were heading for the dream break, R & R in Paris, that wonderful city full of booze and women. . . .

[Leaving Noville, Belgium, on December 20th in a heavy fog, Addor's tank column was blasted off the road by German artillery. He was hit twice by enemy fire, applied a tourniquet to his shattered leg, and heard German soldiers approach and retreat in the dense fog. At last, an American medic found him and carried him by Jeep to a medical unit waiting outside of Bastogne. His next few days were hazy.]

When I finally regained consciousness it was like coming out of a deep sleep. My eyes opened and I saw a neat clean ceiling above me. I looked to my right and there was a guy on a stretcher. The olive drab Army blanket was pulled over his head. There was a yellow Army Quartermaster tag tied to his big toe on his right foot that stuck out from the bottom of the blanket. He was dead. He was Quartermaster material now.

This did not bother me, except I felt sorry for whoever it was. I looked to my left and saw the same thing, another dead guy with a yellow tag. Now this bothered me. Somehow I found the strength to lift my head up to look around the room. It was full of dead men with yellow tags on their big toe. I looked down and sure enough there was a Quartermaster tag on my toe too. I took another look and realized I was in a temporary morgue. Now this shook me up a good bit. I hollered. In a second an Army nurse stuck her head in the door. When she saw me her face turned as white as her uniform. She told me, "Don't move. I'll be right back!" . . .

[The nurse hooked him up to a bottle of plasma, orderlies lifted him onto a table, and a field doctor took over. At this point, Addor mercifully blacked out again, and did not know where he was or what was happening until he woke up in Paris, at a French hospital run by the U.S. Army.]

I was rolled into the building and down a long corridor. I looked up and saw silver tinsel and many different colored Christmas balls hanging down from the ceiling. As we turned a corner there was a large cardboard Santa smiling at me. . . .

I wondered what day it was and was about to ask my pusher when we arrived at the side of a real hospital bed with snow-white sheets. . . .

[A doctor examined the festering wound.]

My leg was eased down and the doctor came over to me with a worried look on his face. He was trying to tell me something but couldn't find the words. I said, "Gangrene?" The worried look left and he answered yes. Before he could say anything else, I responded with, "I guess it will have to come off." He said yes, he would have to amputate it the first thing in the morning. He said he was sorry to have to make such an operation on Christmas day, but the gangrene was spreading and the leg had to be removed as soon as possible. I now knew what day or night it was. It was Christmas Eve, 1944.

He apologized again and said he would send the chaplain to see me. . . . It didn't take long for the chaplain to come. We talked a bit and we said a prayer together and then he left. He could see my morale was OK. It's no fun losing a leg on any day, but . . . I guess my spirits were up for a couple of reasons. One, I had almost died on that Belgium pasture and had even come to in a morgue. Now I was safe and was going to live. I thanked God that he had been with me and helped me to safety and back into his wonderful world.[8]

1944

Heavy Hearts

Second Lieutenant Richard Wellbrock's B-24 was blown
out of the German skies and crashed behind enemy lines. Force-marched
from one POW camp to another, Wellbrock ended up in Moosburg, twenty miles
northeast of Munich. On Red Cross paper, he managed to keep a secret diary,
in the form of letters to his wife and two-year-old son, Kent.
The following letter is from that diary.

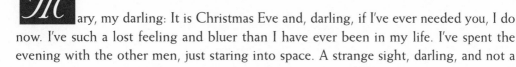

Mary, my darling: It is Christmas Eve and, darling, if I've ever needed you, I do now. I've such a lost feeling and bluer than I have ever been in my life. I've spent the evening with the other men, just staring into space. A strange sight, darling, and not a

pretty one, of 17 men in old clothes, heavy hearts, and hungry, bitter forlorn faces, as they think of home, etc. "Peace on Earth, Good Will to Men" is hard for me to visualize. I only hope this bitterness will fade, but I've seen too many sights and too many men's souls to ever be quite the same. I still wake up in the middle of the night with nightmares. Some of the men who have been down two years wake up screaming, so the nights don't lack interest.

Wellbrock's final letter from Moosburg was dated April 30, 1945. The American flag flew over the liberated camp, and he was headed home. He ended his final entry with these lines.

I hope and pray that Kent will never have to keep a record such as this and that man, in his little weak mind, at last has learned that wars can only cause suffering.[9]

1944

Nuts!

*In the turmoil of the Battle of the Bulge,
Division Commander General Anthony McAuliffe sent this morale-boosting
Christmas message to the men of the 101st Airborne Division. The message
to his surrounded troops included his famous one-word retort to the
German commander, who had demanded that McAuliffe surrender.*

Headquarters 101st Airborne Division
Office of the Division Commander
24 December 1944

What's Merry about all this, you ask? We're fighting—it's cold—we aren't home. All true but what has the proud Eagle Division accomplished with its worthy comrades of the 10th Armored Division, the 705th Tank Destroyer Battalion and all the rest? Just this: We have stopped cold everything that has been thrown at us from the North, East, South and West. . . . The Germans actually did surround us, their radios blared our doom. Their Commander demanded our surrender in the following impudent arrogance:

December 22nd, 1944
To the U.S.A. Commander of the encircled town of Bastogne.

The fortune of war is changing. This time the U.S.A. forces in and near Bastogne have been encircled by strong German armored units. More German armored units have crossed the river Ortheuville, have taken Marche and reached St. Hubert by passing through Hombres-Sibret-Tillet. Libramont is in German hands.

There is only one possibility to save the encircled U.S.A. troops from total annihilation: that is the honorable surrender of the encircled town. In order to think it over a term of two hours will be granted beginning with the presentation of this note.

If this proposal should be rejected one German Artillery Corps and six heavy A.A. Battalions are ready to annihilate the U.S.A. troops in and near Bastogne. The order for firing will be given immediately after this two hours term.

All the serious civilian losses caused by this Artillery fire would not correspond with the well known American humanity.

The German Commander

The German Commander received the following reply:
22 December 1944
To the German Commander:
    NUTS!

The American Commander

Allied Troops are counterattacking in force. We continue to hold Bastogne. By holding Bastogne we assure the success of the Allied Armies. We know that our Division Commander, General Taylor, will say: "Well Done!"

We are giving our country and our loved ones at home a worthy Christmas present, and being privileged to take part in this gallant feat of arms are truly making for ourselves a Merry Christmas.

McAULIFFE,
Commanding[10]

1945

The Ships Came in, the Ships Sailed Out

*By Christmas 1945, the American Red Cross volunteers in England
knew they would be going home. Alice Finney, one of the girls with the
Clubmobile Unit stationed at Southampton docks, enclosed this verse with a tiny
model of the* Queen Elizabeth, *as a stocking gift memento to her wartime
friend, Rosemary Langheldt.*

Alice's Christmas Poem

Christmas Stocking December 1945
To Rosie

 May I give to you this souvenir
To recall to you in a future year
Long nights spent slaving on the docks—
Feet encased in numerous socks,
Hands grown numb, noses red—
Long johns under, hoods on head.

The ships came in, the ships sailed out;
We served the men as they stood about.
Coffee and donuts, our steady diet—
But with them we stymied many a riot.
We made them laugh, we made them smile;
We made them gripe, and forget the "heil."

From these ships and men we learned a lot—
Some of it good, some of it rot.
But down on those docks we saw our boys
As they really are—full of noise,
Full of jokes, full of bad, full of good;
Living war as Americans would; . . . [11]

1945

Cold As Mischief

*At the White House, President Harry Truman prepared to address
the country and light the White House tree for the first peacetime Christmas
celebration since the U.S. entered the war in 1941. His wife and daughter traveled
on ahead to Independence, Missouri, for the holidays. Lonely for them, the
president sent this letter to his 17-year-old daughter, Margaret.*

D ear Margie:

I just now went out and took a walk. It is cold as mischief. I looked
over the Christmas tree, and walked around the back yard—four Secret
Service men and two policemen came along—to keep me from slipping
on the ice I guess. A crowd did collect at the back fence. So I guess
they were right.

The stage is set up south of the fountain, and one of the pine trees
down by the fence is all decorated, and I have to light it and make a
speech to the nation tomorrow at 5:16 P.M.

Hope to see you the next day. Kiss Mamma and tell all your aunts & uncles hello, and call up your country grandma and say hello to your city one.

Lots of love, Dad[12]

1945

A Doll That Would Make Her Eyes Pop

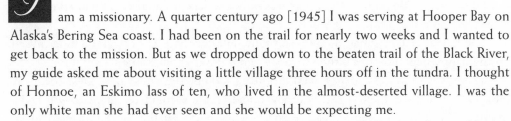

Father Paul C. O'Connor, who served at a Jesuit mission in Alaska in 1945, later shared his memories of giving a slightly delayed, but joyfully received, Christmas present.

I am a missionary. A quarter century ago [1945] I was serving at Hooper Bay on Alaska's Bering Sea coast. I had been on the trail for nearly two weeks and I wanted to get back to the mission. But as we dropped down to the beaten trail of the Black River, my guide asked me about visiting a little village three hours off in the tundra. I thought of Honnoe, an Eskimo lass of ten, who lived in the almost-deserted village. I was the only white man she had ever seen and she would be expecting me.

I turned my dogs off the river, up through some tortuous willows and into a blanket of fog smothering the trailless tundra.

On we traveled at a good clip for three hours, and I knew if the fog did not lift we would be spending the night on the tundra. Then we heard the barking of dogs that led us to our village.

As my assistant removed our food box, I walked up and was greeted with a shy, little smile from Honnoe. She told me that she had been waiting for me for a long time.

I slipped some English walnuts into her hand, which I called "big peanuts" in Eskimo.

Little Honnoe and her aged mother were the only ones in the village. She had arrived late in her mother's life, and here in this tiny village I doubt if she met more than ten strange faces a year. Soon she was showing me her crude toys, including a doll she had made for herself.

I remarked that if she came to the mission I would give her a doll that would make her eyes pop. It was an oft-made offer, for I dearly loved to give dolls to these little tykes. The year slipped by and soon the Christmas season arrived. It was a busy time for me, with confessions for the hundreds of people who arrived by dog team. With three Masses, sermons, decorations, a Christmas play and other holiday affairs, I was one distracted missionary.

I did notice little Honnoe, but hers was only one face in hundreds. I had completely forgotten about my promise of a doll.

The day after Christmas shone beautifully and clearly. I was congratulating myself on the happy departure of all the visitors when a timid knock came to my door.

There was Honnoe and her aged mother. I indulged in small talk, gave them my blessing and wished them a safe journey home. They seemed reluctant to go, and I thought of the long journey ahead of them. They had probably never traveled so far from home.

Then it came to me in a flash—the doll that would make her eyes pop! This tiny girl had come a good two-day journey just to make me keep my promise.

Anguish struck me. I had given away a hundred or more presents and, of course, the dolls were the first to go. I was in trouble, and as I rushed upstairs I asked the angels to help me out of my predicament.

My heart was in my mouth as I looked over a bunch of toys, all broken discards. It was then I spied a carton back against the wall completely forgotten in the frenzied confusion of Christmas. I reached for it, ripped off the wrapping to behold a beautifully made rag doll. She was at least three feet tall with flaxen curls, a prize for any girl.

I hid the doll in the back of my cassock and slowly descended the stairs with hands empty and faced my little maiden.

I said in a slow and measured voice that I had no small dolls, but would this do? As I produced her gift, Honnoe's eyes bulged and her thin arms hugged the doll with all her might.

Making children happy is the supreme joy in life but this was something special. The look of gratitude in that little girl's eyes will live with me forever. She put the doll on her back, Eskimo style, and then solemnly walked up and down the room, patting it as real mothers do.

Her mother could hardly believe I would part with such a grand doll, but Honnoe knew it was hers completely. As she left she beamed with joy. In limpid Eskimo, she said, "Father, you make me so happy."

But I was the happy one that day.[13]

1950

I Wonder

Gene Symonds, a reporter for United Press International,
sent the following from Korea on Christmas Eve.

Christmas eve here is a machine gun sitting on the
edge of your foxhole with the bolt back ready to go.
It's a pale, full moon casting grotesque shadows
among the fierce, rugged mountain peaks around you.
It's your buddy crouching in the bottom of a
freezing dugout
with a blanket around his shoulders to smoke a cigarette . . .

Out there, across those mountain peaks,
a few miles away, are the Communists.
They have been building up a long time
and tonight would be a nice time for them to strike . . .
The talk, what there is of it, is all of home:
"I wonder what the folks will be doing tonight?"
and "I wonder what Mary got the kids for Christmas?"

There's a thin layer of snow on everything
and you can feel the ground tighten up as it freezes . . .

 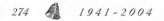

Driving back from the front the cold bites deeper into
your flesh and you feel sorry for the lonely MP's
guarding bridges and roads.
Some of them are permitted to have fires
if they are far enough back from the front . . .

There are not many refugees on the roads tonight.
They have stopped wherever they could for the night
in homes . . . in barns and in stables.[14]

1950s

Santa Clausing

*Gwenda Hayes Holaday of Boone, North Carolina,
recalled Christmas mischief in the foothills of the Blue Ridge mountains.*

I grew up in Wilkes County and we used to go "Santa Clausing" at Christmas.
It was a lot like Trick or Treat, and neighbors would give us candy. If they didn't, we
would trick them by taking their corn shucks.[15]

1950s
Christmas Cheer

*Bernice L. Couch of Winston-Salem, North Carolina,
shared her story about the Mason jar mystery.*

ome Christmas we just went out in the woods, chopped down a tree, broke off holly branches, shot mistletoe out of tree tops, and pulled up running cedar. I remember being out with Grandpa and I was pulling up running cedar and found a Mason jar full of water. Couldn't figure why a new jar would be in the woods so I asked Grandpa. He took the jar and mumbled something 'bout Christmas cheer. Course I didn't know about moonshiners then, and I was so excited bringing in Christmas decorations I forgot all about the jar.[16]

1952

I'll Violate Somebody's Border

*This poem by C.P. Donnel, Jr., appeared in the
December 27, 1952, issue of the* Saturday Evening Post. *It described how
Santa Claus braved a no-fly zone over Russia to deliver a Cold War Christmas gift.*

If Santa Is a Little Late Tonight

hile Santa was shuffling his last-minute mail,

He came on a note that was scrawled
In a faraway land, in a little girl's hand,
    In a language he hardly recalled.
Not an elf made a sound as he scanned it and frowned,
    Then he leaped to his feet with a shout,
And he held out the screed for his workers to read.
    "By Blitzen!" they cheered. "Smuggled out!"

Mrs. Santa said firmly, "This calls for a trip
    You must make up your mind to forgo.
With the reindeer and pack you're a setup for flak
    If you fly at a sensible low.
While their radar and planes make their stratosphere lanes
    Uncertain and hazardous channels,
You're too old."
Here the saint interrupted, "I ain't,
    And I'll thank you to fetch my red flannels.

"For a summons like this I have waited for years,
    While I smoldered continually with
The desire to shame certain people who claim
    I'm a decadent, capitalist myth.
Moreover, I'm riled that this resolute child
    Cannot openly send in her order.
Though I seldom intrude, I am now in the mood,
    Where I'll violate somebody's border."

He was ready to leave when his wife hurried up:
    "I have charted your route on this map.

Fly on oxygen, pray, for two-thirds of the way,
    And avoid the Siberian trap.
Then here, at this town, you will start to drop down
    Till you spot the great Petrovitch Dam.
Level off by degrees, and watch out for tall trees....
    Are you listening?"
                Said Santa, "Yes, Ma'am."

"Tell the world," Santa barked, "of my
earnest request
    For no public excitement or fuss
If I'm tardy tonight. You may label this
flight
    Operation Priority Plus.
I will show certain folks who's a fable
and hoax."
    Then, as spry as a two-month-old pup,
He scrambled aboard, and he boomed
as he soared,
    "One doll, extra large, coming up!"[17]

"*Merry Christmas to all, and to all a good-night*"
Drawing by Thomas Nast

1960

A Big Supply of Fireworks

*A native of Alabama, Sue Spencer was married to a mining engineer,
who worked on a titanium-mining project in Sierra Leone. At the time
she wrote this letter, the three oldest Spencer children were in the states finishing their
schooling; the two younger boys were in Africa with their parents.*

Gbangbama
Christmas, 1960

Dear Lolly and Suzy,

Another sad Christmas with three-fifths of my children absent, a thin homemade Christmas tree with tarnished decorations and hot, miserable weather. But Tom and Rob enjoyed it. With no other children to make odious comparisons, they didn't realize they had a frugal Christmas. For their chief present I bought a big supply of fireworks in Freetown, left over from Guy Fawkes Day which the English celebrate in November. Fireworks, properly used, are the finest present boys can get. Properly used means for parents to ignore how, when and where they will be fired. I told Tom and Rob that they were big boys now and could be trusted to shoot fireworks sensibly; then I retired behind a brick wall for the next few days. They blasted away until the last infernal device was used up, singeing the cat, igniting Mr. Beattie's verandah, setting fire to the grass and grazing the head of Mr. Ryter with one erratic rocket. The worst casualty was a few burned fingers for Rob. Tom being older and wiser let him put off the most daring shots. . . .

Every Yuletide the people come up the hill from the village to sing and dance for us and hold out their hands for their Christmas dash. After about the twentieth group of dancers our dashes get pretty meager. A group is outside now dancing around Rob chanting and rattling their shake-shakes. Every now and then I can hear the word "manager, manager, manager" in their chant. They are probably singing, "The manager is an old slob. He gave us only two bob." Two bob is twenty-eight cents and that is exactly what he gave the last group.

Love, Mama[18]

1960s

Sweetest of Presents

*Michael McFee wrote this poem about a tasty treat
that heralded the beginning of Christmas for
a Blue Ridge mountain boy.*

Yule Log

Just before Christmas, every year,
dad's rich friend Winston would send one
packed in dry ice, in a special box
stamped *Biltmore Dairy* in dark green cursive.

We'd bear it to the kitchen counter
and juggle the smoking ice into the sink
and slowly unroll the frozen paper
around this first and sweetest of presents:

a yule log made of *Premium* ice cream.
Its chocolate rind looked exactly like bark,
down to the scattered nut-knots;
its pith was a plug of creamy butter pecan

so authentic it almost had rings.
Mom held the long knife under the spigot
until it was finally hot enough
for Dad to slice a piece for each of us,

a thin section from this section
of the tree of endless good cheer and luck
and wealth enjoyed at the Estate.
But we weren't jealous, there in the kitchen

of our home built of skinny logs
on land owned long ago by George Vanderbilt;
as dry-ice fog tried to sneak
cheap melodrama into the scene we simply
stood on the verge of Christmas
then filled our empty spoons and lifted them
and burned that log in our mouths,
its cold fire falling, filling our aching chests.[19]

1963

Gone is the Black Mourning Crepe

Although the mourning for President Kennedy,
who was assassinated on November 22, had continued long afterward,
the Christmas season marked a time to look ahead.
In her diary, Lady Bird Johnson showed that she was prepared
to celebrate Lyndon Johnson's first Christmas in office.

onday, December 23, the White House. Gone is the black mourning crepe that swathed the great crystal chandeliers in the State Rooms and draped the high doorways. The flags, at half-mast this long month, now rise—and with them my spirits.

The sense of pall that held the house in hushed quiet has lifted, and we can begin to turn our eyes to Christmas! The mantels are bright with holly and the house smells of evergreen. I have put my small wardrobe of black dresses, worn every day since that day in November, in the back of the closet and put on my Christmas red.[20]

1 9 6 6

There's My Boy!

*Three years later, the war in Vietnam had dragged down the nation's spirits,
and President Johnson's aspirations. This entry in Lady Bird's diary
reflected the tragic times.*

Saturday, *December 24*   After lunch Lyndon and I left in the *Jetstar* . . . to go to
Kelly Air Force Base on a poignant visit for Christmas Eve, to greet wounded GI's who
were returning to Texas.

We landed and met Congressman Henry Gonzalez, and spoke quietly to a small
group who were lined up behind the ropes waiting at the base. The plane came in—an
ambulance plane. Lyndon went aboard and met the men and then came down looking
solemn. We stood at the foot of the steps. . . .

And then they began to file down the steps—twenty evacuees, . . . with bandaged
arms or legs and silent, stunned faces. There was utter stillness—never had the war felt
so close—a strange war. Suddenly, as the first man approached the bottom of the steps,
the small crowd burst into spontaneous applause. And then behind me there was a happy
sound, "There he is, there's my boy!" and a pretty lady brushed past us with: "Please
excuse me, Mr. President." A litter case came down the steps and a young man raised his
head and grinned. . . . They loaded him into a big ambulance in a sort of a hammock,
and his mother sat holding his hand.

The last of the twenty came down, and silently they went their ways and the clapping
died. . . . I felt buffeted by emotions, deep respect for those young men and for an organiza-
tion that could get them all the way from Vietnam to San Antonio within hours of being
wounded, and sympathy for their families and a shattering sympathy for anybody who has
yes's and no's to say about this war—McNamara, Westmoreland, Lyndon....[21]

1967

My Heart is Crying

Bong Son Plains, Vietnam
12/25/67

Dearest Auntie Mame,

It is Christmas Eve in San Francisco—how I wish I could be with you to enjoy it.

A truce has been negotiated, so today we do nothing but lie around. It's raining now, so I am in my tent. Last night one of the Cav's helicopters circled over "the plains" firing different colored flares. It had speakers mounted, so as it flew by I could hear Christmas carols. It was at that time that this intense loneliness hit me. I have saved all the [Christmas] cards I received and just finished rereading them for the third time.

I have, in the past, experienced loneliness, but nothing as intense as the feeling I now have. My heart is crying. I knew that Christmas here would be bad, but not as much as this. Some of the guys are talking to each other, but most are just lying and thinking.

Thank you for the pine branch. When I close my eyes and smell it, I can see your tree [and], in your "penthouse," us together.

I look forward to the day when I board that big jet and come home.
A very Merry Christmas to you, *my* Auntie Mame, and happiest of New Years.
I love you—

Your Nephew,
Dave[22]

1967

We Don't Get Many Treats

This next letter was written by Specialist Fourth Class David Hockett,
Company A, 13th Signal Battalion, 1st Cavalry Division (Airmobile).

[January 1968, Vietnam]
To Cub Scout Pack 508
Saratoga, California

I don't know how to thank you for the wonderful gifts you sent to me and my buddies.

We are located on top of a hill, and it is isolated. The only way in is by chopper, so you can see we don't get many treats such as you sent. After eating C-rations, the popcorn, cake and candy were like gold. The biggest hit was the plastic Christmas tree.

Last week I had a fever and had to spend three days in the medic tent. In the tent sleeping next to me was a 12-year-old Vietnamese boy who had shrapnel in his elbow and shoulder. He was hiding in a bunker with his parents when a grenade exploded, killing all his family. I became friends with him and tried to converse with him in our different languages. When I shared with him the present you sent, he smiled for the first time. He sure got a kick out of the game.

We all hear of protests and riots and get mad. When our buddies die, we wonder why, but we also think of the boys of Den I and Den V and know why this must be done, and we know how lucky we are to live in America.

I pray that none of you will ever have to put on a uniform for hostile reasons.

Your friend,
David Hockett[23]

*Hockman was shipped home after being wounded
on February 1, near Hue during the Tet Offensive.*

1 9 6 9

I'll Be Twice as Alert!

*This third letter was written by Sergeant Raymond Wahl,
who served at Chu Lai as a radio Teletype operator for Headquarters Battery,
American Division Artillery.*

23 Dec. 69, Mon
Chu Lai, Vietnam

Dear Mom,

I hear you had some snow at home, and that the weather is very cold. I'll bet it'll be a beautiful Christmas. I hope you, Pop, and Len enjoy it. . . .

Well, I'll be spending Christmas Eve in good old bunker 110. I've got guard duty again. The only Mass we're having here for Christmas is the Midnight Mass. I want to try to go to Mass. I should be able to. There's supposed to be a truce, so I'll be twice as alert!

When I found out I had guard duty on the 24th, I remembered a TV show they had on a long time ago. It was the story of how "Silent Night" was composed. Do you remember staying up with me to watch it? At the end of the show, when it's supposed to be many years after the song was composed, it showed several soldiers in Germany going into a church on Xmas Eve. They were in full combat gear, just like I'll be this Christmas Eve. I always wondered what it must be like to be at war and far away from home at Christmas. Now I know. I can imagine how Pop felt during World War II.

When I go into church tomorrow night I'll be sad because I'm so far from home. But I'll also be happy because by being here I'm making sure that you and Pop and Len can be at home, and safe, and can really enjoy Christmas. Knowing that I'm keeping you safe and happy at Christmas will make my Christmas happy too.

Love & XXXXX,
Ray[24]

1970

A Strange and Beautiful Thing

*Specialist Fifth Class Peter Elliott was assigned to Headquarters
and Headquarters Company, 20th Engineer Brigade, which was attached
to the 1st Cavalry Division (Airmobile), based at Bien Hoa. In this letter,
he described some very real Christmas fireworks.*

January 7th, 1971
Dear Family,
I got all the Xmas packages—at least I think I did. The tree was a huge success. I brought it with me to a small firebase where I spent Christmas Eve and Christmas. We

rigged up the lights with dry-cell batteries, and it was the only "formal" tree in the small camp.

Christmas out there was really something. I can hardly tell everything since there was a certain emotion that belies words. At midnight on Xmas Eve, the mortars and tracks and tanks and all the 1st Cavalry artillery sent up an absolutely thunderous barrage of high-altitude flares—all red and green star clusters. Since we were in a valley ringed by 1st Cav positions, it was quite a show. The Cavalry gunners topped it off with a crown of white phosphorus shells fired at an extreme altitude. I believe few people have seen fireworks like these.

Then, when all had quieted and the flares had gone out, the whole area calmed and hushed and we could just hear one of the fire bases start singing "Silent Night." Then it was picked up by the other positions around us and by everyone. It echoed through the valley for a long time and died out slowly. I'm positive it has seldom been sung with more gut feeling and pure homesick emotion—a strange and beautiful thing in this terribly death-ridden land. It is something I will always remember. . . .

Love,
Peter[25]

1985

Jesuits Taken By Surprise

"Christmas at Shadowbrook" appeared in the December 28, 1985,
issue of America. *In this poem, James Finn Cotter captured a transcendent*
Christmas Eve experience at the old Jesuit seminary in Lenox, Connecticut.

Christmas at Shadowbrook

*H*odie Christus natus est shattered the silence
Of our dark winter sleep in the calm seminary
Of stone and timber on a Berkshire hillside,
As the full choir of our Jesuit classmates
Marched into the dormitory with voices booming.
Taken by surprise, we first-year novices
Woke to sudden light and song to realize
It was not morning yet but nearing midnight
With Christmas Mass waiting to be celebrated.

The shepherds in the fields could not have been
More startled when they found themselves surrounded
By a chorus of angels intoning in the sky
"Glory to God in the highest, peace on earth,"
Than we were when we found ourselves awakened
By brother seminarians staring down
And singing to us still resting in our beds.

We lay there stunned and wondered were we dreaming.

The carols fading, we sat up and dressed quickly
To make our way down to the brilliant chapel
Miraculously decked with scrolls of laurel,
Poinsettias, wreaths of evergreen, and holly.
As *Introibo ad altare Dei* rang
Chiming in our ears, we ran toward Bethlehem
To find the Child laid in the manger born
In our young hearts with new joy and good will.

Sipping hot chocolate in the refectory
After Mass, we chuckled at our innocence
And knew that next year we should be the angels
Rousing still drowsy shepherds from their dreams.[26]

1990

A Big Feast, Usually Goat

*Dawn Khalil longed to explore life outside the United States.
In the spring of 1990, she left California to serve as a Peace Corps volunteer
in the Small Enterprise Development Program in Ghanzi (pronounced Gantsi),
a town in Botswana, Africa. At Christmastime, she wrote these letters home.*

21 December 1990

Have been spending some time making flour/salt/water Christmas ornaments. Our Christmas Eve celebration will now be properly decorated. We're chipping in and getting a sheep for the occasion. All of us who are stuck in Gantsi and far from home will be together. Should be fun at John Hardbattle's farm. He's got a nice green yard and a makeshift pool. What more could you ask for in a Christmas far from family? . . .

I asked a few people here what a traditional Botswana Christmas entails. Most people are Christian. Seems they have a big feast, usually goat. . . .

Merry Christmas World

25 December 1990

I'm at John Hardbattle's farm now, sitting next to the pool having my first cup of coffee. It's around 8 A.M. and about 75 degrees. Last night was pretty special. Everyone left work at noon and by 3, there were about 6-7 of us here at the farm. Lamb was cooking and we played volleyball in the pool. Quite a change from a USA Christmas Eve. We had a wonderful dinner for ten.

All afternoon, the people who live on the farm (bushmen) were coming in and out getting ready for their trance dance. John's mother is Basarwa, so he speaks Naro, which is one of the "clicking" languages. After dinner, we went out and joined in to watch the dancing. It was incredible.

Picture this: Warm night, Southern Cross just over the horizon, a storm far off in the distance where you can see the lightning light up the sky every now and then; a fire with about 25 to 30 people sitting around it chanting and clapping; lots of the women had on traditional dress, a dancing skirt made of goat skin and fur, and an apron with all kinds of necklaces of ostrich egg shells, etc; the men wore pants, rolled up to their knees or shorts with dancing rattles tied to their ankles (cocoons which are sewn together with some sort of bead inside to make it rattle). The four medicine men carried fly wisps (made of a gemsbok tail) and danced in a circle around the fire. The dance is a rhythmic stomping. With the rattles on, the clapping and chanting makes quite a scene. The women would get up and dance behind the men. The medicine men would break off and "heal" different people in the crowd. He would put one hand on the person's back, the other on the chest and chant, scream and stomp his feet with the rattles on. After a few people, he would stand up as though he were in some sort of trance and wander around the fire. Women would surround him to be sure he was okay. I saw a couple step into the fire, and have no reaction. Then he would fall, and as John explained, he left his body. The other people massaged him to try to get him back out of the trance. It was something to see.

One of the medicine men "healed" me, stomping away. Afterwards, he stood up, pointed over my shoulder and clicked something. John, who was sitting next to me, laughed and said he was talking to a spirit telling the spirit to stay away! I went back to the house about 1:30 A.M. They kept dancing till it started raining around 3. Apparently, all the different chants and dances mean something.[27]

1990

I'm Never Going To The Beach Again

During Operation Desert Storm, Army Specialist Don Odom
wrote this letter to his girlfriend Kim, describing a surreal experience
in the Saudi Arabian desert.

24 December 90

Dearest Kim,

Well, it's Christmas eve and all is quiet on the western front. I know it's been a couple of weeks since I wrote last, so I'll try to fill you in on what's going on. My platoon was attached to an air cav unit with the 101st Airborne. These are the guys who get to fly all of the fancy helicopters, Apache's, Cobra's, Blackhawks. We travelled north for a couple of weeks to conduct training exercises, so that's why I haven't written. At one point, we were only a few miles from the Iraqi border.

After travelling through the desert for 2 weeks, there is only one thing I can say for certain about this country. There's an awful lot of sand. I'm making a promise, I swear I'm never going to the beach again.

We did get to travel through several Saudi villages. It's pretty amazing how different our cultures are, yet how similar the children at play. I saw a group of young children playing a king-of-the-hill type game on a pile of rubble. Of course the game broke up rather quickly when our convoy stopped for lunch. All the children quickly ran towards us begging for candy. We were mobbed by these dirty little hands reaching up in the air at us. Needless to say, no one got to eat the dessert in their M.R.E.'s for that meal. The kids horded the chocolate brownies and oatmeal cookie bars and ran off to taste their sampling of American food.

We came across another village that was really weird. As we approached the outskirts of the village, the desert was covered with the dead corpses of camels and goats and sheep. They were all just lying there rotting in the sun. We didn't actually go into the village, we just stopped in a grove of trees, almost like an oasis, on the outskirts of the town. We stayed there for the night. As I was laying in my cot, I looked up and saw a goat's leg in the trees above me. How it got there I'll never know. We were supposed to stay in that village for several days, but the next morning we had to pack up and move somewhere else. Lt. Bolluytt told us the village had been wiped out by anthrax, that's why all the animals were dead. I don't remember if anthrax is contagious or not, but if it is, I'll probably be dead by the time you read this letter. . . . ha ha ha. In all seriousness though, there were thousands of flies everywhere, buzzing from one carcass to another and then landing on our food. Pretty unsanitary conditions if you ask me. Some of the guys in the squad are wondering if this village was the result of one of Saddam's bio weapons. My thinking is that if that was the case, we would have heard about it all over the news. I don't know, then again maybe not.

By the time you get this, Christmas will be over and you'll probably be celebrating New Year's. I hope you had a great Christmas, and I'll try to beat the lines at the phone center tomorrow to call and hear your voice.

All my love,
Don[28]

No one in Odom's platoon became ill after the stopover,
and they never learned what killed the animals they saw.

1995

Jedus Bon

*The Gospel of Luke was the first book of the Bible
to be published in Gullah. Gullah is a Creolized English with many words
and grammar forms drawn from African languages. It is still spoken by thousands of
descendants of the former Sea Island slaves in the Southeastern coastal area.*

Jedus Bon

Chapter 2

1: Een dat time, Caesar Augustus been de big leada, de emperor ob de Roman people. E make a law een all de town een de wol weh e habe tority, say, "Ebrybody haffa go ta town fa count by de hed an write down e nyame." 2: Dis been de fus time dey count by de hed, same time Cyrenius de gobna ob Syria country. 3: So den, ebrybody gone fa count by de hed, ta e own town weh e ole people been bon.

4: Now Joseph same fashion gone from Nazrut town een Galilee. E trabel ta de town nyame Betlam een Judea, weh de ole people leada, King David, been bon. Joseph gone dey cause e blongst ta David fambly. 5: E gone fa count by de hed, an Mary gone long wid um. She gage fa married um. An Mary

King James Version

1: And it came to pass in those days, that there went out a decree from Caesar Augustus, that all the world should be taxed.

2: (*And* this taxing was first made when Cyrenius was governor of Syria.)
3: And all went to be taxed, every one into his own city.

4: And Joseph also went up from Galilee, out of the city of Nazareth, into Judaea, unto the city of David, which is called Bethlehem; (because he was of the house and lineage of David:)
5: To be taxed with Mary his espoused wife, being great with child.

been spectin. 6: Same time wen dey been dey, time come fa Mary gone een. 7: She habe boy chile, e fusbon. E wrop um op een clothe wa been teah eenta leetle strip an lay um een a trough, de box weh feed de cow an oda animal. Cause Mary an Joseph beena stay weh de animal sleep. Dey ain't been no room fa dem eenside de bodin house.

6: And so it was, that, while they were there, the days were accomplished that she should be delivered.

7: And she brought forth her firstborn son, and wrapped him in swaddling clothes, and laid him in a manger; because there was no room for them in the inn. [29]

2004
Let There Be Peace

Major Carrie Acree, mother of three young children,
was a first-grade teacher in Grand Junction, Colorado, when her unit—
the 443rd Civil Affairs Battalion (Army Reserve)—was deployed to Iraq in mid-July.
In a town north of Baghdad, Acree and other civil affairs officers worked in a daily
spirit of Christmas, rebuilding schools, bridges, and water-treatment facilities.
Her accomplishments included playing a key role in Operation Amber Waves of Grain—
a humanitarian project involving civil affairs personnel working with Iraqi
neighborhood councils to distribute 280 tons of high-grade wheat seed to
more than 350 local farmers. In her Christmas letter to friends at home,
Acree reflected on the season's true meaning.

December 2004: Merry Christmas!

This month has brought many mixed emotions about deployment, service, and duty. It seems the holidays are always the hardest part of deployment. Holiday traditions are missed and as families gather at home, children wonder why Dad or Mom has to be away. Please pray for me and my family, as well as all soldiers and their families, as we spend this holiday apart.

However, I must say that this Christmas is the first in many years where I haven't had endless errands, shopping, parties, and get-togethers. I have been able to focus on the true meaning of Christmas without all the commercialism and typical holiday stress.

I have received numerous cards and letters from classes and students around the country wishing soldiers a Merry Christmas. Their message is always the same—"Thank you for fighting for us." . . . All I can hope for is that I will in my own small way lead the world to a brighter, more peaceful future. . . .

So even though we are a nation at war, the season's message of "Let there be peace on earth, good will toward men" remains my heartfelt prayer during this holiday season.

Much much love.
Carrie[30]

Touch Hands
By William H. H. Murray

*A*h friends, dear friends, as years go on
  and heads get gray, how fast the guests do go!
Touch hands, touch hands, with those that stay.
Strong hands to weak, old hands to young,
  around the Christmas board, touch hands.
The false forget, the foe forgive,
  for every guest will go and every fire burn low
  and cabin empty stand.
Forget, forgive, for who may say that Christmas day
  may ever come to host or guest again.
Touch hands![1]

Acknowledgments

I give grateful thanks to the authors, publishers, agents, and heirs, whose cooperation and permissions to reprint have made the publication of this book possible. For every selection included I have made every effort to trace the ownership and give proper acknowledgment for its use.

Special thanks—

To Dover Publications, Inc., for their 1978 unabridged republication of the work originally published by Harper & Brothers in 1890 under the title *Thomas Nast's Christmas Drawings from the Human Race*. Many of Mr. Nast's drawings brighten the book.

To Page Dieter, who helped me search his box of old *Harper's New Monthly Magazines*, where we found what appears to be an 1857 Saint Nicholas, drawn by Thomas Nast when he was only 17 years old (page 45).

To my excellent editor, Carolyn Sakowski, and the staff at John F. Blair, Publisher.

To Tony Wyatt, who taught me to use a computer.

And, most of all, special thanks to Bob Martell, who puts up with me at Christmas, and all through the year.

 *Endnotes*

✳ 1600s

1. Philip Barbour, ed., *Complete Works of Captain John Smith* (Chapel Hill: University of North Carolina Press, 1986), Volume 1, 245.
2. William Bradford and Edward Winslow, *Mourt's Relation*, or *Journal of the Plantation at Plymouth* (1622).
3. Samuel Eliot Morison, ed., *Of Plymouth Plantation, 1620-1647 by William Bradford* (New York: Alfred A. Knopf, 1970), 97.
4. From the records of the General Court, Massachusetts Bay Colony, May 11, 1659.
5. Father Louis Hennepin, *Description of Louisiana* (1682), trans. by Marion E. Cross (University of Minnesota Press, 1938). Reprinted with permission of the publisher.
6. Increase Mather, *A Testimony against Several Prophane and Superstitious Customs, Now Practiced by Some in New-England* (London, 1687), 36.

⚓ 1700s

1. "The Further Affidavit of James Blair…," William S. Perry, ed., *Historical Collections Relating to the American Colonial Church* (Hartford, 1870), Vol. 1, 137-38.
2. Cotton Mather, *Diary of Cotton Mather, 1681-[1724]* (Boston).
3. Cotton Mather, *Grace Defended: A Censure on the Ungodliness, By Which the Glorious Grace of God, Is Too Commonly Abused* (Boston, 1712), 20.
4. *Publications of the Pennsylvania German Folklore Society* (1941), Vol. 6, 13-14.
5. "The News-Boy's Christmas and New Year's Verses" [broadside] (Boston, 1770).
6. *The Adams Papers: Diary and Autobiography of John Adams, Volume I, Diary 1755-1770*, edited by L. H. Butterfield, pp. 273-274 (Cambridge, Mass.: The Belknap Press of Harvard University Press, Copyright © 1961 by the Massachusetts Historical Soci-

ety). Reprinted with permission of the publisher.

7. Gilbert Imlay, "The Adventures of Daniel Boone," *A Topographical Description of the Western Territory of North America* (London, 1797), 339-43.

8. Herbert Eugene Bolton, *Fray Juan Crespi, Missionary Explorer on the Pacific Coast, 1769-1774* (University of California Press, 1927), 258-59. Reprinted with permission of the publisher.

9. Hunter Dickinson Farish, ed., *The Journal and Letters of Philip Vickers Fithian, 1773-1774: A Plantation Tutor of the Old Dominion* (Colonial Williamsburg Foundation, 1957), 34, 36, 39-40. Reprinted with permission of the publisher.

10. Frank Moore, ed., *Songs and Ballads of the American Revolution* (New York: D. Appleton & Company, 1855), 150-52.

11. William S. Stryker, *The Battles of Trenton and Princeton* (Boston and New York: Houghton, Mifflin and Company, 1893).

12. William S. Powell, ed., "A Connecticut Soldier Under Washington: Elisha Bostwick's Memoirs," *William and Mary Quarterly* (January 1949), 101-3. Reprinted with permission of the publisher.

13. "Valley Forge, 1777-1778. Diary of Surgeon Albigence Waldo," *Pennsylvania Magazine of History and Biography* (1897), Vol. XXI.

14. Fitzpatrick, John C., ed., *The Writings of George Washington, from the Original Manuscript Sources, 1745-1799* (Washington: U. S. Government Printing Office, 1931-1944), Vol. 10.

15. "Valley Forge, Diary of Surgeon Albigence Waldo."

16. Cake recipe supplied by Mary V. Thompson, Research Specialist, Mount Vernon Ladies' Association.

1800-1851

1. "The Old House of Bethlehem," *Gazette*, (Reading Pa.), January 6, 1849.

2. *The Moravian*, April 30, 1863.

3. Neal Owen Hammon, *My Father, Daniel Boone: The Draper Interviews with Nathan*

Boone (University Press of Kentucky, 1999), 122-24. Reprinted with permission of the publisher.

4. Lewis and Clark Journal entries provided by Park Ranger Sean Johnson, Fort Clatsop National Monument.

5. Ibid.

6. Charles Ball, *Slavery in the United States: A Narrative of the Life and Adventures of Charles Ball, A Black Man* (Lewiston, Pa., 1836), 206-8.

7. "John Quincy Adams Memoirs," *America* (Chicago: Veterans of Foreign Wars of the United States, 1925), Vol. 5, 267.

8. Ross Cox, *Adventures on the Columbia River, Including The Narrative of a Residence of Six Years on the Western Side of the Rocky Mountains Among Various Tribes of Indians Hitherto Unknown* (1832), edited by Edgar I. Stewart and Jane R. Stewart. (Copyright © 1957 by the University of Oklahoma Press). Reprinted with permission of the publisher.

9. *Harper's New Monthly Magazine*, (December 1857), 1-2.

10. *Fifty-Four Years' Recollections of Men and Events in Wisconsin*, by Gen. Albert G. Ellis in Report and Collections of the State Historical Society of Wisconsin, Vol. II, 210-13. Reprinted with permission of the Wisconsin Historical Society.

11. *O-DE-JIT-WA-WIN-NING, or Contes Du Temps Passe, The Memoirs of Elizabeth T. Baird* (Green Bay, Wisc: Dennis Fredrick for Heritage Hill Foundation, 1998), Conte 2, 3-4. Reprinted with permission of the publisher.

12. Mary S. Helm, *Scraps of Early Texas History* (Austin, Tex.: privately printed, 1884).

13. *Republican and Anti-Masonic Expositor* (York, Pa.), December 14, 1830.

14. Harriett Martineau, from a pamphlet distributed by the American Sunday School Union of Boston, 1832.

15. *Memoirs of Gustave Philipp Körner 1809-1896, life-sketches* (Cedar Rapids, Iowa: Thomas J. McCormack, Pub., Torch Press, 1909).

16. *Philadelphia Daily Chronicle*, December 26, 1833.

17. Horace Greeley, *Recollections of a Busy Life* (New York, 1868), 43-44.

18. Reverend A.R. Kremer, "Christmas When I Was a Boy," *Reformed Church Messenger*, December 24, 1896.

19. Reverend Benjamin Bausman, "Our Schoolmaster," *Guardian* (June 1873).

20. Reverend U. Henry Heilman, "Descriptive and Historical Memorials of Heilman Dale," *Lebanon County Historical Society Proceedings* (1909), Vol. 4, 456.

21. *Christian Register* (Boston, Ma.), December 20, 1834.

22. Frederick Douglass, *Autobiographies: Narrative of the Life of Frederick Douglass, an American Slave* [1845]; *My Bondage and My Freedom* [1855]; *Life and Times of Frederick Douglass* [1892]. (New York: Literary Classics of the United States, 1994), 66, 288-90, 593-9.

23. Lewis W. Paine, *Six Years in a Georgia Prison, Narrative of Lewis W. Paine, Who Suffered Imprisonment Six Years in Georgia, for the Crime of Aiding the Escape of a Fellowman from that State, after He had Fled from Slavery, Written by Himself* (New York, 1851), 179-80.

24. Harriet A. Jacobs, *Incidents in the Life of a Slave Girl, Written by Herself*, edited and with an introduction by Jean Fagen Yellin (Cambridge, Mass.: Harvard University Press) 118-120, 277. Copyright © 1987, 2000 by the President and Fellows of Harvard College. Reprinted by permission of the publisher.

25. *The Liberator* (Boston, Ma.), May 26, 1837.

26. Jacobs, *Incidents in the Life of a Slave Girl*, 277.

27. Dr. Edward Warren, *A Doctor's Experiences in Three Continents* (Baltimore, 1885).

28. *Public Ledger* (Philadelphia, Pa.), December 24, 1891.

29. Reverend Benjamin Bausman, "An Old-Time Christmas in a Country Home," *Guardian*, January 1871, 15-16.

30. Matthias Mengel reminiscences, *Weekly Eagle* (Reading, Pa.), December 28, 1895.

31. Osborne Russell, *Journal of a Trapper; or, Nine Years in the Rocky Mountains, 1834-1843*, edited by Aubrey L. Haines (University of Nebraska Press, 1955), 114-15. Reprinted with permission of the publisher.

32. Rufus B. Sage, *Rocky Mountain Life; or, Startling Scenes and Perilous Adventures in the Far West* (New York: R. Worthington Co., 1884), 113.

33. *Spirit of the Times* (Philadelphia, Pa.), December 21, 1842.

34. *Daily Albany Argus*, December 23, 1842.

35. Brevet Captain J. C. Fremont, *Report of the Exploring Expedition to The Rocky Mountains in the Year 1842, and to Oregon and North California in the Years 1843-'44*. Printed by order of the Senate of the United States. (Washington: Gales and Seaton, Printers, 1845).

36. Pierre-Jean DeSmet, S.J., *Oregon Missions and Travels Over the Rocky Mountains in 1845-46*.

Published in 1847.

37.   James H. Simpson, *Report of Explorations across the Great Basin of the Territory of Utah for a Direct Wagon-Route from Camp Floyd to Genoa, in Carson Valley in 1859* (Washington: Government Printing Office, 1876). Appendix Q contains "Journal of Mr. Edward M. Kern of an Exploration of the Mary's or Humboldt River, Carson Lake, and Owens River and Lake, in 1845," 483-44.

38.   *Gazette* (Reading, Pa.), December 20, 1845.

39.   *Gazette* (Reading, Pa.), December 27, 1845.

40.   *Kriss Kringle's Christmas Tree* (Philadelphia: E. Ferrett & Co., 1847), introduction.

41.   *Daily Commercial Journal* (Pittsburgh, Pa.), December 17, 1846.

42.   George R. Stewart, *Ordeal by Hunger: The Story of the Donner Party* (Boston: Houghton Mifflin Company, 1960), 326-27. Copyright © 1936, 1960 and © renewed 1963 by George R. Stewart. Copyright © renewed 1988 by Theodosia B. Stewart. Reprinted by permission of Houghton Mifflin Company. All rights reserved.

43.   Thomas E. Breckenridge, and others, *The Story of a Famous Expedition: The Narrative of Fremont's Retreat from the San Luis Valley* (New York: Cosmopolitan, 1896).

44.   Sallie Hester diary, *The Argonaut*, (1925), Vol. 97.

45.   *Minnesota Chronicle and Register* (St. Paul, Minn.), December 22, 1849.

46.   John Woodhouse Audubon, *A Western Journal, 1849-50* (Cleveland: A. H. Clark, 1906).

47.   Major William Downie, *Hunting for Gold* (San Francisco: California Publishing Company, 1893), 61, 66-68.

48.   Carl I. Wheat, ed., *The Shirley Letters from the California Mines, 1851-1852,* by Louise Amelia Knapp Smith Clappe (New York: Alfred A. Knopf, Inc., copyright © 1949), 102-6. Used by permission of Alfred A. Knopf, a division of Random House, Inc.

❧

1851-1865

1.   Roach and Eggleston Family Papers (#2614), Southern Historical Collection, Wilson Library, The University of North Carolina at Chapel Hill.

2. *Daily Journal* (Wilmington, N.C.), December 23, 1851.

3. Letter courtesy of Barbara Bowen. Mrs. Mortimer quoted from Favell Lee Mortimer, *Reading Without Tears: or, A Pleasant Mode of Learning to Read*, (New York: Harper & Brothers, 1857).

4. Whipple Papers, Oklahoma Historical Society Research Division. Reprinted with permission.

5. *Daily Times* (New York, N.Y.), December 26, 1855.

6. Roach and Eggleston Family Papers.

7. Caja Munch, *The Strange American Way: Letters of Caja Munch from Wiota, Wisconsin, 1855-1859*. ©. Reprinted by permission of The University of Wisconsin Press.

8. Carrie Williams diary, Gold Flat, Nevada County, California, 1858-64, Yale Collection of Western Americana, Beinecke Rare Book and Manuscript Library.

9. Thomas Dyer, *To Raise Myself a Little: Amelia Akehurst Lines* (Athens: The University of Georgia Press, 1982), 171, 122. Reprinted courtesy of Hargrett Rare Book and Manuscript Library / University of Georgia Libraries.

10. *The Negro in Virginia* (Winston-Salem, N.C.: John F. Blair, Publisher, 1994), 96.

11. Ibid., 97-8.

12. Ibid., 98.

13. Ibid., 97.

14. Belinda Hurmence, ed., *Before Freedom, When I Just Can Remember: Twenty-seven Oral Histories of Former South Carolina Slaves* (Winston-Salem, N.C.: John F. Blair, Publisher, 1989), 37.

15. Solomon Northrup, *Twelve Years a Slave: The Narrative of Solomon Northrup, a Citizen of New York, Kidnapped in Washington City in 1841 and rescued in 1853, from a Cotton Plantation near the Red River in Louisiana* (Auburn, N.Y.: Derby and Miller, 1853), 216-17.

16. William John Grayson, *The Hireling and the Slave, Chicora, and Other Poems* (Charleston: McCarter, 1856), 52.

17. *Missionary* (Pittsburgh, Pa.), January 5, 1859.

18. *Chicago Tribune*, December 24, 1859.

19. William H. Brewer, *Up and Down California in 1860-1864*. Fourth Edition. Edited/translated by Francis Farquhar. Copyright © 1949. The Regents of the University of

California. With permission.

20. *New York Clipper*, March 16, 1861.

21. Margaret Mitchell, *Gone with the Wind* (New York: Macmillan Publishing Company,1936), 3.

22. Mills Lane, *Dear Mother: "Don't grieve about me. If I get killed, I'll only be dead.": Letters from Georgia Soldiers in the Civil War* (Savannah: The Beehive Press, 1977), 89-90. Courtesy of Georgia Archives.

23. Dyer, *To Raise Myself*, 209.

24. Courtesy of Mary Jane Bird, his great-granddaughter.

25. Lane, *Dear Mother: don't grieve*, 206.

26. Brewer, *Up and Down California*, chap. 7.

27. *Bloomington Pantagraph* (Bloomington, Ill.), December 22, 1862.

28. *Herald and Free Press* (Norristown, Pa.), December 30, 1862.

29. Minrose Gwin, ed., *A Woman's Civil War: A Diary with Reminiscences of the War, from March 1862*, by Cornelia Peake McDonald (Madison: The University of Wisconsin Press, © 1992), 99-105. Reprinted by permission of the University of Wisconsin Press.

30. William Bircher, *Drummer-Boy's Diary: Comprising Four Years of Service with the Second Regiment Minnesota Veteran Volunteers: 1861-1865* (St. Paul, Minn.: St. Paul Book and Stationary Company, 1889), 52.

31. Donald H. Wickman, ed., *Letters to Vermont: From Her Civil War Soldier Correspondents to the Home Press, Volume I* (Bennington, Vt.: Images from the Past, Inc., 1998), 134, 135. Reprinted courtesy of Images from the Past.

32. Kate Cumming, *A Journal of Hospital Life in the Confederate Army of Tennessee: from the Battle of Shiloh to the End of the War* (Louisville, Ky.: John P. Morton & Co., 1866), 54, 117-18.

33. Henry Wadsworth Longfellow, *Flower-De-Luce* (Boston: Ticknor and Fields, 1867).

34. Mary D. Robertson, ed., *A Confederate Lady Comes of Age: The Journal of Pauline DeCaradeuc Heyward, 1863-1888* (Columbia, S. C.: University of South Carolina Press, 1992), 28-29. Reprinted with permission of the publisher.

35. Bircher, *Drummer-Boy*, 92-93.

36. From the diary of Robert Watson. Reprinted with permission of the Florida State Archives.

37. Charles F. Bryan, Jr. and Nelson D. Lankford, editors, *Eye of the Storm: a Civil War Odyssey, Written and Illustrated by Robert Knox Sneden* (New York: Free Press, 2000), 174-75. Reprinted with permission of the publisher.

38. Sara Agnes Rice Pryor, *My Day, Reminiscences of a Long Life* (New York: The Macmillan Company, 1909).

39. Virginia Matzke Adams, ed., *On the Altar of Freedom: A Black Soldier's Civil War Letters from the Front*, by Corporal James Henry Gooding (Amherst: The University of Massachusetts Press, 1991) 94-96. Reprinted with permission of the publisher.

40. John Q. Anderson, ed., *Brokenburn: The Journal of Kate Stone, 1861-1868* (Baton Rouge: Louisiana State University Press, 1955), 269. Reprinted with permission of the publisher.

41. *Cincinnati Daily Enquirer*, December 25, 1863.

42. *Frank Leslie's Illustrated Newspaper*, January 9, 1864.

43. Frederick W. Seward, *Reminiscences of a War-Time Statesman and Diplomat 1830-1915* (New York: G.P. Putnam's Sons, 1916).

44. Mary Boykin Chestnut, *A Diary from Dixie, as Written by Mary Boykin Chestnut, Wife of James Chestnut, Jr., United States Senator from South Carolina, 1859-1861, and Afterward an Aide to Jefferson Davis and a Brigadier-General in the Confederate Army* (New York: D. Appleton and Company, 1905).

45. Carl Sandburg, *Abraham Lincoln, The War Years* (New York: Harcourt, Brace & Company, 1939), Vol. 3, 634-35.

46. Bircher, *Drummer-Boy's Diary*, 153-56

47. Robertson, *A Confederate Lady*, 61-62

48. John Buckly Bacon diary, *Wisconsin Then and Now*. Reprinted with permission of the Wisconsin Historical Society.

49. George W. Peck, "How Private Peck Put Down the Rebellion," *Wisconsin Then and Now*. Reprinted with permission of the Wisconsin Historical Society.

50. *Sunday Dispatch* (Philadelphia, Pa.), December 25, 1864.

51. Charles Alfred Humphreys, *Field, Camp, Hospital and Prison in the Civil War, 1864-1865* (Boston: George H. Ellis Co., 1918).

52. La Salle Corbell Pickett, *Pickett and His Men* (1899), Vol. 6, 4.

53. Cumming, *Journal of Hospital Life*, 158.

54. Bryan and Lankford, *Eye of the Storm*, 296-98.

♣

1865-1899

1. *Richmond* (Va.) *Daily Whig*, December 27, 1865.

2. *Galena Weekly Gazette* (Galena, Ill.), December 26, 1865.

3. *The Milwaukee Sentinel* (Milwaukee, Wis.), December 26, 1866.

4. *Western Missionary* (Dayton, Ohio), January 18, 1866.

5. *North American* (Philadelphia, Pa.), December 23, 1867.

6. Dyer, *To Raise Myself*, 228-29.

7. *Daily Rocky Mountain News* (Denver, Colo.), December 22, 1869.

8. *Miners' Journal* (Pottsville, Pa.), January 1, 1870.

9. Traditional spirituals, composers unknown.

10. "Christmas Dinner on the Upper Brazos in 1872," *West Texas Historical Association Year-book* (October 1938), Vol. 14, 83. Reprinted with permission.

11. *Ottawa Free Trader* (Ottawa, Ill.), December 20, 1873.

12. Henry Ward Beecher, *Pittsburgh Gazette*, December 26, 1874.

13. *Daily Rocky Mountain News*, 1874.

14. *Examiner and Express* (Lancaster, Pa.), December 28, 1876.

15. *The Miner* (Georgetown, Colo.), December 22, 1877.

16. Oblinger Manuscript Collection, Nebraska State Historical Society.

17. *Milwaukee Sentinel*, December 20, 1880.

18. F. W. Woolworth, excerpts from unfinished autobiography, edited by Edward Mott Wolley, *McClure's Magazine* (1925).

19. Booker T. Washington, *Up from Slavery, An Autobiography* (©1900, 1901), 132-35.

20. Andrew Waters, *On Jordan's Stormy Banks* (Winston-Salem, N.C.: John F. Blair, Publisher), 141-42.

21. Isabella Maud Rittenhouse, *Maud*, Richard Lee Stout, ed. (New York: The Macmillan

Company, 1939), 48-49, 155.

22. Anne Ellis, *The Life of an Ordinary Woman*, 34-35. Copyright 1929 by Anne Ellis, © renewed 1957 by Neita Carey and Earl E. Ellis. Reprinted by permission of Houghton Mifflin Company. All rights reserved.

23. William Augustus Croffut, *Detroit Post and Tribune*, December 1882.

24. Susan Anna Brown, "A Word About Christmas," *The Century Magazine*, December 1883.

25. *Milwaukee Sentinel*, December 23, 1883.

26. Courtesy of Suanne F. Holtman, The Texas Cowboys' Christmas Ball Association, Anson, Texas.

27. Ellis, *Life of an Ordinary Woman*, 52.

28. Keller, Helen, *The Story of My Life* (Garden City, N.Y.: International Collectors Library American Headquarters, 1905), 39-41, 176-77, 288-89.

29. F.W. Woolworth unfinished autobiography.

30. Ann Banks, ed., *First-Person America* (New York: Alfred A. Knopf, 1980), 19. Reprinted with permission.

31. "Christmas Greeting," from Alford Brothers Steam Laundry flyer, 1892.

32. Taken from wholesaler's 1892 catalog.

33. Rittenhouse, *Maud*, 568-69.

34. *Champaign County Gazette* (Champaign, Ill.), December 27, 1893.

35. *The New York Times*, December 26, 1895.

36. "Biltmore Thrown Open," *The New York Times*, December 26, 1895.

37. *Asheville Citizen* (Asheville, N.C.), December 25, 1895.

38. Dena J. Epstein, ed., *I Came a Stranger: The Story of a Hull-House Girl*, by Hilda Satt Polacheck (Urbana and Chicago: University of Illinois Press, 1989), 51-52. Copyright 1989 by the Board of Trustees of the University of Illinois. Used with permission of the University of Illinois Press.

39. Jack London, "To the Man on the Trail," *Overland Monthly*, Vol. 33, January 1899.

40. Ellis, *Life of an Ordinary Woman*, 190.

41. *The Memoirs of Herbert Hoover, Years of Adventure, 1874-1920*, Vol. 1. Herbert Hoover Handwritten Drafts, Box No. 1, Herbert Hoover Presidential Library and Museum, West Branch, Iowa. Reprinted with permission.

1900-1940

1. Menu for German House restaurant in Idaho Springs, Colo., 1900.
2. Harva Hachten, *The Flavor of Wisconsin: An Informal History of Food and Eating in the Badger State* (Madison: Wisconsin Historical Society Press, 1981), 102. Reprinted with permission of the Wisconsin Historical Society.
3. *North American* (Philadelphia, Pa.), December 22, 1900.
4. *Theodore Roosevelt's Letters to His Children* (New York: Charles Scribner's Sons, 1919).
5. Telegram from Orville Wright, Kitty Hawk, N.C., to Milton Wright, Dayton, Ohio, December 17, 1903.
6. R.W.B. Lewis and Nancy Lewis, ed., *The Letters of Edith Wharton* (New York: Charles Scribner's Sons, 1988), 100-101. Reprinted by permission of the Estate of Edith Wharton and the Watkins/Loomis Agency.
7. Katharine Ball Ripley, *Sand in My Shoes* (Asheboro, N.C.: Down Home Press, 1995), 198.
8. Anna C. McDonald, "Memoirs." Courtesy of Dorothy McDonald, daughter-in-law.
9. *The Record* (Philadelphia, Pa.), December 25, 1913.
10. Harrison Salisbury, "The Victorian City in the Midwest," in *Growing Up in Minnesota: Ten Writers Remember Their Childhoods*, edited by Chester G. Anderson (University of Minnesota Press, 1976), 68-70. Reprinted with permission of the publisher.
11. Voit Gilmore, *The Pilot* (Southern Pines, N.C.), January 2, 2004, C6. Reprinted with permission of the author.
12. Lillian Smith, *Memory of a Large Christmas* (New York: W. W. Norton & Company, Inc., Copyright © and renewed 1990 by Lillian Smith), 58-64. Used by permission of W. W. Norton & Company, Inc.
13. Courtesy of Sarah Watkins Cooke, Colfax, N.C.
14. Countee Cullen Papers, Amistad Research Center at Tulane University. With permission.
15. Nils Granlund telegram to Lucille LeSueur, December 25, 1924.
16. Calvin Coolidge Presidential Library. Reprinted with permission of The Calvin

Coolidge Memorial Foundation.

17. "Christmas at the White House," *Citizen* (Washington, D.C.), December 26, 1930.

18. Robert Peters, *Crunching Gravel: Growing up in the Thirties* (San Francisco: Mercury House, Incorporated, 1988), 54-55. Reprinted by permission of author and publisher.

19. Sue McCoy, Jill Dean and Maggie Dewey; Diana Balio, eds., *Yarns of Wisconsin* (Madison, Wisc.: Wisconsin Trails/Tamarack Press, 1978), 224.

20. Jay Parini and Richard Brown, *A Vermont Christmas* (New York: Little, Brown and Company, 1988). Reprinted with permission of the publisher.

21. Robert Cohen, *Dear Mrs. Roosevelt: Letters from Children of the Great Depression* (Chapel Hill, N.C.: University of North Carolina Press, © 2002), 151,152-54, 157, 159-60, 161. Used by permission of the publisher.

22. Shirley Schoonover, "Route 1, Box 111, Aurora," *Growing Up in Minnesota: Ten Writers Remember Their Childhoods*, edited by Chester G. Anderson (University of Minnesota Press, 1976), 153-54. Reprinted with permission of the publisher.

1941-2004

1. Elizabeth M. Norman, *We Band of Angels: The Untold Story of American Nurses Trapped on Bataan by the Japanese* (New York: Pocket Books, 1999), 23. Copyright © 1999 by Elizabeth M. Norman; Maps copyright © 1999 by David Lindroth, Inc. Used by permission of Random House, Inc.

2. On display in the Bataan March collection of the Deming Luna Mimbres Museum, Deming, New Mexico. Reprinted with permission of the museum.

3. Franklin Delano Roosevelt, national radio broadcast, December 24, 1942.

4. Eleanor Roosevelt, "My Day," *Poughkeepsie New Yorker*, December 25, 1942.

5. Olive Nowak, "A Busload of Strangers," *Good Housekeeping* (December 1993), 42.

6. Norman, *We Band of Angels*, 181.

7. Rosemary Norwalk, *Dearest Ones, A True World War II Love Story* (New York: John Wiley & Sons, Inc., © 1999), 101-5. Reprinted with permission of John Wiley & Sons, Inc.

8. Don Addor, *Noville Outpost to Bastogne: My Last Battle* (Canada: Trafford, 2004), 59-64.

Reprinted with permission of the author.

9. Richard Wellbrock, *War Letters: Extraordinary Correspondence from American Wars*, edited by Andrew Carroll (New York: Scribner, 2001), 278. Reprinted with permission.

10. General Anthony McAuliffe, message to the men of 101st Airborne Division, December 24, 1944, RG 407.

11. Norwalk, *Dearest Ones*, 217-18.

12. President Harry Truman, letter to Margaret Truman, December 23, 1941.

13. Father Kenneth Ryan, ed., *The Catholic Digest Christmas Book* (St. Paul, Minnesota: Carillon Books, 1977), 77-78. Reprinted with permission of the Society of Jesus— Oregon Province.

14. United Press International. Reprinted with permission. Valeo Clearance License 3.5981.4611056-65674.

15. Jan Kiefer, writer and compiler, *A North Carolina Christmas* (Englewood, Colo.: Westcliffe Publishers, Inc., 1996), 40. Reprinted with permission of the publisher.

16. Ibid., 24.

17. *The Saturday Evening Post*, © 1952. Renewed. Used with permission.

18. Sue Spencer, *African Creeks I Have Been Up* (New York: David McKay Company, Inc., 1963), 201-3. Reprinted with permission of the author.

19. Michael McFee, "Yule Log," *Earthly*. By permission of Carnegie Mellon University Press © 2001.

20. Claudia Johnson, *A White House Diary* (New York: Holt, Rinehart and Winston, 1970), 20. Reprinted with permission of the Lyndon Baines Johnson Library.

21. Ibid., 464-65.

22. David Bowman, from *Dear America: Letters Home from Vietnam*, edited by Bernard Edelman for the New York Vietnam Veterans Memorial Commission (W. W. Norton & Company, 1985; currently available in a trade paperback edition, W. W. Norton & Company, 1986), 250-51. Reprinted with permission of the editor.

23. David Hockett, ibid., 212-13.

24. Raymond Wahl, ibid., 240-50.

25. Peter Elliott, ibid., 253-4.

26. James Finn Cotter, "Christmas at Shadowbrook," *America*, December 28, 1985: 467. Reprinted with permission of the author.

27. Dawn Khalil, *Letters from Botswana: A Peace Corps Odyssey* (Cranston, R. I.: The Writers' Collective, 2003), 109-10. Reprinted with permission of the author.

28. Don Odom, from *War Letters: Extraordinary Correspondence from American Wars*, edited by Andrew Carroll (Scribner, 2001): 482-83. Reprinted with permission.

29. *De Good Nyews Bout Jedus Christ Wa Luke Write: The Gospel according to Luke in Gullah, Sea Island Creole, with marginal text of the King James Version* (American Bible Society © 1995), 9-10. Reprinted with permission of the publisher.

30. Major Carrie Acree, "Letters From War," *The P.E.O. Record*, January-February 2005: 8. Reprinted with permission of the author.

Epilogue

1. William Henry Harrison Murray (1840-1904), from "John Norton's Vagabond."

Index